The Workings of the Household

Family Life Series

Edited by Martin Richards, Ann Oakley, Christina Hardyment and Jackie Burgoyne

Published

Janet Finch, *Family Obligations and Social Change*
Lydia Morris, *The Workings of the Household*
Philip Pacey, *Family Art*

Forthcoming

David Clark and Douglas Haldane, *Wedlocked?*
Miriam David, *Mum's the Word: Relations between Families and Schools*
Jean La Fontaine, *Child Sexual Abuse*
Ann Phoenix, *Young Mothers*

The Workings of the Household

A US–UK Comparison

Lydia Morris

Polity Press

First published 1990 by Polity Press
in association with Basil Blackwell

Editorial office:
Polity Press, 65 Bridge Street,
Cambridge CB2 1UR, UK

Marketing and production:
Basil Blackwell Ltd
108 Cowley Road, Oxford OX4 1JF, UK

Basil Blackwell Inc.
3 Cambridge Center
Cambridge, MA 02142, USA

ISBN 0 7456 0441 2
ISBN 0 7456 0442 0 (pbk)

British Library Cataloguing in Publication Data
A CIP catalogue record for this book is available from the British Library.

Library of Congress Cataloging in Publication Data
A CIP catalogue record for this book is available from the Library
of Congress.

Typeset in 10 on 12 pt Baskerville
by Downdell Ltd, Oxford
Printed in Great Britain by
T.J. Press (Padstow) Ltd, Padstow, Cornwall.

Contents

1	Introduction	1
2	Male Unemployment	22
3	The Variable Experience of Male Unemployment	42
4	Employment for Women	60
5	The Division of Domestic Labour	80
6	Household Finance	103
7	Women's Unemployment	123
8	Young People and the Household	147
9	The Household in Social Context	165
10	Conclusion	189
	References	198
	Index	211

Dedicated to C. C. Harris

1   *Introduction*

The last two decades have seen deep-seated change in the economies of advanced industrial societies. Levels of employment have fallen dramatically, the composition of the work-force has altered, and there have been shifts in emphasis from full-time to part-time employment, from male to female labour, from manufacturing to services and from secure to casualized work. After a twenty-year period of high and stable levels of employment, one of the most fundamental bases of post-war society has been shaken: full male employment can no longer be taken for granted.

While industrial decline in the UK and US meant increasing rates of male job loss and unemployment, married women have been drawn into the labour force in ever-growing numbers, largely to occupy positions in the expanding service sector. Thus, not only have the structures of the British and American economies changed, but the gender roles that have traditionally been associated with advanced industrial society seem also to have been challenged.

This book is about the organization of the household and its internal dynamics, viewed in the context of the social and economic environment in which it is located. Its purpose is to ask how changes in the market for labour interact with the way in which men and women organize their domestic lives and structure their relationships. How do household members use their time and labour to secure the means of survival? What different sources of income combine in the household economy? How do individual and collective interests interact? What implications do different combinations of income source have for men's and women's respective roles and domestic relationships? How far do established patterns of gender identity and their supporting ideologies constrain the organization of domestic life? In what ways and through what mechanisms is the household–labour market link established, maintained or transformed?

Why the Household?

Questions of this kind have conspired to bring about an increased awareness of the household as an important focus for social scientific research.
High levels of unemployment have made paid work an unsatisfactory basis
for conceptualizing social structure, and research into unpaid work has
assumed correspondingly greater significance. Attention has accordingly
turned towards the household; the site of much of the work – domestic
labour, self-provisioning, child care and so on – carried out beyond the
confines of the work-place.

In addition to these specifically work-related interests are topics more
directly concerned with the nature of life and relationships within the
household, that is with domestic organization, which is inextricably linked
to gender relations and the domestic division of labour. The household,
seen as the theatre of many aspects of the relationship between men and
women, is the obvious place in which to investigate the effects of male
unemployment, and the impact of changing labour-force patterns, especially
the increased employment of married women.

A concern with the household has also emerged in a rather different
context; from the province of 'family sociology'. Anthropological work has
for some time been at pains to emphasize the conceptual difference between
the family and the household,[1] whilst in our own society the residential
arrangements commonly associated with the nuclear family have often
blinded us to this distinction. Nevertheless, it is both possible and advisable
to differentiate between, on the one hand, types of household composition
and patterns of residence, and on the other, nuclear and extended family
relations from which no residential pattern necessarily follows.

This move becomes particularly significant in the light of recent enthusiasm for 'household' research since it means, at least potentially, that household composition and formation will not be taken as given and can
themselves become topics of investigation. As a result, the residential unit
will the more easily be placed in its social, economic and kinship setting,
and, as we shall see, this development is of crucial importance in attempts
to research into 'household effects' of economic change.

There are a number of difficulties, however, that arise when researchers
attempt to realize the promise of the household approach, not least of which
is that of identifying a relevant literature. The potential field is so broad
that it is rare to find all possible aspects of the perspective combined in one

---

[1] An example of an anthropological discussion of the distinction in a research context is to
be found in Solien (1960). For a discussion of the domestic group see Goody (1972), and for a
conceptual discussion of family and household see Harris (1983: 41).

study. What we have is rather a collection of non-comparable studies that tend to focus on specific areas of interest within the household – unemployment, domestic labour, household finance, power and decision making, self-provisioning, labour market position and so on – but which are in no way cumulative or even mutually informing.

The work required to bind these studies together has only relatively recently begun and the present volume attempts such a task of integration. It draws on recent material from both the UK and the US, looking at similarities and differences in the experience of economic change at the level of the household, but seeking first to identify the nature of that change, and so to provide a background for the discussion which follows.

Household and Economy

In modern capitalist society the household has usually, though not necessarily, been composed of people related by kinship and marriage, and has often, though by no means always, coincided with the nuclear family made up of a married or cohabiting couple and their offspring. This arrangement, the nuclear family household, has tended to be accompanied by a traditional division of labour between the sexes, which gives the woman primary responsibility for securing the means of household survival; its daily and generational reproduction.

It was with reference to this setting that the notion of a 'family wage' developed – the idea of a sole (male) earner providing for the (nuclear) family by selling his labour in the market for a wage sufficient to maintain a wife and children. Thus the basis of our understanding of contemporary family life arguably depends upon a grasp of the relationship between the household unit and the structure and organization of the demand for waged labour.

The emergence of a privatized, nuclear family as a basis for domestic organization can largely be understood (though not explained) with reference to the historical processes that led to the separation of place of residence from place of work, the segregation of domestic labour from industrial labour, and the consequent development of a particular kind of relationship between the household and the productive enterprise (see Harris, 1983; Lopata et al., 1986; Oakley, 1974; Pahl, 1984).

The organization of, and participation in, paid work necessarily plays a major part in the internal dynamic of the household. In the early stages of industrialization, paid labour became available to men on increasingly preferential terms (see Brenner and Ramas, 1984; Lewis, 1984; Lopata et al., 1986), and men's superior position in the labour market both fostered, and was in turn reinforced by, the notion of the male bread-winner.

It was in this context that the concept of the 'family wage' was popularized, representing a claim for payment that would enable a man to maintain a wife and children; a claim common to both British and American trade unions (Land, 1976; Ware, 1977). The economic logic of this position is that the wage should provide sufficient income to sustain a wife whose domestic services transform that wage into the means of subsistence,[2] whilst also guaranteeing the social and biological reproduction of the next generation, the future labour-force. The demand for a family wage thus carried with it the assumption that the married woman would not need or wish to seek employment. It was backed both by male trade union pressure and an associated ideology concerning gender roles.

The Nuclear Family Household in Industrial Society

The earliest theoretical perspective to contain an approach to the relationship between household and economy was the functional theory of the family, which based its analysis on the identification of necessary 'social functions'. This perspective argues that the basic institutions of society must somehow fit together in a way consistent with the achievement of these functions, and it is the emphasis on this relationship between society's basic institutions and functions that is of interest to us here.

The most prominent theorist in this field was Talcott Parsons, who has argued (1949) that the nuclear family, with its structural isolation (that is, the nuclear family *household*) is the family form best suited to the social institutions of industrial societies. A related body of literature sprang forth debating the validity of this view, much of it based on a misunderstanding of the term 'structural isolation'. This debate has been reviewed by Harris (1983) and will not be detailed here. The point of central importance is that this 'structural isolation' of the nuclear family household, that is its existence as a *residential* unit, should not be taken to imply the absence of kin linkages across household boundaries, the importance of which will be discussed later in this book.

The existence of the nuclear family in a structurally separate household arrangement was one of the factors that Parsons saw as functional for industrial society, facilitating 'occupationally induced geographic mobility'. The necessary assumptions here are that only one member of the nuclear

---

[2] This argument has been explored in an extensive literature which has come to be known as the 'domestic labour debate', reviewed and summarized in Harris (1983).

family will be in paid employment, and that *primary* ties of obligation and loyalty will be contained within that unit.

The notion of sex-role specialization grew out of this position, and Parsons' most contentious argument has been his conferment on the wife of the expressive (that is supportive) role, and on the husband the instrumental (that is dominant) role. This argument is not one of biological determinism, however, as has sometimes been suggested (for example Edgell, 1980: 18), but rather concerns a view of the arrangement most suited to the functional requirements of industrial society. If differentiation and specialization within the nuclear family household is the most efficient arrangement in terms of the economic system, and given the need for employed members of the household to be relatively unconstrained in the performance of their paid work away from the home, then childbearing and rearing will necessarily make women more likely to assume or be accorded the expressive, rather than the instrumental role.

Parsons was, however, aware of the inevitable strains built into this arrangement, and as Harris (1983: 61) observes, Parsons' *Essays in Sociological Theory* 'make all the "modern", "feminist" points about the imprisonment of the wife in domestic tasks, her exclusion from the occupational sphere, the small amount of domestic assistance she receives from her husband and the negative effects on her psychic health'.

Thus, the functional fit between the household and the economic system seems in the case of industrial society to be achieved at women's expense.

Capitalism and Domestic Labour

A much more recent body of literature, which has come to be known as the domestic labour debate,[3] has grown out of an essentially feminist concern to extend a Marxist perspective to the analysis of domestic labour and an understanding of sexual divisions in society. The position that has emerged has much in common with the functionalist approach outlined above; ironically so since Parsons has become the *bête noire* of many feminists. There are two fundamental questions to be answered within the terms of this framework:

1 What is the nature of the economic relationship between the household and the capitalist system?
2 What was the process by which specialized gender roles and a sexual division of labour emerged?

[3] For a review see Molyneux (1979).

The answer to the first of these questions is complementary to the functionalist view of developments in the household in terms of the efficiency of the economic system. Focusing specifically on domestic labour the Marxist-feminist perspective has been concerned to argue that the work performed within the home was part of a wider division of labour which was functional for capital. Leaving aside the technial debate that ensued about whether domestic labour could be seen as *productive* in the strictly Marxist sense, and how one might set about measuring the contribution of domestic labour to the *value* of labour power, the major contribution of this literature has been to demonstrate the role of domestic labour in the daily and generational reproduction of labour power.

Since industrial society has been increasingly dependent upon a population of workers forced to sell their labour in the open market for a wage, then a corollary of this arrangement is the need for some system whereby the wage is transformed into the means of subsistence. This role came to be performed by domestic labour, which produces use-values consumed within the household. Ironically, the lower the income given over to this end, the greater the input of domestic labour must be in order to ensure the survival of household members, and hence tomorrow's labour-force, and this argument comes across clearly in discussions of the household effects of unemployment.

More generally this latter point is of significance for employers, since the value added to the wage by the domestic labour that transforms it into the means of subsistence holds the amount paid to the workers below that required to reproduce their labour power. Domestic labour comes free, except in so far as the wage contains some element intended to permit the maintenance of a spouse and children – the 'family wage' traditionally fought for by male trade unionists. Even granted this, additional labour is still required to turn the wage into consumable form, and this labour receives no monetary reward, only subsistence.

The second question to be posed in the analysis of domestic labour is how it came about that women and not men were held principally responsible for these tasks. The answer, however, is not to be found in abstract theorizing but rather in an account of the historical processes that led to the reduced presence of women and children in the paid labour force.

The Employment Society

Prior to industrialization the majority of the population in both the UK and US was confined to rural areas. The household was largely responsible for satisfying its own requirements of food, clothing and shelter, and of necessity operated as a production unit, with the home as the location of production. The household economy was often augmented by earnings from trade, and with the introduction of the putting-out system, by paid labour in the home. Employment for pay outside the home served simply to supplement this essentially domestic enterprise.

Capital industrialization revolutionized the domestic or household organization of production, and there grew up a population no longer able to look to agriculture for its principal means of survival. Changes in farming techniques, population growth and the development of a factory system of production laid the foundations for large industrial towns peopled by rural migrants who were totally dependent on the wage for their livelihood. They had lost control of the means of production, and as a result were compelled to sell their labour on the open market.

Initially the new industrial household depended on male, female and child earners, and indeed in both the US and UK there are examples of how the family was imported into the factory as a means of disciplining the workforce (see Prude, 1983, for a US example and Anderson, 1971, for a UK study). Married women, however, became increasingly disadvantaged in the market for labour. The gradual exclusion of children from the workplace meant constraints on the labour time and resources of the household, with women carrying the major child-care burden. This situation was exacerbated both by protective legislation, which limited women's hours of employment, and by the exclusionist strategies of some of the skilled, male-dominated trade unions (Brenner and Ramas, 1984).

Despite such developments, the notion of a family wage has been challenged by a number of writers (see Barrett and McIntosh, 1980; Land, 1981). It is argued that the image of a sole male breadwinner was 'ideological' in the sense that it represented a view of social relations that did not correspond to the 'facts' of economic and domestic life, and expressly served the interests of a particular social group, that is the skilled male working class. More generally, it has been pointed out that the wages system cannot ensure the needs of households at all stages in their development (Land, 1981). Thus the idea of a family wage neglects the contribution made by married women and their offspring to the household income, the vagaries of the market for male labour and the inability of low-paid workers to honour the obligations implied by the 'breadwinner' role, as well as the state's eventual intervention in offering some support.

It seems then that women's financial dependence on men was never fully established in all households, and nor was men's reliability ever fully assured. Clearly the viability of what we shall term the 'traditional' model of gender relations embodied in the idea of a family wage will depend on the availability of employment for men at a wage sufficient to cater for the demands of the nuclear family, and men's readiness to meet these demands. It is a model that is challenged by the growth of employment for married women, and by high rates of long-term unemployment for men, both of which have been recent features of the British and American economies.

The Discovery of Unemployment

The emergence of the 'employment' society in which a majority of the population depended for survival on paid labour – whether their own or their spouses – necessarily carried within it the threat of an 'unemployment' society. Unemployment was a phenomenon that did not exist in its current sense until industrialization was firmly established. The term was coined in the 1820s[4] and could have meaning only in a society in which a large section of the population earned a living by selling its labour power. It was still some time, however, before the capacity of the new industrial economy to generate sufficient employment was to be thrown into doubt, and by then male identity had become firmly bound up with paid employment.

In a social climate that emphasized individual endeavour, unemployment and poverty were at first attributed to indolence on the part of their victims, and it was not until the turn of the century that an alternative view took hold. The weakness of the early explanations of unemployment was that in times of expansion the 'work-shy' were miraculously absorbed into the employed population. It was partly as a result of this anomaly that influential figures in both Britain and America gradually began to recognize the *social* origins of unemployment.[5]

Beveridge's view of unemployment as 'a problem of industry' (1909) marks this shift in thinking. It is a view that prevailed in both the UK and US throughout the unprecedented unemployment levels of the inter-war years. In Britain the workless reached a peak of 15.3 per cent in 1932, and in the US in the same year rose to 22.3 per cent. The average levels throughout the 1920s and 1930s were 9.4 and 9.2 per cent, respectively (figures adjusted for comparison from Ashton, 1986: 32–3). During World War Two unemployment fell to almost negligible proportions[6] and the post-war period began with an endeavour by the governments of both Britain and America to do all that was possible to prevent a return to the conditions of the 1930s.

---

[4] See Ashton (1986: 27) for details.

[5] That is, explanation at the level of the individual was inadequate, and had to be sought in the prevailing economic conditions of the time.

[6] UK 0.5 per cent and US 1.2 per cent for 1944 (Hughes and Perlman, 1984: 146, 158).

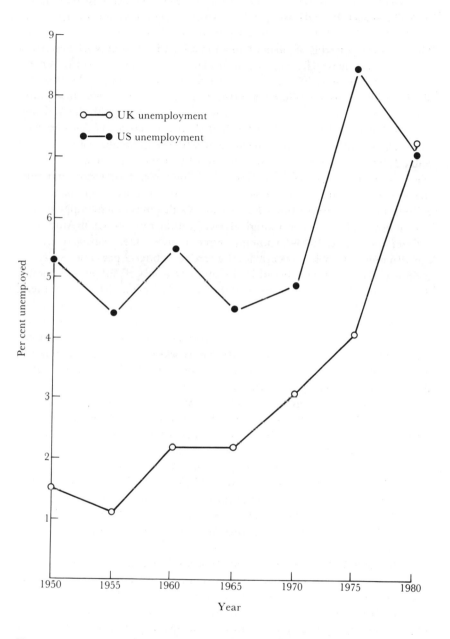

Figure 1.1 UK and US unemployment, 1950–1980
Source: D. E. Ashton (1986: 32–3).

The Post-war Paradigm

The post-war period is of particular interest for the present work because it is the time during which a number of fundamental values governing current ideas about everyday life were established. Amongst them is the commitment to full (male) employment. Hughes and Perlman (1984) have summarized the characteristics of the post-war economy for both the UK and the US. They note that in 1944 the British government's White Paper on employment policy stated as a primary aim 'the maintenance of a high and stable level of employment'. Similarly the 1946 Employment Act in the US was designed 'to promote maximum employment, production and purchasing power', and thus to provide 'useful opportunities for those able, willing and seeking to work'. For a time, both governments appeared to have considerable success, though Britain rather more so than America.

Over the period 1948–66 unemployment in the UK averaged 1.7 per cent. In only 5 of these 19 years did the rate rise above 2 per cent. Although 1966 was the year that ushered in the end of the era of 'full employment', the prior two decades had established the ideal of a job for all (male) workers, which came to be a taken-for-granted aspect of social and economic life. The phenomenon had lasted long enough for workers who entered the labour market in 1948 to be almost half-way through their working life before the change began, and for a new generation of workers to have grown to adulthood socialized in an environment that fostered the belief that mass unemployment would never be seen again (see figure 1.1).

Whilst full employment was widely accepted as a post-war policy goal in the US it had to compete with other policy aims (see Hughes and Perlman, 1984: 161) and unstable levels over the last four decades have not produced such a rigid distinction in the experience and socialization of different cohorts of workers as in the UK. During the 11 years from 1947 to 1957 the overall US average lay between 4 and 4.5 per cent, though between 1957 and 1964 the figure was to rise to almost 6.4 per cent (Ashton, 1986: 32–3). Since 1970 the rate has risen fairly consistently, with low points in 1973 and 1979 and a recent fall to 5.3 per cent in June 1988 (*Unemployment Bulletin*, 28, 1988) (figure 1.2).

Thus, the full employment society was never as convincingly realized in the US as in the UK and popular expectations would perhaps have been less optimistic. In contrast to Britain's two decades of full employment, America had only one, followed by a seven- to eight-year period of relatively high unemployment, and a second but shorter period of full employment (Hughes and Perlman, 1984: 161). Recent levels of unemployment, however, have not been as high in America as in the UK, and, as we shall

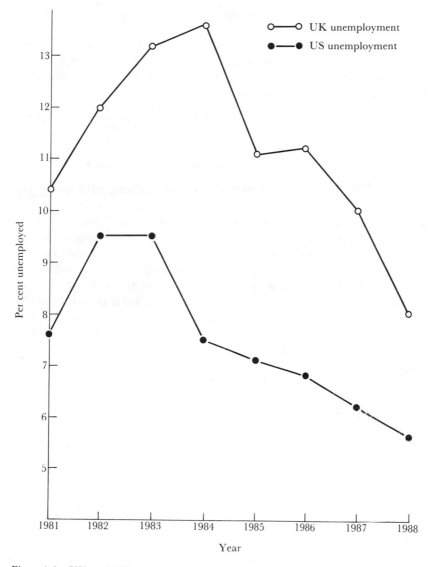

Figure 1.2   UK and US unemployment, 1981–1988
Source: D. E. Ashton (1986: 32–3); 1985–6 figures from the *ILO Yearbook of Labour Statistics*; 1987–8 figures from the *Unemployment Bulletin*, Autumn 1988, Unemployment Unit, London.

see in chapter 2, the duration of unemployment in the States is commonly much shorter. In terms of patterns of employment and unemployment, then, Britain has had a history of more marked extremes than the US, but the general features of the post-war era have been broadly similar in both countries.

A number of changes were underway in both the UK and US by the end of the fifties that came to challenge the feasibility of full (male) employment, and gradually to undermine the taken-for-granted status it had acquired. The changes had three major manifestations:

1 A shift in the nature of industrial activity away from manufacturing and into services.
2 A failure of job creation to keep pace with growth in the labour-force.
3 An increase in labour-force participation of married women.

As Dex (1985) points out, these changes have not been sudden. Between 1940 and 1960 there was a decline in UK manufacturing employment from 39 to 35 per cent and an increase in services from 38 to 45 per cent. In the US the manufacturing decline was from 30 to 25 per cent, with an increase from 41 to 58 per cent in services. These figures represent more than just sectoral shifts, however. There have been accompanying changes in the kinds of jobs available and in the kinds of worker employed. In both societies the move has been away from well-paid, full-time jobs in manufacturing to low-paid, often part-time jobs in services. The job loss has been largely from industries employing a predominantly male labour-force, whilst the newly created service employment has tended to favour married women.

Women's Labour

Post-war growth of women's employment in the UK and US has been similar in many respects. Although women were quickly replaced from their short-lived experience in the traditional areas of male employment after World War Two, jobs soon became available in the expanding service sector. Many women never returned to their previous way of life and others joined the labour force for the first time (see figure 1.3).

In Britain the number of female employees rose from 33.6 per cent in 1948 to 41.7 per cent in 1980, and whilst married women made up 38 per cent of the 1951 female work-force, by 1971 the figure had risen to 63 per cent (Dex, 1985: 3), and was fairly stable thereafter, reaching 64 per cent in 1985 (*General Household Survey*, table 6.24). American data show the same trend. Labour-force participation for all women rose steadily between 1940 and 1972, from 27.4 to 43.7 per cent, reaching 55.4 per cent in 1987 (*Bureau of Labour Statistics*). The proportion of these women who were married rose over the same period from 14.7 to 41.5 per cent (Hesse, 1979:

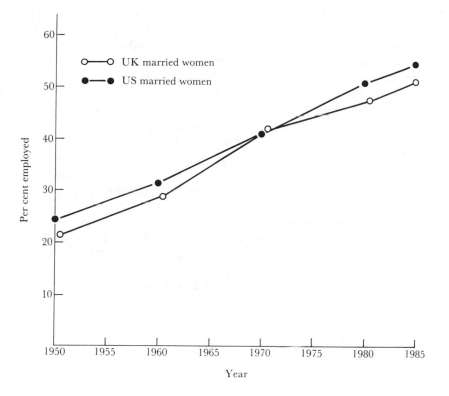

Figure 1.3 Married women's labour-force activity rates for the UK and US, 1950–1985

Source: Up to 1981, Mallier and Rosser (1986: 28); UK 1985 from the *General Household Survey* (1987: table 6.16); US 1985 from the *Bureau of Labour Statistics*, Washington DC.

53), and currently stands at 55.8 per cent (*Bureau of Labour Statistics*). We should note, however, that whilst labour-force participation rates for white American women aged between 20 and 44 have risen consistently since 1966, black female labour-force rates have levelled off in recent years (Mott, 1979).

In both countries, women are concentrated in the same areas of employment. Reviewing data from the UK Women and Employment Survey and the US National Longitudinal Survey of Labour Market Experience, Dex and Shaw (1986: 30) report that in 1980 among younger women in the UK 63.9 per cent had their last job in services, and 65.2 per cent in the US. For older women the proportions were respectively 55.6 and 60.3 per cent. Within the category of women's labour there is, however, substantial variation. For example, although in both countries service sector expansion has also meant a growth in part-time jobs (Dex, 1986: 5; Ashton, 1986: 90), the employment of women as part-time workers is lower in the US than the UK, where numbers rose from 33 per cent of employed women in 1971 to 42 per cent in 1981 (Dex, 1985: 5). Only 25 per cent of women workers in America were employed part time in 1980 (Dex and Shaw, 1986: 25).

Whilst British women in their 40s and 50s are more likely to be in employment than American women of the same age (94.4 vs. 74.7 per cent, Dex and Shaw, 1986: 29), a much greater proportion of the former group are in part-time jobs. For younger American women in their late 20s and early 30s employment is much more common than in the older age group, though slightly fewer are employed than in Britain. The American group is, however, more likely to be employed full time than its British counterpart, and to work far more through the period of family formation. In general they show a much stronger attachment to the labour-force when they do work, despite their lower representation (68.9 per cent in the US vs. 76.7 per cent in the UK, Dex and Shaw, 1986: 29; Dex, 1985: 95). Dex, however, confirms that women in both countries continue to occupy a generally inferior position in the labour market, although their *presence* in the labour-force has been growing.

This weak labour market position is partly responsible for the growth in women's jobs, which often offer a cheap means of expanding or restructuring employment. It also leaves women vulnerable to job loss. Ironically, as the size of the female labour-force increases and women's employment becomes the norm, then the phenomenon of women's unemployment becomes more visible and its impact more marked. Thus, despite the increase in women's employment, unemployment is by no means an exclusively male problem.

Household Effects

Attempts to translate the effect of recent economic change into an understanding of domestic life and gender relations is by no means straightforward. Some preliminary indication of the difficulties is perhaps best provided by a selection of brief case studies.

Case 1

Mr and Mrs Atkins are aged 52 and 54. Mr Atkins was made redundant from an unskilled job in the steel industry ten years ago, but after a short spell out of work he found factory employment through the influence of his wife's uncle. After two years he was redundant again, his age and short period of service with the firm leaving him vulnerable to job loss. Mrs Atkins has held a part-time job as a cleaner since their youngest child reached school age 13 years ago, working in the evenings when her husband was available for child care. This work continued until Mr Atkins's second redundancy, when she finally left the job because he felt unhappy about her working when he was unemployed, added to which her earnings were offset against his claim for benefit. Mrs Atkins handles all the finances for the household; her husband hands over the benefit cheque, receiving back pocket money when she judges there are sufficient funds. All domestic chores are performed by Mrs Atkins, and this was mutually agreed by the couple. Mr Atkins spends as much time as possible out of the home during the day, walking or fishing to leave his wife to her chores and occasional visits to family and friends.

In this case the man's unemployment was quickly followed by his wife's withdrawal from work, for reasons related to benefit rulings, the inadequacy of her earnings as a sole income and the power of local prescriptions about gender roles. The subsequent arrangement of domestic life has, in fact, continued to reflect beliefs about gender roles which are more appropriate to their previous circumstances.

Case 2

Mr and Mrs Baker are both aged 33 and have two school-age children. Mrs Baker now works full time in a supervisory sales job from which she was able to take maternity leave for the birth of her children. She has relied on her mother who lives nearby for child care. Her husband is currently employed as a driver for a local bus company. Although he has experienced a series of redundancies over the last ten years, he has never spent more than one week without work, usually drawing on contacts with previous employers or workmates to identify new opportunities if a job comes to an end. The couple have a joint bank account from which Mrs Baker draws sufficient money to purchase basic household supplies, whilst Mr Baker is responsible for the payment of major bills. They consult each other over any significant personal expenditure. Mr Baker regularly contributes to the general cleaning, cooking and tidying in the home although responsibility for planning meals and washing and ironing clothes lies with Mrs Baker. The couple characterize their marriage as one of complete sharing. Much of their spare time is spent together in the home, on which they have expended a good deal of labour and money.

This couple have been more fortunate than Mr and Mrs Atkins in that despite several job losses for Mr Baker both he and his wife have been able to maintain virtual continuity of employment. Younger than the Atkins, they seem less bound by conventional gender roles, and their relative affluence allows them greater flexibility in the handling of their finances. There is, nevertheless, a recognizable vestige of traditional gender responsibilities in the organization of their domestic life.

Case 3

Mr and Mrs Charlton are aged 28 and 29 and have a young child. Mr Charlton has a history of broken employment, often called back to work for the same firm when their orders warrant extra labour, and between periods of formal employment he is often introduced to odd jobs by ex-workmates. He attributes his ability to find work to his skill as a welder, to his reputation as a hard worker and to his wide network of social contacts. Nevertheless, he has been unable to sustain unbroken employment over the last ten years. His wife, meanwhile, has been employed part time on the evening shift by a mail-order firm. Like her husband, she has had spells without work, the longest being after the birth of their child, but her old employer has always called her back eventually when there has been a gap in their staffing. Whenever possible, Mrs Charlton has continued to work during her husband's spells of unemployment, using her wage to augment the allowance she receives from his earnings or his unemployment benefit. She believes they would not survive without her wage, while her husband sees it as providing 'extras'. Mrs Charlton carries the responsibility for planning meals and paying regular bills, except for the mortgage, and she is also fully responsible for domestic chores. Her husband agrees to her paid work only as long as she is able to maintain her obligations in the home.

This couple is less securely placed in the labour market than the Bakers, and Mr Charlton has experienced a number of periods without paid work. Despite his wife's continued employment at such times, her job and her earnings are seen as in some way secondary to his, and the organization of their domestic life continues to adhere to traditional gender norms.

These three case studies are taken from a town in the north-east of England that has experienced severe economic decline with the fall off in heavy manufacturing since the sixties. There are, however, aspects of each case that typify changes occurring both in the structure of employment and in the relations between men and women in both the UK and US. They offer only a hint of the possible variations in the arrangements of one household across time, or between households at any given moment. So what are the conceptual and theoretical tools available to social scientists for understanding this variety whilst also forming conclusions about the nature and direction of social change?

Household Divisions of Labour

We began this chapter with a brief consideration of the relationship between the household and the economy in early capitalist society. This relationship came to be one of complementarity, based to a great extent on a division of labour between the sexes. Although the division was never completely impermeable and the poorest households remained dependent on women's earnings in addition to those of the man, by the early 20th century the traditional model of the male worker earning a family wage for the maintenance of a nuclear family household was clearly identifiable.

An ideology supporting the notion of the dependent wife, at least as an ideal, had become firmly established, and persists to the present day. Yet as we have seen, over the last 50 years married women's participation in paid employment in both the UK and US has risen dramatically, and sociologists have increasingly directed their attention to the effects of such change on the organization of domestic life. One attempt to provide a framework for the study of these effects is the 'New Home Economics', an American approach propounded by Gary Becker. Becker's argument (1981: 15) is that within the household each person 'maximizes utility' by choosing the optimal allocation of time between the market and household sectors. The relative allocation between household members is then seen in terms of comparative advantage, with those best placed in the market specializing completely there, and vice versa for the household. He adds, however, that: 'Although the sharp sexual division of labour in all societies between the household and market sectors is partly due to the gain from specialized investments, it is also partly due to intrinsic differences between the sexes' (1981: 21).

For Becker, such differences are a source of patterns of comparative advantage between the sexes, which lead to female specialization in domestic time and labour, and also to lower market wages. This argument is somewhat reminiscent of the Parsonian view of specialization we discussed earlier.

Berk (1985: 23–35) has outlined the problems associated with Becker's approach to household labour, noting a number of unacceptable assumptions. Perhaps the most important of these is the very idea of the household as a consensually operating unit. In its simplest form the model is based on a 'single utility' function for the household. In other words, it depends on an acceptance of individual decisions being made on the basis of household rather than personal well-being. This assumption would not hold if, for example, a wife is driven into the market sector because of lack of access to her husband's earnings, a circumstance outlined more fully in chapter 6.

To deal with the possibility of inequity Becker introduces the notions of selfishness and altruism, and further suggests that: 'Malfeasance could sometimes be detected . . . by invading the privacy of members (of the household) to gather evidence on the fidelity of their behaviour to the interests of the household.' None of these moves take account of the problem of the differential distribution of power within the household, over resources or behaviour, and nor does the model provide a framework for the study of how decisions within the home are actually arrived at. Similarly, there is no treatment of tastes and preferences, which are held constant across time and across classes. In this connection, Hannan (1982) has pointed out that the examination of cultural effects, for example, would of necessity involve questions about the distribution of preferences between and within populations. Geerken and Gove (1983: 26) also argue that the household does not operate only by rational calculative responses to its environment, since that environment is in part constituted by societal norms affecting behaviour. Hannan's point is that these norms may differ between different sections of the population, thus, as Geerken and Gove point out, there can be a range of responses to similar sets of circumstances.

Berk (1985: 31) also queries the absence from Becker's model of normative and institutional constraints on individuals' activities both inside and outside the home. This presents a problem if calculations are being made on the basis of the worth of a person's time in the market sector as opposed to the household. The weakness of such an approach is, she argues, that: 'the lower "value" of women's time can "justify" a one-sided division of household labour. That is, *because* women earn lower wages, it is argued, their greater time spent in household labour is "appropriate".'

Geerken and Gove (1983: 58) have, in addition, argued that a neglect of tastes and preferences can render the equally unsatisfactory account that the woman is held in the housewife role only by either the needs and desires of husband and children, or by lack of opportunity in the market.

Changing Conditions

As Ben-Porath (1982) has pointed out, the intention of Becker's work was to develop a theory of very broad applicability, and specifically one able to contain the recent rapid changes taking place in advanced industrial societies. Among the changes calling for explanation that Ben-Porath identifies is the increased labour-force participation of women, and especially married women.

Although, as we have seen, one aspect of Becker's argument is that biological differences contribute strongly to an explanation of the traditional, 'sole male earner' household pattern, he does not wish to argue that sex roles are unresponsive to market forces. Thus, higher market wages for women (or presumably job loss for men) will change the allocation of women's time. This leaves us unclear about whether biological characteristics 'explain' sex roles and lower market wages, or whether the wage structure determines sex roles (Ben-Porath, 1982: 53).

Causal direction is similarly vague in another aspect of women's employment considered by Becker (1981). He attributes an upward trend in the divorce rate to an increase in the earning capacity of women. His argument is that high-wage women: 'gain less from marriage than other women do because higher earnings reduce the demand for children and the advantages of the sexual division of labour in marriage' (1981: 231). However, he also argues that a higher divorce rate will lead to an increase in the earning ability of women in that divorced women will invest more in work experience and as a result will command a higher wage. They will be free to do so because of the absence of certain of the domestic constraints that come with marriage.

The question that must accompany women's increased market time, or indeed male job loss, is whether there follows any increase in the household time allocation of the man. The only means Becker has of explaining the absence of such adjustment within the terms of his model is by reference to altruism and selfishness. As long as selfish members have a vested interest in the system as a whole, then the argument is they would themselves suffer from any selfish behaviour, and so will refrain. This is not entirely convincing when it comes to domestic labour, or in the matter of the allocation of financial resources. An unequal system may continue to function at the disutility (personal cost) of the woman alone, because of the superior power wielded by the man, or because gender ideology deems it appropriate.

Household Strategies

The household strategies perspective, which shares certain features of the New Home Economics, has been taken up and developed relatively recently in the UK. Although the notion has its roots in much earlier studies of third-world and ghetto poverty, the source of the current wave of UK 'strategy' research has been an attempt to understand recent economic change by rethinking 'work'. Gershuny (1977, 1979) was a central figure in the development of this perspective and his early writing made a connection between jobs lost in 'formal' employment as a result of world recession, improved manufacturing productivity and high-cost services; and a reclamation of areas of work by the household in the form of 'self-provisioning'.

Gershuny was largely concerned to understand aggregate shifts, however, whilst Ray Pahl was meanwhile speculating on related changes in household production and consumption, asking how we might understand the organization of time and labour by an examination of changing work patterns. It was proposed that changes in the nature of work could be analysed in terms of shifts between three sectors of the economy (Gershuny and Pahl, 1979, 1980). Thus, as formal opportunities for employment dwindled, people would be freed from the 'realm of necessity' (Pahl, 1980: 17) to achieve an 'autonomous' mix in the use of their labour.

The reorganization of work, both paid and unpaid, was assumed to be occurring not simply between sectors and between households, but *within* the home. Household members were, according to early speculation, assessing their situation, their prospects and their needs, and working out an appropriate strategy:

> No longer do we have . . . a universal sex-linked division between the male 'chief earner' in the formal economy and his unpaid and dependent wife engaged in unremunerated housework. Nor is there such a rigidly sex-linked division of labour between men and women in the practice of domestic work.   (Gershuny and Pahl, 1981: 86)

Thus, the scene was set for speculation and research about precisely how the organization of life at the level of the household was changing, or to use Pahl's terminology, how households were developing 'new ways of getting work done'. Like Becker (1981), Pahl (1984) was concerned to investigate the nature and sources of labour harnessed by different households in their efforts to maintain a given standard of living; in other words, the household work strategy: 'The best use of resources for getting by under given social and economic conditions' (1984: 20), to be defined later in the same work as: 'how households allocate their collective effort to getting all the work that they define has, or feel needs, to be done.' (1984: 113).

As with Becker's work, the 'household strategy' perspective suffers somewhat from taking the household as an unproblematic unit for analysis, whilst the voluntarism implied as well as the implicit assumption of consensual decision making are somewhat misleading when we come to consider the limitations on household or individual choice. In the event, the options available to households in their responses to economic change prove to be fairly narrow, as subsequent chapters will show. This invites some examination of the processes by which strategies are arrived at, and the limitations under which they are constructed.

Thus, there are two senses in which the 'use of resources' or 'household strategy' approach is unsatisfactory. Firstly, it implies that the household may be treated as a consensually operating unit, with equitable access to and use of resources. In fact, both power within the household and material resources may be differentially distributed. The distribution may well be related to labour market strengths and weaknesses, but may also come to act back upon behaviour in the labour market. Thus the 'household' outcome in terms of the use of time and labour will be intricately related to the internal dynamic of household relations.

Secondly, the voluntarism implied by the household approach distracts attention away from the constraints under which outcomes are constructed, which may derive, for example, from the nature of the market for labour, state policy on income tax and income support, cultural and ideological influences embodied in local social practice and so on. Thus, further progress in our understanding of the experience of recent economic change at the level of the household requires a more detailed examination of the components involved in the construction of a household strategy, and the processes by which they emerge.

Inside the household the critical areas are: (a) the organization of domestic labour and (b) the management and control of household finance, and both of these aspects of domestic life may be related to the labour market activities and prospects of different household members, as we shall demonstrate. In focusing attention on the internal characteristics of the household, however, we should not neglect to take account of external influences. The nature of opportunities available to household members, for example, will vary by virtue of the characteristics of the local market for labour, and the individual strengths and weaknesses within that market.

We must therefore examine the position of the household and its members in the local labour market, and uncover the way in which that position is influenced by relationships within the home, and access to opportunities through networks of contact that may extend beyond household boundaries. In addition, we must identify constraints imposed by the nature of the social, ideological and statutory environment in which the household is located; constraints which will define and limit the options available to any given household. We begin our inquiry into household experience of change with an examination of the particular case of male unemployment, and its impact on relations within the home.

2 Male Unemployment

This chapter attempts to construct from available material for both Britain and America the general effects of male unemployment on relationships within the household. Despite a tendency in the literature on unemployment to focus on the psychological condition of individual (male) workers, there is a growing body of material which is concerned to make the point that the individual workers are members of households and families, and that others may suffer both materially and psychologically as a result of unemployment. In short, relationships within the home may be disrupted.

Concern with the effects of unemployment on marital and household relationships dates back in both the US and UK to the thirties and forties, and there are some remarkable studies from this era that provide a useful starting point for our discussion. Although such work has been criticized for its emphasis on male unemployment, this is partly to be explained by an overpowering cultural and ideological climate that accepted what I have termed the 'traditional' sexual division of labour as normal, and in many ways desirable. This convention turns out to be an important factor in the reported findings of research; ideas about what constitute appropriate male and female roles affect the way in which unemployment is experienced. It is also a factor whose presence diminishes the utility of approaches to domestic organization that focus principally on the allocation of time and labour power.

Findings of Early Research on Unemployment

1 E. W. Bakke In the 1930s Bakke embarked on a piece of research in Greenwich with the aim of studying working-class adjustment to male unemployment in a 'normal working-class community in which urban industrial problems were exemplified'. Little of his early work specifically examines relationships within the family, although we are given some hints of their deterioration in such statements as: 'Even my family is beginning to think I'm not trying so I can't talk with them any more' (1935: 66).

In the detail reported we also find signs of women's role in stretching inadequate income, children poorly fed and clothed, and men's problems in disposing of time on their hands, but there are also indications that different categories of worker may react differently. For the young, work had not yet become the 'cornerstone of their whole life'; and the unskilled, more accustomed to casual employment, seemed likely to adjust more easily. Unemployment will clearly vary according to a number of other factors from family circumstances and material resources, to dominant work-based ideas about gender roles and the source of personal identity.

Reference was made in Bakke's study to the importance in some homes of the wife's earnings, and to the problems that might result from this dependence: 'It's getting me under to see the wife supporting us and me who is supposed to be the head of the family and doing nothing but look for work. . . . You have to work to keep your self-respect' (pp. 69–70).

Bakke states: 'Practically every man who had a family showed evidence of the blow his self-confidence had suffered from the fact that the traditional head of the family was not able to perform his normal function. . . . "It's hell when a man can't even support his own family" ' (p. 70).

These findings are repeated when Bakke further develops his work in the American industrial town of New Haven (1940b: 116): 'So well established is the functioning of the male chief breadwinner that any departure from the norm usually called for some explanation or rationalization. The role has assumed a greater than economic significance. A man's status in the family and in the community is definitely coupled with his exercising that role successfully.'

The family features more prominently and is treated more systematically in the later writing (1940a and 1940b). In Bakke's discussion of the family as an economic unit, for example, we learn that the mother commonly becomes the 'administrative officer' of financial planning and management (1940b: 141), responsible for apportioning inadequate income and 'stretching resources'. Spending on clothing and recreational activity was the first and commonest reduction. The importance of developing family solidarity in these circumstances is emphasized, and we learn that women as the key economizers may bear the brunt of their children's criticisms.

The importance of older children's contributions to income is noted, as well as the possibility of a wife's employment, but the incidence of gainfully employed women seemed to vary substantially between different ethnic groups, with 40 per cent of black wives, but only 10 per cent of foreign-born wives, and 15 per cent of white native born wives earning. The use of credit was also found to vary according to ethnic identity, as did the use (and presumably availability) of savings, which additionally turned out to be skill related. It was reported that the unskilled were entirely dependent for loans on other family members rather than formal institutions. Jewish and Italian workers seemed to have most extra-familial support, which contributed to internal stability. Another area of variety was the degree of rigidity maintained between the roles of husband and wife. Greater rigidity (chiefly in families of non-American origin) seemed to produce greater conflict.

Bakke (1940a) is at pains to stress the problems attached to generalization, but nevertheless puts forward the idea of a cycle of adjustment through discernible stages from initial stability, through disorganization, to ultimate adjustment. At worst, he speculates: 'Unemployment may damage the satisfaction involved in mutual association, may decrease the mutual respect, regard and affection of members and substitute negative attitudes and reactions, thus removing incentives to, and lubricants for adjustment' (p. 157).

Stress and strain start to erode the customary mutual consideration and regard, but in other senses the hold of custom is strong. Although the wife may develop additional sources of income, often through work in the home, initially: 'both husband and wife feel that any thoroughgoing redistribution of domestic duties somehow is not a proper procedure' (p. 183).

Later attempts by the couple to draw up a new division of labour seem often to result in conflict. The wife is more than ever in command of resources, supplementary earners become resentful, parent–child relations deteriorate, the man loses status within the family, and relinquishes all recreational activities outside the home: 'The family is now thrown in upon itself where conflict and confusion dominate and established relationship patterns have disintegrated' (p. 209).

Mutual blame and the absence of attraction also characterize this stage of disorganization, but once the attempt to hold on to past customs has been abandoned, then readjustment is argued to be achievable.

2 M. Komarovsky   The nature of family relationships in the face of male unemployment is the specific focus of another American study, published at around the same time as Bakke's later research. Komarovsky's *The Unemployed Man and his Family* (1940), though firmly located within the social psychological tradition, does not confine itself to the individual but examines a relationship: that between 'the man's role as economic provider of the family and his authority within the family' (p. 1).

The study aimed to focus on a specific group of workers and to secure homogeneity within the achieved sample of 59. To this end the men selected were all native-born Protestants who were skilled manual or white-collar workers in nuclear family households in which the father had been unemployed for at least one year. The sample was therefore of a higher economic and occupational status, and more homogeneous, than the mixture of workers on whom Bakke's research was based. The study was located in a 'large industrial city just outside of New York'.

It is interesting that an explicit concern with homogeneity permits the inclusion of both skilled manual and white-collar workers, and this suggests that class or occupational cultures differ less between these two groupings than one might expect in, for example, the UK. Class culture was not an issue given explicit attention, although underlying analysis is the idea of a work based gender identity that is disrupted by male unemployment. This perspective is quite close to some of Bakke's work, but with neither writer can we be sure that the associations reported are class specific.

Komarovsky found that in 13 out of 58 cases unemployment lowered the status and therefore the authority of the husband in relation to his wife. Her comment is that this: 'may appear to indicate that being a provider plays some, but after all only a small part, in determining the prestige and powers of a husband' (p. 24).

The manner in which loss of status occurred turns out to have varied between three outcomes: the crystallization of a prior inferior status; the breakdown of a more or less coercive control; and the weakened authority of a husband over a none the less loving wife (pp. 24–5). It was also the case that the unemployed man's status, whilst more precarious with his wife than with young children, was most vulnerable with adolescent children. We should note, however, that instances of marital separation and of wage-earning wives were excluded from the sample.

As in Bakke's study, Komarovsky found that with unemployment the wife tended to assume command of the household income, and that for men this meant two things: the loss of self-respect or status that attached to the role of provider; and the loss of the instrumental power conferred by control over resources. Also comparable to Bakke's findings was the significance of periodic casual earnings in bolstering the man's morale, and the depressing effect that a wife's paid employment could have.

The question of the man's contribution to labour within the home was also found to be problematic in some cases: 'Housework is so closely identified with the woman's rather than the man's role in the family that performing it is a symbol of [male] degradation' (p. 44).

The husband's criticism of his wife's housekeeping and child-rearing practice could also be a source of conflict. This was not always the case, however, and at least one couple shared domestic labour and enjoyed increased companionship in unemployment.

Komarovsky explains differences of this kind by reference to the attitudes and cultural patterns established prior to job loss. This is consistent with Bakke's view that: 'Unemployment is a complex phenomenon which acts as a disturbing irritant upon the practices and relationships customary to a particular family. The problems raised by unemployment were injected into a situation the major factors of which were already active' (Bakke, 1940a: 228).

The central consideration for studies of unemployment was expressed by Komarovsky as follows: 'The extent to which work was the means of self-expression for the man, and the extent to which his self-esteem was identified with his socio-economic status or his role of the family provider' (p. 74).

3 The Pilgrim Trust   One further early study that we should mention here is a report to the Pilgrim Trust (1938) on a study of unemployment in six British towns experiencing differing degrees of affluence and decline. A random sample was drawn of 1086 workers, unemployed for at least a year, and 760 men and 120 women were eventually interviewed. The study is unusual in its inclusion of a section on women's unemployment, which we consider separately later in this book. The report makes the important statement, however, that unemployment affects women not just directly but in their position as the wives of unemployed men. Male unemployment and its social importance must be considered in terms of families: 'on the man in the queue there may depend a large family at home which is, perhaps, more affected than he is himself by his state of prolonged unemployment' (p. 43), and the women and children at home are referred to as the 'shadows behind the queue' (p. 45). At the time of writing there were 250,000 long-term unemployed in England and Wales. The problem was consequently felt by 270,000 young children and 170,000 wives, 'whose burden is perhaps the heaviest of all' (p. 46).

Reporting on women's roles within households experiencing male unemployment, the study makes explicit a number of the points that crop up incidentally in Bakke's and Komarovsky's work: 'In most unemployed families the parents and particularly the wives, bear the burden of want, and in many cases were literally starving themselves in order to feed and clothe the children reasonably well' (p. 112).

In about a third of families the wife was suffering from anaemia and/or nervous debility, whilst in a quarter of families children were suffering ill health attributable in part to 'growing up in an atmosphere of strain'. The report makes the vital point that: 'the application of a poverty standard to the family income as a whole does not necessarily give a fair picture of the position of each of its members' (p. 110), and goes on to add that poverty is not associated only with unemployment.

An issue that appears in different guises throughout the work is the variability of the experience of unemployment. One source of difference is the woman's skill as manager of scarce resources and the readiness of household members to: 'curtail any form of outside interest involving a cost of more than a penny or two' (p. 104).

This may have proved problematic in some areas; for example in Liverpool it was found that gambling provided a valuable means of social contact and focus of interest for men. As with the other studies referred to above, the importance of casual earnings (for example from lodgers) and odd jobs for the unemployed is stressed, and such income would perhaps go some way to financing social intercourse for the men, although we are not told this.

Areas differed in other respects than male social interaction, and one of the valuable contributions of this report in considering six different towns is to draw attention to the possible influence of different labour market conditions on the way households experience unemployment, and on their differing access to resources.

We learn, for example, that in Crook fuel was obtainable through 'coal picking', that in Liverpool with its busy port the opportunity for casual work was more likely, and the duration of unemployment shorter than, for example, in Leicester. It is also noted that the general level of prosperity in Leicester, however, made it relatively easy for younger members of the family to get work, while in Blackburn a tradition of both male and female employment meant that the probability of a wife as principal earner was higher than elsewhere. It may also be that an established tradition of female earning reduces the blow to the male ego. Another illustration of difference is that for every year of long-term unemployment suffered in Deptford there were 260 years in the Rhondda (Pilgrim Trust, 1938: 43).

Variety between households was also noted in connection with the stage of development the household had reached. Thus the poorest homes were those with large numbers of dependent children. This was the situation for the 25–44 age range; whilst between 45 and 54, earnings of older children improved the standard of living, which fell again between 55 and 64. This latter group were also noted as facing particularly poor employment prospects. Although these sources of difference were not followed through in detailed accounts of household experience, they provide an important advance on the image of a homogeneous army of 'the unemployed'.

The Challenge to Household Relations

The works referred to above have in common a focus on male unemployment within the skilled and unskilled working class, a tendency also present in contemporary research and largely to be accounted for by the high concentration of joblessness in these sections of the population. The findings reported may thus represent a distinctively working-class pattern. It is certainly true of both the US and UK that the higher the occupational status, the lower the vulnerability to unemployment. If we consider, for example, the unskilled and semi-skilled, Ashton (1986: 51) quotes figures for 1982 that show that these workers in the UK made up 18 per cent of the work-force but 41 per cent of the male unemployed, whilst in the US male operatives, non-farm and construction labourers experienced unemployment rates of 21.6 per cent as against an overall rate of 10.9 per cent.

A number of general points emerge from the studies we have so far considered and provide a basis for understanding and further investigating the household effects of male joblessness for the working-class population. The first major factor is the challenge to the man's status within the home, since a cultural and economic pattern that stresses the male provider role means that unemployment may undermine a man's gender identity and self-respect and sometimes, in consequence, his source of authority within the home.

The psychological significance of the man's ability to provide a household income may, however, be distinguished from the instrumental significance of the power of disposal over income in ensuring control within the home; the capacity to enforce decisions and secure response. A tendency for the wife to assume control of finance in cases of male unemployment emerged from all the studies reported. This will have the effect of placing instrumental power in the hands of the woman, as well as possibly further eroding the man's status within the household. Clearly the arrangement is a potential source of conflict, although ideally we need information about the way finances were organized prior to unemployment, and more detail about the handling of money thereafter, to marshall a convincing argument about the effects of job loss.

We should be cautious in viewing the woman's position of notional controller as a privileged one, however, since what is also clear is that with this position goes responsibility for budgeting with insufficient funds, stretching income and adding to its value by additional labour. This point is made in a body of writing that has come to be known as the 'domestic labour debate' (for review see Molyneux, 1979), and emphasizes the importance of domestic labour in turning household income into subsistence. Clearly, if income falls, such labour must increase, and a woman's skills in this area can be a critical factor in determining a household's standard of living, as will the co-operation of household members in reducing their personal calls on that income. A woman's notional control could, for example, be challenged by unpredictable demands for cash from an unreasonable husband.

Analysis of this kind must take care to separate out the effects of unemployment from the effects of poverty, however, for a number of the issues raised above will be as valid for low-wage households as for jobless households. One consequence of the increased importance of the woman's financial role when her husband is unemployed is that arguably the intensity and importance of her sphere of activity is enhanced at a time when her husband's major sphere of activity and his *raison d'être* have been removed. A further problem area associated with this shift in the relative positions of the man and woman is that domestic labour becomes an area of contention. The assumption of domestic work by the man may injure his self-esteem further and disrupt his wife's routine, whilst his failure to take on domestic duties may lead to resentment from his wife. These are problems to which we shall return.

One final and important fact to emerge from the early studies was that despite their focus on predominantly working-class populations, and despite the generalized tendencies detailed above, there is still some scope for variation in the experience of, and responses to, unemployment. Sources of variation identified in early research have been ethnic identity, position in the labour market, access to casual employment, the nature of the local labour market, stage in the life-cycle, older children's earnings, wife's employment and the importance of work as a source of identity. One of the aims of this following chapter will be to examine specific data relating to these differences, and particularly to identify contrasts between the US and UK populations. Firstly, however, we must turn to more recent data on unemployment, to seek confirmation of the general tendencies identified so far, and to locate any signs of change.

Male Breadwinners

One possible source of strain popularly assumed to cause difficulties in household relations is the importance to male identity of the breadwinner role. In both the UK and US there has been speculation that changing views about the importance of work and a relaxing of gender role stereotypes will ease the strain of unemployment (Pahl, 1980; Pahl and Gershuny, 1981; Thomas et al., 1980). Despite this 'optimism', contemporary studies of working-class and white-collar populations reassert the idea of the breadwinner role as an important source of male identity and status within the household. Wilcocke and Franke (1963: 86), in a study of non-managerial staff from five varied plant shut-downs in the US, cite as a common sentiment the remark 'It's hard to keep wearing the pants in your family when you're not making no money', stating: 'They have seen their authority as head of the family slip away when they no longer provide support.'

Similarly, research with redundant workers from British Steel in South Wales (Morris, 1985a: 408) found a strong feeling on the part of both men and women that it is the man's place to be the main wage-earner, and that any other arrangement will necessarily be in some sense stressful for one or both partners. The same feelings were recorded in research among working-class households in the north-east of England, and expressed in statements such as: 'We're brought up to believe in work. It's what the man does; the man's the breadwinner' and 'He feels guilty because he's a man and should be working. You can't change that can you?' (Morris, 1987b: 98).

Role Swap

One significant area of change for both American and British society since the Depression years, however, has been the dramatic rise in employment for married women (for details see chapter 4). In both countries service-sector employment for women has been increasing whilst manufacturing employment for men has simultaneously fallen. Among early popular reactions to these changes in the composition of the labour-force was the assumption that women were taking over from men as principal earners. Such translation of aggregate statistics into household arrangement needs closer inspection, however.

The central questions to be posed are as follows:

1 How is work outside the household distributed among its members?
2 How is work within the household distributed among its members?
3 What is the relationship between these two divisions of labour?

This is to distinguish between the sexual division of labour in paid work outside the home, and the division of domestic labour, or unpaid work, inside the home.

In the UK we find that the wife of an unemployed man is less than half as likely as the wife of a man in employment to have a job herself. The pattern has been described as a process of polarization between working and work-less households (Pahl, 1984; Morris, 1987d), and the tendency appears to have increased over time. In 1973, 55 per cent of the wives of employed men were themselves in paid work, and 34 per cent of the wives of unemployed men. By 1986 the figures were respectively 67 and 24 per cent (GHS, 1986, table 8.23, p. 105). In other words, the likelihood of the wife of an unemployed man being out of work herself has increased, whilst the incidence of wives earning when husbands are also earning has risen.

In the US the pattern is similar but the trend seems to be in the opposite direction. The proportion of wives employed while husbands are unemployed is substantially lower than in the UK; at 19.5 per cent in 1983 (*Monthly Labour Review*, 1984, vol. 107, no. 12) in contrast to a British figure of 30 per cent for the same year. Unlike the UK, however, where the percentage is falling, the US percentage has risen from 17.8 per cent in 1970, although the proportion of wives of working men who are themselves employed has risen more steeply; from 50.8 per cent in 1970 to 64.9 per cent in 1983.

In summary, the tendency for the wives of employed men to have jobs is higher than for the wives of unemployed men, and is rising in both the UK and US, though more steeply in the latter country. The tendency for the wives of unemployed men in the UK to be employed themselves has fallen, whilst in the US the proportion has been rising. Nevertheless it is still more common in the US for a woman whose husband has no job to be unemployed herself than is the case for the UK. Oddly, specific studies of unemployment in the two countries do not seem to reflect these differences. In the UK much work has placed emphasis on the fact that wives are likely to fall out of employment if their husband's unemployment persists (see for example Bell and McKee, 1985; Morris, 1985a, 1987b, 1987c), whilst American studies have often noted the tendency for wives to assume employment when husbands are out of work (see for example Buss et al., 1983: 70; Schlozman and Verba, 1979: 48; Thomas et al., 1980: 520; Wilcocke and Franke, 1963: 77).

Our references to early literature suggested that the challenge to a man's status that comes with unemployment would be intensified if his wife was earning. Although the woman as breadwinner was not a majority solution to male unemployment in either the UK or US, Morris (1985a: 407) reports some isolated instances in the course of research with redundant steel-workers, quoting one man who states:

> While I was out of work I felt I wasn't playing a part in things, ashamed that I wasn't keeping my family. I suppose tension would have been worse if the wife hadn't been working, but I'd spend sleepless nights, I'd get up and come downstairs sometimes, at three in the morning, worrying that I'm the man and it's my job to see that everything's right between these four walls. If it's not then it's my fault.

More recent research in the north-east of England (Morris, 1987c: 94) recorded comments from men about the viability of role reversal, such as: 'It's not possible and it's not natural, I suppose it's class if you come down to it. For the working class it's our system, worked out over hundreds of years, and you can't change it' and 'If a woman gets a job well it's awkward. Men don't like it. It knocks their ego down a bit.'

Another recent study by Jane Wheelock (1986), again focusing on working-class male unemployment, looks specifically at female bread-winner homes, summing up the position among the more traditional cases with the quotation: 'He's a man and a man should be out working.'

These sentiments seem remarkably close to the general impression gleaned from much earlier studies during the Depression years.

Men at Home

One aspect of role reversal that is of interest regardless of the employment status of the woman is the division of domestic labour. An obvious problem posed by unemployment for men is the likelihood of their spending much longer periods of time about the house. In the US, for example, Wilcocke and Franke (1963: 86) mention withdrawal from recreational activities and group contact, and the gradual process of separation of the unemployed workers and their families from the rest of society. The question confronting the men is how their new time in the home is to be spent; they are now, at least potentially, available for domestic labour.

The general tendency in both the UK and US seems to be against the assumption of domestic chores by unemployed men, however. Berk (1985), investigating the apportionment of work in American households, reports on a sample of 748 wives and 358 husbands, covering a wide variety of occupational statuses, and with a level of 17 per cent unemployment among the men. Unfortunately this subsample was not singled out for special attention, but the study does state: 'When one or more factors motivates the husband to withdraw from the labour force (i.e. to work fewer hours), household work is still not the alternative activity to which he is likely to turn his attention' (p. 109). Later in the book we learn that attempts to analyse allocation of time to employment and to household tasks: 'ran afoul of a few "outlier" couples where the husbands were unemployed and did virtually no household labour' (p. 129). They were dropped from the analysis.

A large-scale survey in the UK carried out by Pahl (1984), using inter-views with 730 households on the Isle of Sheppey, reported similar findings. Contrary to popular expectations at the time of research, the common response to male unemployment was not an increase in domestic labour, and in fact the share of domestic work taken by unemployed men is slightly lower than the average for the employed men in the sample (p. 273). We get some idea of how and why this situation might arise from several small-scale studies of unemployment in the UK that have specifically addressed this issue.

In *Workless*, Marsden (1982) discusses the possibility of the unemployed man becoming a housewife. This was a study of unemployment among the skilled and unskilled working class, and although the findings are not presented systematically, a number of important points emerge. We find a general identification of domestic labour as women's work, and a certain amount of defensiveness from women who do not wish to surrender their role, and regard male participation as inappropriate: 'Well it's a woman's job really, isn't it?' (p. 119).

In addition to contention about who should perform domestic labour, the very presence of the man in the home seemed likely to generate tensions and create more work. These findings have been confirmed by other studies.

Bell and McKee (1985: 397) in a small scale study of working class, male unemployment in Birmingham (UK) quote the following comment:

> Sometimes he gets me mad when he's sat in and I'm doing it [the housework] and you've got to keep asking him to move. I mean he just can't sit in the kitchen while I do in here and then come in here while I'm doing the kitchen. . . . In the end I told him I'd give him two quid and I said 'just clear off to the pub'. I said 'I've had enough, just get out of my way so I can get it done.'

Morris (1985c) reports other difficulties: 'It was alright for something to do, but just sort of when I felt like it. She'd keep on at me to get it done straight away and I couldn't see the point' (p. 10). Enthusiasm would wane in the face of a wife who found her routine disrupted and the work not up to her standards: 'It got me down in the end. I'd have a go then she'd come and do it all again anyway' (p. 11), whilst the possible strain on the woman taking the role of main earner is revealed in the comment: 'It wouldn't work. He wouldn't stand it and there'd be more quarrels than it's worth, I'd rather do the work myself. I couldn't stand the strain' (p. 10).

Although these comments convey something of the sentiments against male domestic involvement in traditional working-class society, as well as the problems that might arise between husband and wife, there clearly are homes in which a change in male behaviour occurs as a result of unemployment. How to assess the degree of change, and how to deal with variety in responses, both methodologically and interpretively, has been the focus of two small-scale British studies.

Two Small-scale Studies

1 Redundant steel workers   Morris (1985a: 408) deals with the problem firstly by deriving from her data culturally established spheres of responsibility that guide the division of labour within each home. She goes on to observe that some men will offer help in the 'women's sphere' more readily than others, but nevertheless identifies a core domain of female domestic activity, and asks to what extent there has been any blurring of boundaries in terms of actual behaviour. On this basis she develops a fourfold typology:

(a) Traditional – in which the man offers occasional help in specific areas of domestic labour, notably preparation of food, transport for shopping, help with dishes and playing with children (for short periods).
(b) Traditional-rigid – in which there is no evidence of flexibility in the man's general orientation, nor any actual blurring of boundaries between male and female spheres of responsibility.
(c) Traditional-flexible – in which men have shown a significant degree of adaptability at some point since unemployment but in which domestic organization is nevertheless based on traditional patterns.
(d) Renegotiated – in which the man assumes responsibility for a substantial number of tasks traditionally regarded as 'female', although one can still identify a remnant of the traditional division of labour.

Morris's sample of 40 redundant steel-workers contained 26 men who had experienced significant unemployment since redundancy (the rest quickly found other employment). It is clear that a number of men reacted to unemployment by slightly increasing their contribution to domestic labour but without significantly departing from the traditionally established pattern. In other words, there may be an increase in general tidying about the house, help with the dishes and possibly with food preparation. This seems to have occurred mainly where the woman is gainfully employed, but in no way represented a major assumption of domestic responsibility on the part of the man, and was in almost all cases viewed as a temporary arrangement. On the other hand, in certain cases where the wife lost her own job at the same time as her husband's redundancy there was a contraction in the man's contribution to domestic labour because the wife was then considered to be fully available to carry out such labour herself.

One may, however, see an increase in male participation in domestic labour, but again within the traditional framework outlined, in cases where the woman is not gainfully employed, and usually as a response to boredom on the part of the man. This pattern is likely to be short lived for two reasons. On the one hand the woman usually finds interference disruptive of her own routine, and judges the standard of work performed by her husband to be too low. On the other hand, often in the face of irritation on the part of their wives, men soon tire of domestic work, and anyway seem reluctant to make a commitment to regularly performing particular tasks.

A third and final pattern of response to unemployment on the part of men takes the form of an extreme reaction against any surrender of the traditional division of labour, which will be maintained by their creating some surrogate form of work. Many took on the task of completing major structural alterations to the house – a popular use of redundancy payments – and/or performing tasks for particular individual clients, for which some form of payment – not necessarily in cash – will be made. Alternatively, a man may accept paid employment that is not declared to the welfare authorities. In most cases such bouts of employment are short term and unpredictable. In a few rare instances they will be full time and long term. Slightly more common is a pattern of odd-jobbing which may be for an employer, or an individual client. Whatever the specific circumstances, considerable attempts were made to adhere to a domestic pattern evolved prior to unemployment.

More generally, it was found (Morris, 1985b) that resistance to assuming domestic duties was greater where the man was involved in a predominantly male social network with a high potential for developing and enforcing group norms. Thus:

> The association between social activity and the division of domestic labour for both men and women is quite marked, with a concentration of rigidity in the division of domestic labour coinciding with a collective social pattern for both men and women whilst, conversely, flexibility is highest where social contact is individualistic. (p. 335)

Even the flexible couples, however, retained a clearly recognizable traditional core in the organization of domestic work.

2 Female breadwinners   A particularly helpful, and somewhat unusual British study advances the enquiry into male domestic labour considerably, by adopting a typology similar to that proposed by Morris, but applying it to a very particular sample of households. Wheelock (1986) examines 40 working-class households in which the man is unemployed and the woman employed, though with hours varying from less than 5 to 30 per week. Emphasizing that this arrangement is far from typical of households suffering male unemployment, Wheelock constructs a benchmark against which to assess the division of domestic labour for this particular collection of couples, organizing the data around a core of female tasks. On this basis she develops a typology of traditional-rigid, traditional-flexible, sharing and exchange.

Wheelock finds the sample to be evenly distributed across the four types, which means that even in cases of the wife's employment and husband's unemployment, half adhere to an essentially traditional pattern for domestic labour. The author, however, stresses the potential for adjustment, noting: 'It is . . . very striking that half the couples have distinctly non-traditional forms of organisation for family work, while only a quarter of the sample fall into the traditional-rigid category.'

What is also striking is that the degree of change seems to be closely related to the number of hours worked by the wife (cf. Morris, 1985; Pahl, 1984), which suggests that male employment status may be the wrong focus for our attention.

To resolve the question of the man's assumption of domestic work in unemployment we must turn to individual histories, and look not simply at the division of domestic labour during unemployment, but ask how far men had changed their behaviour as a result of job loss, even if the change is simply from traditional-rigid to traditional-flexible. Wheelock's conclusion here is that there is substantial evidence of change on these grounds, with 20 households moving in a 'non-traditional' direction, and six of these showing a substantial degree of change (1987: 125). We should note, however, that in three households there was movement in the opposite direction – 'regressive change' (p. 126) – and that more generally the degree of change was related to some extent to the woman's hours in employment.

Quantitative Findings

Other recent research on a larger scale has also looked at reverse role households and found 'a substantial redistribution of all household tasks from wives to husbands . . . but . . . even here, women still do more than men' (Laite and Halfpenny, 1987: 229).

Thus, whilst at a gross level we might argue that male unemployment does not produce a reversal of roles either through a majority of women assuming paid employment, or through a majority of men assuming substantial domestic tasks, the evidence suggests a potential for change that may be described (Morris, 1985a: 400) either as a minor adaptation permitting the maintenance of pre-existing sex roles, or as rather the first step in a long process of renegotiation in the domestic division of labour, prompted by a restructuring of the economy. Which of these two interpretations is correct remains open to speculation and debate.

Further progress has been made, however, with data from 1983–4 time budget research (Gershuny et al., 1986). Unemployed men were found to carry out three times as much routine domestic work as men in employment, but less than the non-employed women they were living with.

Reporting on the same data, Thomas et al. (1985) note that the contribution of unemployed men to domestic work fell below that of non-employed and part-time employed women, but above that of women employed full time.

These findings seem at variance with Pahl's data (1984), which suggest that the sexual division of domestic labour is more marked with male unemployment. Definitive conclusions would, however, require longitudinal data on change in individual households, not just a static measurement. Certainly Morris's work suggests that there can be slight shifts perceived by the man as highly significant but which still leave a fairly rigid gender division of labour. We should also bear in mind the possibility of regional cultural variations according to the class composition and work-force characteristics and traditions in particular areas, and Massey (1984) has argued that the contrasts are considerable.

Although the detailed evidence cited has been almost exclusively British it has echoes in statements on the US from Thomas et al. (1980: 522) to the effect that homes where sex roles are more rigidly defined experience the greatest difficulty when the husband is unemployed. Powell and Driscoll (1973), in a study of middle-class unemployment, found the presence of a man in the home who does not participate in domestic tasks to place a strain on husband–wife relations. The same study, however, found that over a period of time couples passed through stages of adjustment to unemployment, and eventually sex role distinctions were reduced with corresponding improvements in marital relations. If adjustment only takes place over the long term, then one would expect less adaptation in the US than in the UK as a result of the more commonly short-term nature of unemployment.

Long-term unemployment has always formed a larger proportion of total unemployment in Britain than in the US. Between 1973 and 1983 the proportion of the unemployed out of work for 12 months or more varied from 13.7 per cent (1975) to 36.2 per cent (1983) in the UK, whilst the lowest and highest proportions in the US were 3.3 per cent (1973) and 13.3 per cent (1983) (Ashton, 1986: 95–6). Correspondingly, the incidence of short-term unemployment in the US is much higher. Spells of unemployment lasting less than five weeks made up proportions of the total which varied from 22.2 per cent (1973) to 8.6 per cent (1982) in Britain, and from 51.0 per cent (1973) to 33.3 per cent (1983) in the US, suggesting a higher rate of movement between jobs in the latter case. In other words, the US generates a high turnover of short-term jobs, and whilst in Britain job security is higher, long-term unemployment is a more common experience.

Thus the British data on the minimal domestic adjustments that follow male unemployment are sufficient to sound a note of caution when assessing suggestions of greater adaptation in the US. Given the generally shorter duration of American unemployment we must be sceptical of speculation about the adaptive potential of working-class families that claims to identify: 'changes in sex-role stereotyping, such that unemployment and a working wife is not so great a threat to the husband's self-esteem, and families are consequently able to adapt to changes brought on by male unemployment' (Thomas et al., 1980: 523). The statement certainly sits oddly against the low proportion of employed wives with unemployed husbands in the US, which as we noted is lower even than the UK, although now rising.

Household Finance and Unemployment

Conceptions of the financial strain imposed by unemployment are some-what varied. Though Thomas et al. (1980) are in no doubt voicing widely held views, which are in some sense accurate, when they state for the US that: 'For the majority of the population today, society has provided a financial floor beneath which they are not allowed to sink' (p. 520), such a view underestimates the substantial strains imposed by a reduction of income. It is perhaps significant that the article in which this statement is made reports on a study of unemployed professionals who may have had considerable resources to call upon in unemployment.

Within working-class homes one effect of unemployment consistently reported is the shortage of money, which is argued to create tensions within marriage and to enforce sacrifices from all household members. Wilcocke and Franke (1963), in their survey of non-managerial unemployment in the US, note the universality of financial problems, though indicating variations of degree. They report the need to cut back not only on luxuries but on what had previously been considered to be necessities, thus incor-porating a notion of relative deprivation that seems to be absent from the view expressed by Thomas et al.

Wilcocke and Franke found a large majority had dipped into and often exhausted their savings, and cite cases of the sale of personal property, and moves to less expensive accommodation. They concede, however, that these more drastic responses were uncommon during the first year when adjustment rather took the form of day-to-day economizing: 46 per cent cut back on necessities, 30 per cent reduced spending across the board and 24 per cent reduced recreational spending. Reductions increased with duration of employment, and although severance pay had an important ameliorating effect, this was only short term. Again, then, we might expect the American and British accounts to vary as duration of employment varies.

The position adopted by Thomas et al. (1980) argues that the systems of welfare that have been introduced since the Depression years serve to secure the living standards of the unemployed. Research in the UK has come to challenge this view, arguing that recent developments give cause for concern about the living standards of the unemployed. Bradshaw et al. (1983) examine income, expenditure and availability of consumer durables, making a distinction between long-term, medium-term and short-term unemployment (over 52 weeks, 14–52 weeks or 13 weeks and less). These homes were then compared with households of employed men. In concluding their study the authors state: 'the cumulative weight of evidence suggests that the living standards of the long-term unemployed are lower than those in short-term unemployment and that the living standards of both are below those of the poorest families in work'.

Popay (1985: 181) notes that a quarter of unemployed people on supplementary benefit were in arrears with rents, rates or mortgages. She also states that research has indicated that poor families try to make ends meet by cutting back on food. Overall consumption has been found to be low, meals monotonous and nutritional balance lacking.

Finance and Marital Strain

Marsden's book *Workless* (1982) notes the importance of casual earnings for the unemployed man, because this means he need not take from his wife to finance whatever social life he may try to maintain (p. 140). This seems to indicate that benefit payments went to the woman, while the man's illicit earnings were under his personal power of disposal. We also learn that such earnings may be used to make minor contributions to housekeeping money.

Morris's research on redundant steel-workers looks systematically at these questions. In dealing with household finance she makes the distinction (1984a: 494) between *household income*, the total income of all household members, and *domestic income*, that proportion of household income available for spending on collective needs.

The research was carried out in South Wales, where there seemed to be a normative prescription to the effect that during unemployment benefit payments should be given over entirely to 'domestic income' (that is, spending on collective needs) and this money was usually in the hands of the wife. Surprisingly, however, all but three of the 21 cases using this method had had the same arrangement prior to redundancy. Thus female control of income must be associated with some factor other than unemployment, which was effective prior to the man's job loss. Morris suggests that this other factor may simply be scarcity of resources, for large numbers of children and/or low wages can produce the same effect. This would mean that with male unemployment we may simply be witnessing a strengthening of an already existing tendency for minimal income to be managed by the wife, a suggestion that was seen to emerge from the early studies of unemployment reviewed at the start of this chapter.

We can explain the pattern by arguing that when resources are limited and close budgeting required it is most easily deal with by one person, that is by 'unitary control' of income. Given the need to place priority on basic requirements such as food, heating and accommodation, and given a sexual division of labour that associates the woman with the domestic sphere, she is the person most appropriate to manage resources. One obvious implication of this system is the absence of any formal access to money for the man. In other words, when income is low (for example in benefit-dependent homes) it is likely that all income is turned over to domestic income, and no allocation will be made for the man's spending.

In South Wales, and many other working-class areas, there is a strong pattern of male social activity that requires financial expenditure, and is regarded by women as being somehow necessary for men: 'Well I've got the house and the children. I don't really like to go out. But it's different for a man' (p. 504); 'I never go out myself except for a special do, but men need to really don't they. It's different for a woman, she sees her friends anyway. If he couldn't go out he just wouldn't see anyone' (p. 505).

The burden of decision making about areas of spending can clearly be a heavy one, added to the increase in domestic labour necessary to stretch inadequate income by mending clothes, shopping selectively, cooking cheaply, economizing on fuel. Marital harmony can depend on how well a wife does this and how readily her husband accepts her decisions:

> If you're a good manager they think you're the bank of England. It's not a question of me deciding if we can afford it. If he wants it he's got to have it. . . . But some days I'd come down and he'd just be sitting in the chair. By the end of the day I couldn't stand it any longer, I'd take a pound out of my purse and say 'Look just take this and get out . . .' (p. 506)

Such instances lie behind the argument that a neglected area of unemployment studies is the disproportionate burden borne by the wife.

Summary

We have found in this chapter that, despite a growth in women's employment, role reversal, that is employment for the wife, is not a common

solution to problems faced by households experiencing male unempl⌐
ment. In the US it occurs rather less often than in the UK, and in eitʰⁱⁱ
country additional problems tend to follow in its wake. Such findings must
place some doubt on the validity of an approach to the sexual division of
labour based on assumptions about the rational deployment of labour
resources within the household. Thus the comparative advantage (Becker,
1981) and flexible strategies (Pahl, 1980) perspectives are not entirely
convincing. The problems posed by male unemployment are all related to
issues concerning the internal dynamics and organization of the household,
and a simple deployment of labour approach alone is not adequate for
complete understanding. Male unemployment seems to pose three distinct
problems:

1 A challenge to gender identities that had previously revolved around the
   man as main provider.
2 The adjustment by household members to a reduced income, in the
   majority of cases managed by women who often bear a disproportionate
   burden of the loss.
3 The disruption, and possible renegotiation of responsibility for domestic
   labour.

These problems all apply to the experience of unemployment in both the
UK and US, though with minor differences, notably that unemployment in
the US is of generally shorter duration, and long-term adaptation will be
called for in only a minority of the homes affected.

More generally, however, it is clear that there is room for considerable
variation in responses to unemployment at the level of the household.
Research has tended to focus on that class that has the highest experience of
unemployment, and on the household organization most likely to be undermined by unemployment, that is the nuclear family household. Even so
there are signs of considerable variety. There will be differences in experience and responses within this group, and between this and other social
groupings, and in many cases their explanation will lie outside the boundaries of the household. The next chapter will explore the source and nature
of variety in unemployment, and will place particular emphasis on contrasts
between Britain and America.

3 The Variable Experience of Male Unemployment

The previous chapter attempted to identify some general features of the experience of unemployment. Through reference to current literature for both the UK and US, as well as historical works dating back to the thirties and forties, there emerged an image, albeit a patchy one, of the commonest household effects of male unemployment. There are a number of problems implicit in such an exercise, especially if part of the objective is to introduce an element of comparison. On a practical level one encounters the difficulties of using studies not designed for comparability in attempts to identify similarities and differences between regions, countries or social groups. An additional but related problem is the tendency for studies of unemployment to concern themselves with the skilled and unskilled white working class, which limits the range of possibilities and the scope of recorded variation.

Differences in the degree of exposure to unemployment, that is duration, vulnerability, distribution by race and class, and so on, as well as evidence of variety in individual experiences, suggest that the search for a general picture will inevitably be in some sense a frustrated endeavour. This chapter, then, rather than seeking to make general statements, will examine the literature available that offers some insight into sources of difference in household responses to male unemployment. Although aggregate information on employment and unemployment trends tells us little about the experience of individuals and members of their households, such statistics can provide data on the social and economic context in which that experience occurs. They may well prove to be an underexploited key to variations in the experience of unemployment.

Our data in the introductory chapter have highlighted differences between the UK and US in, for example, average duration of unemployment and the extent of short-term employment, although the two countries have in common patterns of vulnerability in youth and old age, and among ethnic minority groups. Such information suggests that the experience of unemployment may vary with position in the labour market both in terms of class background and prospects for future employment, material resources for survival, the existence of a similarly placed reference group, the development of subcultural norms to deal with unemployment, and the degree of localization or spatial concentration.

Differences that may be traced back to social structural factors will, however, be cross-cut by other influences, notably position in the life-course, such that the experience of unemployment will be coloured by the characteristics of the household in which it occurs, not least in terms of the number and variety of people involved. An expanding body of literature is now concerned to make the point that more than one person is affected by job loss, that many male workers have dependants, and members of their household may suffer both materially and psychologically, with relationships in the home being disrupted. These are important factors in our understanding of household variations in the effects of unemployment.

Dependants

One obvious source of variety will be the nature and structure of the household in which unemployment occurs, although this can in turn be related to class and/or ethnicity. Popay (1985) has summarized statistical evidence concerning the numbers and types of families affected by male unemployment in the UK. Prefacing her argument with the note that official figures are an underestimate of unemployment rates, she firstly states that married men are less likely to become unemployed than single, widowed or divorced men (8 per cent in 1981 compared with 14 per cent for the single group). However, if married men alone are considered, then the unemployment rate is higher for those with dependent children. In 1981 married men without children constituted 20 per cent of unemployed men, whilst those with children accounted for 34 per cent.

Other important points made in this article are that although the unmarried are at greatest risk of unemployment, married men with children are more likely to remain out of work long term (Popay, 1985: 177), and that as UK unemployment rose, fathers of large families experienced a sharp rise in vulnerability as compared to fathers of smaller families. In December 1980 there were 0.75 million children in households with a husband/father receiving benefit because of unemployment. By 1983 the figure had risen to

1.2 million. This may of course be a class effect, for family size increases as we move down the class ladder, as does vulnerability to unemployment.

The pattern of vulnerability is markedly different in the US, however. Of married couples with no earners, only 8.1 per cent have dependent children in contrast to 48.5 per cent of all married couples (cf. Schlozman and Verba, 1979). The concentration of unemployment in marriage, then, is where there are no dependent children (MLR, 1984, December, vol. 107, no. 12). Similarly, while 3.4 per cent of married couples with a husband earning have four children under 18, this is true of only 1.4 per cent of couples with no earners (MLR, 1984, December, vol. 107, no. 12).

In the UK the general pattern was reversed. In 1984 66 per cent of unemployed married men had dependent children, in contrast to 56 per cent of employed married men, whilst 6 per cent of unemployed married men had four or more children and only 2 per cent of employed married men. There have been attempts to explain these concentrations by looking at the incentive/disincentive effects of benefit. In the UK benefit rises with additional children, whilst in the US the welfare system extends to households with an unemployed father in only 23 out of 50 states.

Life-cycle and Unemployment

It is no surprise, in view of the data above, that one approach to the variable impact of unemployment has been to look at the significance of stage in the life-cycle. The argument here is that most individuals in negotiating a path through their biological and social development will enter into various states of co-operation with, and incur numerous obligations towards, a number of other individuals, principally parents, mate(s) and children. The implications carried by specific events for the social groupings that emerge will vary with different types of decisions and problems characterizing particular stages of life-cycle development. Thus at each stage the individual, family or household will be confronted by different sorts of demands and will be in a position to martial different kinds of resources to meet them.

Pahl (1984) makes this point in his book *Divisions of Labour*, which sets out to document the 'work strategies' of households on the Isle of Sheppey. The study posed the questions: what sorts of labour do household members perform, and what sorts of labour do they call upon? He makes the point that the household is a constantly changing unit, and that the work provided by, and supplied to, different households is mediated by the intervening variable of stage in the domestic cycle.

A similar point has been made by other writers with specific reference to the effects of unemployment. Fagin (1984), focusing on the nuclear family household, argues that the impact of unemployment will be different at different stages in the life-cycle, and that problems will be greatest and experienced most frequently in transitional phases of development. He cites examples such as changes in the marital relationship through delayed entry to the next stage in the cycle; the erosion of a marriage as the woman demands more assistance with young children; the man's feelings of exclusion on the birth of children; and his loss of authority over older children. In his analysis Fagin repeats the point made by earlier writers (see Komarovsky, 1940) that unemployment simply brings out existing strengths and weaknesses in the family, but suggests through case studies that these may be related to stage in the cycle. Jackson's argument (1986) follows similar lines: 'Family responsibilities will vary with the structure of the family (whether the man is head of the household, how many dependent children he has and what are their ages), and will in turn alter the effect of unemployment on psychological health.' He reports on a study of unskilled and semi-skilled men in England and Wales, carried out in 1982, which makes some interesting findings on financial strain and life-cycle development.

This work has been published by Warr and Jackson (1984), who note that the biggest drop in income was experienced by married men under 35 without dependants, and by those who are divorced or separated. These groups received less than half their previous income. The smallest drop to only two-thirds was experienced by single men under 20 years, and married men with preschool children. This, says Jackson, may be because means-tested supplementary benefit (now income support) rises with number of dependants, but despite this, married men with young children report the highest level of money worries. It is not surprising, then, that this group showed a high employment commitment, although Jackson suggests this may be as much a psychological need to fill the breadwinner role as a purely financial need. The finding nevertheless is a caution against explaining high levels of unemployment in large nuclear families by the disincentive effects of the benefit system.

In his work Jackson makes the observation that financial stress is the result of imbalance between needs and resources, and may vary between countries according to how benefit systems accommodate family structures. Reporting on research in the US, Moen (1979) investigates the possibility that duration of unemployment may be affected by stage in the life-cycle, periods without work being shorter where work incentive because of financial need is greater, that is where there are young children present. The data seem not to support this suggestion, for the number of children was unrelated to *duration* of unemployment for male family heads, and both male and female household heads were more likely to have extended periods of unemployment when there were no other income earners in the home (p. 566).

The Life-cycle and the Labour Market

Moen's article does take an important step towards broadening the speculation and debate about life-cycle effects by implying a relationship between the life-cycle and position in the labour market. Moen argues: 'The relationship between life-cycle stage and the duration of unemployment for both men and women reflects both the absence of job seniority and job skills by young parents. At the very time when financial need may be greatest (when children are under 6) unemployed family heads lack the skills required for rapid reemployment.'

Morris (1987a) makes a similar point from research in the north-east of England. She argues against the limitations of too rigid a use of notions of domestic or family cycle and the implication of a stable model of progression within which changes in economic and social life are accommodated, and through which they are mediated. The suggestion is that attention should be focused less exclusively on the internal dynamic or 'requirements' of family or household development, but rather on the external constraints imposed, especially in periods of economic change, on the very form and nature of that development.

Her argument is that the way members of different households perceive and respond to their situation will differ according to position in the family and domestic cycle, not simply because of constraints peculiar to that position, but also because of the changing attitudes and expectations towards work and gender roles brought about by different experiences in the labour market. By a series of case studies Morris argues that established patterns of inter- and intra-generational progression have been disrupted by changes in opportunities for employment, and that at different stages of development households will be facing different labour market conditions, with different prospects of employment, and occupying different positions in the housing market. As a result a newly married man in his early twenties may be denied the possibility of treading the same path through the life-course as that taken by his father; the timing and manner of entry into different life-cycle stages and relationships between generations may be radically altered. Some aspects of such change are illustrated by the comments of an unemployed 24-year-old man in the north-east of England:

> If we're stuck over a bill I'll go to my parents. My dad's retired now, and I don't like to have to ask him. I should be helping him out. All

his kids are on the dole, and in a way he's worried about it more than we are. My dad's worked all his life and he thinks we should have a chance to do the same. . . . I've always thought of my dad as working. I wasn't proud of it at the time but when I look back I am. He worked hard to bring me up, and what am I doing? Living off the state. And my kids can only look at me and their memory will be of me sitting about the house all day in an armchair like an old man, and they'll know the state's brought them up, not me.   (p. 200)

Bound up with this image of the father–child relationship is both a notion of duty to one's children, the obligation to provide for them through one's own labour and an image of gender identity.

There remains, however, the possibility that these expectations could change given a high level of long-term unemployment among the young; that is if an alternative view of how to organize family and domestic relations grew up that was not work related. This question draws attention to the significance of yet another variable, duration of unemployment, which may be age related and thus coincide with, or bring influence to bear on, the nature of household structure and domestic organization through the life-cycle.

Duration of Unemployment

Whilst the UK and US share a tendency for unemployment to be concentrated among the young and the old, long-term unemployment has always made up a larger proportion of the unemployed in Britain. The US generates a high turnover of short-term jobs in relation to the UK, where job security has to date been stronger and where long-term unemployment is more of a problem.

Warr and Jackson (1984) have investigated some of the correlates of age and duration of unemployment, finding that length of unemployment is associated with deteriorating health, increased financial strain and the decreased probability of a wife's employment. The results relating to financial strain may partly be explained by the concentration of unemployment in Britain among the low paid (see chapter 1) who are also likely to have the largest number of dependants, class and family size being correlated nationally. It is, however, among the youngest workers, many without dependants and experiencing less financial strain, that duration of unemployment is longest, but this will have implications for household formation that have yet to be fully investigated. It is perhaps within this group that one would expect change in dominant values and gender role behaviour, although Morris (1987a) has suggested, on the basis of research in the north-east of England, that the birth of children seems to encourage a shoring up of established ideas about gender.

Although Warr and Jackson indicate that stress will be greatest for the middle age range with dependants, these people are at least more favourably placed than other age groups in the search for work. This is partly to be attributed to the possession of relevant skills and experience, as well as the increased significance of informal access to employment in times of job scarcity (see Morris, 1984b, 1987c, 1987d). Thus whilst the middle age ranges of married men with dependants may suffer most stress with unemployment, they have a better chance of finding work, and whilst younger single workers without dependants may be less stressed, and possibly most likely to develop an alternative value system, they are likely to be inhibited in household and family formation.

The general picture in the US will be similar in that long-term unemployment is highest among the young, but there are a number of contrasting points to be made. It is generally the case, as we noted in chapter 1, that unemployment is less likely to be long term, and is more evenly distributed throughout the population, showing a much lower concentration among low-paid workers than in the UK. This is partly to be interpreted as an indication of greater insecurity among those in employment. The result for the unemployed may, however, be less stress and a more limited duration out of work. We should bear in mind, however, that a man's unemployment benefit in the US will be terminated after a maximum of 26 weeks (*Social Security Bulletin*, 1986) and there is no equivalent to the UK supplementary benefit, though 23 of the 50 states pay Aid to Families with Dependent Children (AFDC) where the father is unemployed. It may be, then, that despite shorter durations, unemployment is much more stressful financially in the US than in the UK, especially since job loss is likely to be a repeated experience. The wider distribution of unemployment in the US population may, however, mean that sufferers are less affected by feelings of failure, inadequacy and social stigma.

Social Class and Unemployment

Clearly we may expect differences between social classes and occupational categories in vulnerability to, and duration of unemployment. Although, as we have pointed out, the US has a wider distribution of unemployment than the UK, the pattern of vulnerability in both countries is similar. The most badly affected groups are the young, old, unskilled and semi-skilled, women and blacks. When it comes to understanding the experience of unemployment, distribution by class may affect perceptions of unemployment, and social classes may differ both materially and culturally in their ability to deal with the experience.

As we have noted, specialized studies have tended to concentrate on the white, working-class male, but there is some material available that concerns itself with midde-class and professional unemployment. This may, at least in the UK, be a response to the fact that recent economic decline has had some impact on all social groupings, not just on the traditionally vulnerable groups. Comparisons are difficult in the absence of data specifically designed for such a purpose, but the same general themes arise in work on middle-class households as on working-class homes.

Berthoud (1979), in a study of 636 unemployed professionals and executives in the UK, noted feelings of inadequacy in failure to provide for families, and constraints on socializing as a result of reduced income. These feelings were found to worsen over time, especially when prospects of re-employment were poor. Poverty as such was due less to an absolute shortage of funds than to the degree of disruption of previous styles and standards of living. Of those without an employed spouse, 14 per cent of the sample had an income of less than a quarter of previous earnings, and 53 per cent less than half. These figures should be compared with Warr and Jackson's findings (1984) among the semi-skilled and unskilled unemployed that 9 per cent had an income of less than a quarter and 31 per cent of less than a half of previous earnings. In other words, the unemployed working class suffer less of a reduction, but this is because of lower previous earnings, which presumably means they have fewer resources to draw upon.

It is significant that 53 per cent of the Berthoud (middle-class) sample reported drawing on savings or capital, and 40 per cent of the men had earning wives (82 per cent of the women had earning husbands). Of those whose spouse was in employment, 18 per cent had an income of less than half of previous earnings. If an unemployed professional male is married to a professional woman she would be less likely to give up her career because of benefit disincentives than a woman in unrewarding, poorly paid work. Such a reversal of the traditional 'breadwinning' role will lead to other problems, however, given the reported feelings of inadequacy through failure to meet family responsibilities. One might expect less attachment to traditional roles with non-manual, middle-class employment, in contrast to the high degree of gender segregation associated with working-class culture, but a number of studies (Edgell, 1980; Pahl, 1971) call this assumption into question.

Some evidence on general household responses, gender roles and marital relations in cases of male professional unemployment in the US is provided in a study by Powell and Driscoll (1973). The authors report on discussions with 25 male unemployed scientists and engineers, and interviews with an additional 50 male professionals. They present their findings with reference to four stages: relaxation and relief; concerted effort; vacillation and doubt; malaise and cynicism. In the first phase they note that family relations remain normal, and in the second phase state, at least for those with previous experience of unemployment: 'When it was possible for the wives to work this reversal of roles was handled smoothly' (p. 21).

By stage three, however, they argue that family relations are 'severely impaired' with marital relations under heavy strain:

> Seeing her husband fail to obtain a job and then apparently fall into periods of no activity at all, a wife badgers her husband to try harder, or begins to doubt his ability and transmits these concerns to him. Already doubting himself and wondering if he will ever find a job, the husband often responds acrimoniously to well-intentioned queries about how things are going and what should be done if he doesn't soon find a job.

Powell and Driscoll also note that where the man is not actively seeking work but still expects his wife to do all the domestic work then these problems are exacerbated: 'In homes where the roles are strictly defined the difficulties were most severe. The problems intensified when the wife considers going back to work' (p. 23). This statement is in marked contrast to the 'smooth handling' referred to in an earlier phase, and suggests a response to unemployment not dissimilar to that of working-class couples.

The strain on the wife reported in this US study is confirmed in a British study of the wives of the managerial unemployed. Jean Hartley (1987) reports on interviews with 18 wives of unemployed middle and senior managers in 1975–6. Six wives worked part time and one worked intermittently, two worked full time, and nine were housewives. Describing this sample Hartley states: 'with hardly any exception, we see here the traditional middle class marriage with employment centred husband and home centred wife, and the acceptance of the hidden contract' (p. 123).

This term is used by Gowler and Legge (1978) to denote a commitment by the wife to further her husband's career and contain domestic distractions. The arrangement is described by Finch (1983) as being 'married to the job' and is a peculiarly middle-class phenomenon.

Wives tended to have ambivalent feelings about this arrangement, and as a result some expressed relief at their husband's unemployment and the chance to spend time together. Contrary to the view found in some studies of working-class unemployment (Bell and McKee, 1985; Morris, 1985a) that a male presence in the home leads to conflict, many women enjoyed their husband's company, though a few felt that he interfered with established routine. None felt the husband should have to partake in housework, though some resented the extra chores his presence brought. Whilst none of the men took over domestic work, most did increase their participation. With the exception of only two couples, no dramatic role reversal occurred and couples maintained the relationship they had prior to unemployment. Hartley raises the interesting question of who in such circumstances 'supports the supporters' (p. 134), a topic that invites some consideration of the social world in which the household is located.

In general it seems that apart from the different nature of financial strain – changed life-style rather than absolute hardship among professionals – working-class and middle-class households have remarkably similar experiences of unemployment. The major difference seems to be the extent to which a wife's identity depends upon her husband's career; a middle-class pattern. The indications are that similar difficulties arise in both the US and UK so that in seeking to identify differences within populations we would need to refer to questions of the duration of unemployment, the degree of support available from family and friends, the extent to which the job was the sole basis of identity, the previous experience of unemployment, and the extent to which it is a familiar and non-stigmatized condition in particular social settings.

Whilst one would predict differences on most of these dimensions, there is insufficient evidence for categorical statements. In general one might expect middle-class unemployment to represent a greater challenge to identity, more social stigma, less locally available support (because of a tendency to geographical mobility) but possibly more material support and access to savings. Powell and Driscoll reported better adjustment among professionals who had previous experience of unemployment, and such experience would be more common among the working class, as would the presence of family and friends who previously or currently shared the experience. Moral support might also be more available within the working class, and feelings of stigmatization would probably be reduced, though access to material resources would be more limited. Personal identification with manual work seems less likely than with professional employment but, nevertheless, across classes it seems true that male gender identity is bound up with paid work.

All of the problems noted seem to have repercussions on marital relations which are broadly similar whatever the social class – though with room for variation. In seeking class contrasts, however, it should not be forgotten that within the working class one finds substantial variation, and that industrial decline in both America and Britain has meant a first-time experience of unemployment for members of the skilled white working class currently in middle age, and firmly conditioned into the ideal of full employment.

The Black Family and Unemployment

The question of variable responses to unemployment is further complicated by the introduction of racial or ethnic differences. Debate about the nature of black family structure and its causes has been running in the US for some time, especially since the publication of the now notorious Moynihan report (1965) on the 'disorganization' or 'deterioration' of the black family. The debate revolves around the question of whether the high rate of female-headed households among the black American population is due to a black subculture or is simply the result of economic constraints that produce an effect at odds with the values, ambitions and beliefs about marriage held by the black and white populations alike.

Staples (1985) has compiled some interesting data on this question. His argument is that the ideology of most blacks is 'in the direction of traditional family forms' (p. 1006) despite the increase over the last 30 years of black female headship. The majority of adult black women over 14 were separated, divorced, widowed or never married, whilst the rate of 'failure' of black marriages is much higher than for white marriages. Two out of three black marriages will eventually dissolve, in contrast to one out of two white marriages. The 'deterioration' of the black family noted by Moynihan has been argued by others (for example Stack, 1974) to be a rational response to deteriorating economic conditions.

Staples (1985) argues that whilst black culture applauds traditional gender roles, notably motherhood for women with the man as provider, the economic position of the black American male is such that he is often unable to perform this role. He cites a study by Joe and Yu (1984) that concludes that 46 per cent of the 8.8 million black men of working age were not in the labour-force, added to which there are a half million more black women over the age of 14 than black men. Staples goes on to argue not only that employment problems have been associated with marital disruption (see Hampton, 1980), but that the more successful black males tend to marry outside the race. Black women are, as a result, choosing to have children and raise them alone, encouraged by a welfare system that in 27 states requires men to be absent from the home for the payment of AFDC.

Joe and Yu (1984) illustrate the scale and direction of change in the circumstances of black families by noting that 75 per cent of black men were working in 1960 and black families headed by women accounted for 21 per cent of all black families that year. By 1982 only 54 per cent of black men were in the labour-force and 42 per cent of all black families were headed by women. Female headed families are in the same study, projected to be 59 per cent of all black families with children by 1990, when almost

75 per cent of black children will be living in these families and 70 per cent of blacks with incomes below poverty level will belong to these families.

This argument does not preclude the possibility that whilst the reason for female headship in the black population is the weak labour market position of the black male, a justificatory set of values can grow up around these circumstances. This process is sharply illustrated by Liebow's book *Tally's Corner* (1967). His argument is that black marriage breaks down or never takes place due to economic strain, but as a means of concealing this failure the black male population evolves a protective set of values that places emphasis on individual freedom, sexual infidelity and drinking, all of which are inimical to marriage. The cause of breakdown then becomes not only failure to provide for wife and children (p. 215) but a catalogue of highly praised 'manly flaws' (p. 116).

These same issues have received much less attention in the UK, where the presence of a black population has a shorter history. There has, however, been an increase in single parenthood and especially in the black population (see chapter 8), which suggests the argument set out above may carry some weight. Unemployment among black youth is disproportionately high in both the UK and US; respectively 22.8 and 23.2 per cent in 1982. Although the benefit system in the UK does not require the absence of the man as in some American states, the rate will be more generous for single parents, whilst single parenthood ensures eligibility independent of the man, and also means a high priority ranking for public-sector housing.

Black Networks

Another aspect of black family structure that has figured in an American literature on poverty rather than unemployment *per se*, has focused on 'survival strategies', an approach close to the perspective more recently developed in the UK by Ray Pahl (1984). The notion was introduced in a literature concerned with third-world or ghetto poverty (Lomnitz, 1977; Peattie, 1968; Stack, 1974) that documents the routinized flow of information and aid across household boundaries. The central argument is that unreliable or non-existent employment opportunities for men produce conditions conducive to the development of elaborate female-centred networks of mutual support. Such networks have been taken to characterize the poor black population of the US and are often cited to counter the alleged 'disorganization' (Moynihan, 1965) of the black family.

It is thus unsurprising that American literature on the extended family and patterns of aid tends to focus on the black population. Hofferth (1984: 795) reports that in 1976 7 per cent of white and 20 per cent of black husband–wife families with children were extended (that is included other relatives in the household). She sets out to explore the conditions under which kin ties are important, focusing specifically on socio-economic need.

Hofferth cites a number of studies that have shown stronger kin ties among blacks than among whites (Allen, 1979; Angel and Tienda, 1982; Hays and Mindel, 1973; Soldo and Lauriate, 1976) and notes their role in shaping strategies for coping with poverty. Stack's work provides an illustration of how important such supportive networks can be: 'In the flats the responsibility for providing food, care, clothing and shelter, and for socializing children within domestic networks can be spread over several households' (p. 90).

Hofferth's argument, however, is that race is not the crucial feature in such patterns of support, but single parenthood. This we have already seen to be associated with male unemployment rather than simply with a cultural tendency. It nevertheless remains likely that some kind of legitimating or justificatory position is likely to emerge, especially where there are high concentrations of black unemployment. A highly developed network of mutual aid that spans household boundaries may thus be seen as a cultural adaptation to economic stress. It may not, however, be ethnically specific.

Social Support

Research focusing specifically on male unemployment and not confined to the black population has developed the idea of a network of mutual support as one component in the 'household response'. Speculation about the possibility of the informal sector of the economy providing an alternative to formal employment (Pahl, 1980) has long since been abandoned. Nevertheless, there are a variety of ways in which social networks can operate as a channel for informal aid, or earning opportunities, which become especially important for households facing male unemployment and/or reduced income. The availability of such assistance or its absence can be a significant influence on the manner in which a household deals with unemployment (Morris, 1987b).

We saw in chapter 2 that different network patterns have been found to be associated with differing degrees of male involvement in domestic labour (Morris, 1984a, 1985b). The same research also reports that sources of informal income for men varied from odd jobs for neighbours in return for a flagon of beer, payment for odd-jobbing, assistance from male relatives, occasional days or weeks work for a local employer 'off the books' (that is undeclared), or more rarely long-term undeclared unemployment. Such earnings usually finance some social activity for the man, although they may be used to meet a household emergency.

For women, common sources of additional income are mail-order commission, selling parties or child minding for friends or relatives. The use of the income is invariably to increase housekeeping money or for spending on children. Common to both men and women is the access to resources by virtue of membership of a network of contacts, and the wider it stretches the greater the opportunities will be.

The network can therefore be a differentiating influence between households by virtue of the resources it offers. There is very little systematic research into this area but a number of studies contain indicative comment or data. McKee (1987) in a study of the households of white working-class males, summarizes her findings thus:

> It has been shown that there is considerable diversity amongst unemployed households in their degree of access to resources. Some households could depend on considerable support from their families, and the range of resources provided was extensive and freely offered and accepted. There were examples of cohesive, mutually supporting households and networks, and examples of isolated, fragmented households' (p. 114)

Marsden (1982: 114–15) documents the kinds of aid and understanding that flow between working-class men in an area of high unemployment with a tradition of collective male social contact, though he makes the important point that: 'Any flow of cash from men in work to the workless on skid row was probably small, and remained in the men's world to subsidize drinking.' Similar exchanges of aid passed between women, but was directed to the task of providing for basic household needs (p. 116, cf. Morris, 1985b).

Binns and Mars (1984) have begun to investigate the nature of differences in social support patterns, contrasting the relatively full social life with reciprocal obligations and expectations sometimes superseding extended kin relations of the young, and the relative social isolation of the older unemployed. As with other research, the mother–daughter tie is identified as an enduring source of material help with, for example, food, clothes and household items, and an emphasis is placed on the local nature of such connections. It becomes clear, however, that even in exchanges between kin there is a considerable variety. Some couples expressed a preference for formal agencies of support, either as a wish to conceal need from kin or in appreciation of their similarly reduced circumstances.

Like most of the research on support networks, Binns and Mars fall short of any clear categorization of types or explicit attempts at explanation. They do, however, offer some important insights, notably their reference to:

> involvement in an extended chain of sociability providing access to a network which can offer emotional, symbolic and perhaps material

support within a shared cultural environment. Such networks help to sustain shared definitions of priorities which give primacy or at least legitimacy to non-work-oriented relationships and activities. These then become uniting forces within the networks – which display sub-cultural features. (p. 686)

This statement is useful since it draws attention to the importance of proximity, both social and geographical, in the generation of mutual support and a sustaining counter-ideology for the unemployed. It suggests, however, that we might expect to find class differences and locality differ-ences – and certainly many cases where social stigma and isolation may accompany unemployment.

Berthoud's (1979) study of middle-class unemployment gives hints of diversity which are not developed. For example, two different respondents are quoted as follows: 'I did not want to tell any of my friends if I could help it, so we became very isolated' and 'Friends are very good but it makes a difference when you can't pull your weight' (p. 23).

Powell and Driscoll (1973), writing on middle-class unemployment in the US, note that previous experience of being out of work can make adjust-ment easier. Those who had been unemployed in the past were more open about telling others and more able to adopt appropriate job search strategies. It is generally observed, however, that at least in the early stages, friends and neighbours were supportive. As time out of work continued, however, relationships with others became restricted to a very few close friends and relatives: 'Though the reasons vary a major factor is that the family altered their life style to accommodate the husband's unemployment. It was easier for them to stay at home than to be with acquaintances whose way of life is now very different from theirs' (p. 25).

Clearly class and locality differences require more systematic investi-gation, and involve complexities that make blanket comparison inappropri-ate. The key focus would seem to be the local social setting – how generally familiar is the experience of unemployment, what traditions of mutual aid exist and what alternative sources of social identity are available. All of these factors will affect the feelings of stigmatization attaching to unemploy-ment, and the sources of both material and psychological support.

Social and Spatial Segregation

One important influence on these sources of variation is the extent to which they correspond to social and or spatial concentrations of unemployment. Payne (1987), using data from the UK General Household Survey, has demonstrated a tendency for unemployment to be concentrated within families, and has offered some possible explanations – a limited job-getting network, employer discrimination, and discouragement and low motivation, which will be greater the more family members are out of work.

Morris (1987d) has examined the role of social networks, and the process of what she terms the social segregation of the long-term unemployed, in research in the north-east of England. Her argument is that a spatial concentration of the long-term unemployed has come about as a result of their disadvantaged position in the housing market. This clustering of the unemployed, together with the tendency for unemployment to be repeated within particular families (Payne, 1987) serves to separate them from informal contacts with the world of work, which are of enhanced significance in times of recession. This pattern of segregation was also found to affect potential for informal aid, which tends to be exchanged between households in similar positions of financial difficulty (cf. Marsden, 1982: 116) rather than across different employment statuses.

There is some comparable research about concentrations of unemployment in the US, in which the significance of race is also apparent. Staples (1985: 1011) for example, notes that: 'The white male teenager ultimately uses his kinship and friend-of-the-family networks more effectively to secure employment, while many black male teenagers who lack such networks drop out or never join the workforce.'

Schlozman and Verba (1979: 45) report that 10 per cent of working men and 12 per cent of working women, in contrast with 32 per cent of unemployed men and 31 per cent of unemployed women know many other people who are out of work. There is an additional striking contrast between blacks and whites. Nine per cent of employed whites as opposed to 27 per cent of employed blacks have many friends who are out of work. The analogous figures for the unemployed are 27 per cent of whites as opposed to 42 per cent of blacks. The authors state: 'In view of the degree of residential segregation in our metropolitan areas and the astronomically high rates of unemployment among minority youth this is perhaps not surprising' (p. 45).

Localized familiarity with and acceptance of high levels of unemployment and the associated problems is likely to affect the experience of hardship and the propensity for the formation of supportive networks.

Networks as a Source of Variety

Whilst it seems apparent that family structure is shaped by economic conditions, and that financial hardship can enhance the strength of kin ties, there is clearly more work to be done on the specific nature of exchanges across household boundaries, across and within class groups and employment statuses, and within ethnic populations. Before leaving this topic, however, it is worth noting that social networks do not simply function as potential sources of material and psychological support, but can influence the very nature of the marital relationship. This argument was popularized by Elizabeth Bott (1957) whose work provided a new way of thinking about the internal organization of the elementary family and the social world in which it is located, postulating an association between the type of social network of the couple and the organization of their domestic and leisure activities.

Morris (1985b) has applied these ideas to a study of male redundant steel workers in South Wales, arguing that where there are numerous linkages between the people who make up a social network, then they are more likely to develop shared ideas about appropriate ways of behaving; which are quite likely to extend to prescriptions about marital roles (cf. Fallding, 1961; Harris, 1969). She also suggests that where sexually segregated networks develop, it is likely that local norms will maximize gender difference and that where this is the case the divisions of gender roles that develop will be policed by the social networks.

This reading of the effect of a social network is then illustrated with reference to male resistance to participation in domestic labour, where men are members of a highly developed single-sex network. The tradition of collective and sexually segregated social activity for men then comes part way toward explaining male resistance to the assumption of 'female' domestic tasks, even in the face of unemployment, a resistance that is reduced when the collective dimension of social activity is lacking, and social contact instead is individualistic.

The implication of different network patterns for the organization of household finance and the availability of additional resources in unemployment is also investigated. The argument here is that a high degree of male involvement in domestic life will lower the potential for marital conflict, largely because home-centredness on the part of the man minimizes his personal spending requirements, encourages familiarity with the joint needs of the household, and, thus, where income is low – especially in cases of male unemployment – reduces one major source of disagreement.

Different patterns of social contact will have implications for spending requirements that are more marked among men than women, because male social activity is dependent on spending, taking place in the public rather than the private sphere. Thus, in the case of male unemployment the nature and extent of marital strain may be linked to the degree of male involvement in extra-household networks and the characteristics of those networks (cf. Marsden, 1980). Thus even within the same locality and same occupational class one can expect to find differences between household experiences of male unemployment, and the suggestion here is that the demands or supports embodied in local social networks will form part of an explanation of such difference. Morris (1987b) has illustrated these differences by a series of case studies.

There is the 'profligate spender', whose social commitments are largely independent of, and a threat to, his home life, revolving around a group of drinking friends who operate an elaborate system of mutual aid; the self-financed spender, whose benefit money is all given over to his wife, but who finances his own social activity through illicit earnings, odd-jobbing for members of his extensive social network; and the home-centred husband, whose independent social activity is minimal, much of his recreational activity being family based. Thus the network can become a drain on scarce resources, can become self-sustaining by offering the opportunity to earn or by supplying resources directly. Alternatively, the network can play a minimal part in an essentially home-centred existence.

Summary

The argument in this chapter has been that despite the general features of male unemployment discussed in chapter 2, there is enormous variety in detail to be found in the experiences of different households. Differences will relate to factors such as age, stage in the life course, duration of unemployment, number of children, class membership and orientation to paid employment. In addition, however, are more complex influences that have their origins outside the household and include the resources, facilities and constraints embodied in local social networks. This is a topic discussed more fully in the final chapter.

4 *Employment for Women*

Our two previous chapters have been concerned with the household effects of rising male unemployment, and the extent to which male joblessness demands the reorganization of home life based on traditional assumptions about gender roles. Whilst high levels of male unemployment represent a challenge to traditional models of family life, which cast the man in the role of sole or principal breadwinner, equally challenging has been the virtually simultaneous expansion of married women's participation in paid employment. This expansion is common to both British and American labour markets, and today levels and types of married women's employment are remarkably similar in both countries.

The significance popularly attached to these changes is partly to be understood by virtue of the gendered obligations that emerged from the revolution in work patterns precipitated by industrialization, a process we referred to in chapter 1. Commentators on both British and American history have identified the same basic developments. The introduction of waged labour as the principal means of subsistence in a pre-industrial society where the home was the recognized site of much vital production was followed by the emergence of a perceived separation of spheres with the home as the place in which the labourer recovered from paid work carried out elsewhere (see Bergman, 1986; Brenner and Ramas, 1984; Lopata et al., 1986; Oakley, 1974).[1]

The process by which these 'separate' spheres came to have a gendered identity has yet to be fully understood, but there is general agreement on a number of central points: a relative lack of control by women over repro-duction, an associated constraint upon women's activities, their assumed

[1] The relationship between domestic labour and industrial labour has been exhaustively analysed in a debate termed the domestic labour debate. For a review see Molyneux (1979) and Harris (1983: ch. 10).

responsibility for child care, their growing exclusion from waged labour outside the home, and a subsequent move on the part of male-dominated trade unions to secure male advantage in the labour market.[2] Thus, as Ware (1977: 12) writes of the US:

> The basic demand of the unions . . . was for a living wage, which could enable a man to support his family in comfort and decency. . . . They shared the perception of manhood and womanhood which had become popular during the nineteenth century when industrialization had destroyed the household as a productive unit based on shared activity and substituted the dichotomized world of work which was the domain of men and home now defined as woman's 'natural' sphere.

These sentiments were also evident in the British Trade Union Movement, expressed by a speaker at the 1877 Trades Union Congress as an obligation on the part of male workers to struggle: 'To bring about a condition where their wives would be in their proper sphere – at home – instead of being dragged into competition for livelihood against the great and strong men of the world.'[3]

Changing Work Patterns for Women

Married women in both countries have, however, recently increased their *numerical* strength in the labour-force. For the US, Bergman (1986: 20) reports that the rate of women's labour-force participation has grown almost continually since 1870, rising from 16 to 25 per cent in 1940 (Lopata et al., 1986: 54). From the 1950s onwards the increase in women's employment became much sharper and the rates rose respectively to 39 and 41 per cent in the sixties and seventies, most notably among married women. In 1890 only 4.6 per cent of married women were officially listed as part of the civilian labour force, but by 1940 16.7 per cent of married women were employed, rising to 22 per cent in 1950 and 51.8 per cent in 1982, and currently standing at 55.8 per cent (*Bureau of Labour Statistics*, 1988).

The impact of these changes on married women has been most strongly felt over the last 35 years, since early employment growth was concentrated among single women. Throughout the recent period there has also been a change in the nature of the female work-force. Initially it was older married

---

[2] There is some dispute about the universality of male trade union resistance to women workers. See for discussion Brenner and Ramas (1984). For case studies see Walby (1986).

[3] Quoted in Barrett and McIntosh (1980).

women who were most likely to take up the new opportunities; predominantly women with no pre-school children, but since 1965 mothers of young children have made up an increasing proportion of the female workforce in the US.[4]

Dex (1985: 3–4) has reported broadly similar developments for the UK. In 1881 women constituted 27 per cent of the labour-force, whilst by 1948 the proportion had risen to 33.6 per cent and by 1980 to 41.7 per cent. In 1984 43 per cent of the work-force was made up of women.[5] As we saw with the American figures, the biggest change has been since 1940, but unlike the US we find that up until the present day the largest increase has been for women between the ages of 35 and 54, that is those without young children (Dex, 1985: 4). The changes in Britain, as in the States, translate into a gradual rise in the proportion of the female work-force made up of *married women*, from 38 per cent in 1951, to 63 per cent in 1971 and 64 per cent in 1985 (*GHS*, table 6.24). Whilst this general pattern of growth was similar for both countries, the proportion achieved in the UK has been even higher than in the US, and there are significant differences between the two countries, some of which may be linked to demographic factors.

Demographic Factors

Mallier and Rosser (1987) offer a wealth of comparative data on the significance of demographic change. They begin by observing that: 'economic growth and change cannot be discussed rationally except in the context of population growth, size and distribution' (p. 9).

An examination of these factors reveals considerable differences between the apparently similar changes which have occurred in Britain and the US since the 1940s. In Britain, they note, the proportion of women in the population has remained stable at around 51.5 per cent, and in only one decade this century did the total population rise by more than 10 per cent. In America, by contrast, not until the 1940s was the number of females equal to that of males, though since then the proportion has converged with the British figure. In only one decade did the total population grow by less than 10 per cent, however. Part of an explanation for the growing *proportion* of women workers in the US is therefore their increased presence in the total population, an explanation not applicable to the UK, whilst their rising *numbers* may be partly associated in both countries with general population growth.

---

[4] Figures from Lopata et al. (1986). For a full account of this change see also Bergman (1986).

[5] The most recent figures available are to be found in a report on the 1984 employment census in the *Employment Gazette*, January 1987.

The proportion of women who are married has risen in the 20th century in both countries, though more steeply and from a lower starting point in the UK. Thus, over this period, the female labour-force could only maintain its size or expand by accepting larger proportions of married women. Whilst this is true for both countries it is particularly true for the UK, though both countries also show a *recent* fall in married women as a proportion of the total female population; to 60.3 per cent in the US, in contrast to Britain's 66.5 per cent. The difference is particularly marked in the younger age group with 86 per cent of younger British women married in 1980, as compared with only 72 per cent in the US (Dex and Shaw, 1986: 30). We might therefore expect the rates of married women's employment to be greater in the UK than the US, which was in fact the case.

Dex (1985: 4) draws our attention to an important distinction when she notes that although the changing employment patterns that we have documented may be seen as an increase in married women's paid work it is not women's 'marital status behaviour' that has changed but rather their child-rearing practices. During the course of this century the rate of female fertility has fallen in both the UK and the US, although in neither country has the fall been unremitting. In Britain the decline was from 113.0 to 62.1 per 1000 women aged 15–44 (Mallier and Rosser, 1986: 15), and whilst white American mothers born in the first half of the 19th century averaged more than five children their counterparts in the 20th century average 2.9 (Bergman, 1986: 42).

Despite the demographic contrasts then, the broad picture is one of a growing female work-force, the majority of whom are married, but with a general trend towards fewer births. These broad similarities should not blind us to important differences, both within and between countries. For example, a black British or American woman typically has more children than a white woman (Brown, 1984: 45; Stone, 1983: 36), and we might also expect to find class differences in family size, attitudes towards paid work, labour market commitment, child care practices and husband's employment status. There are, however, some clearly identifiable general trends that should be remarked upon.

Bearing and Caring for Children

Dex and Shaw (1986) have noted a U-shaped employment pattern for both British and American women, with a decline in employment after marriage or child bearing, followed by a rise in the late twenties/early thirties age group to reach a high employment plateau in the forties. For younger American women the pattern appears to be changing, however, with earlier returns to work after child bearing and a greater probability of working between births. Thus: 'Among younger women in their late twenties and early thirties . . . American women were much more likely than British women to be employed' (p. 22).

The difference was one of 20 percentage points for women in their late twenties, but only 10 percentage points for those in the early thirties. There is some evidence of British women's return to work between births but they are far behind American women in this development. These differences may in part be explained by differences in marriage, divorce and child-rearing.

The average American woman is more likely to be divorced, to remain single or to be childless than is a British woman. In 1980 25 per cent of American women in the 26–35 age range had no children in contrast to only 15 per cent of young British women. Among older women the contrast is reversed, with the American women averaging three children, and the British women 2.4. These factors will clearly have some kind of influence on women's employment patterns but not in any obvious and straight-forward manner (Dex and Shaw, 1986: 31). Although younger women in the US are less likely to have children, those who do are nevertheless increasingly entering into paid employment. Bergman (1986: 24) notes that in 1970 24 per cent of married American women with children one year or younger were in the labour-force, whilst by 1985 the figure had risen to almost half. British women appear to be far more constrained.

Child Care

There are striking differences between Britain and America in the child care practices of working women, which can only be fully explained by reference to factors outside of parental control, such as the structure of the market for women's labour and the statutory provisions made for child care needs.

Dex and Shaw (1986) provide us with a systematic comparison between US and UK practices, noting for preschool children that: 'in Great Britain care by husbands is the most common kind of care, involving 50% of the households of young working women and over 33% of the households of older working women. In contrast, only 16% of American husbands care for pre-school children while their wives are at work' (pp. 36–7).

Just over 50 per cent of American women depend on non-relatives for child care in contrast to 33 per cent of British working women, and differences continue as the child grows older. Husbands are generally less involved than at an earlier stage, though their involvement is greater in Britain than the US, American working women remain more highly dependent on extra-familial care, and this will often mean paid care.

American women's greater propensity to purchase child care must be in some part related to the availability of tax relief on child care expenses, a facility denied to British women, though we should note that few mothers recovered more than 20 per cent of costs and lower-income households much less, and that 22 states out of 50 provide no such relief. The higher level of purchased child care may, however, be influenced by the fact that American women are more likely than British women to work in the better paying occupations (Dex and Shaw, 1986: 29), whilst in many states assistance is available to low-income homes for child care costs. A further significant and remarkable factor influencing child care differences between the UK and the US is the very high concentration of British married women who are employed part time.

Part-time Employment

Although part-time employment might be defined as anything less than full time, the official cut-off point in UK statistics is 30 hours per week, and in the US 35 hours. On either basis many more British women work part time than do American women, and in fact Mallier and Rosser (1987: 135) have noted a median close to 20 hours per week among part-time workers in both countries.

The percentage of female employees working part time in Britain has risen from 33.5 per cent in 1971 to 42 per cent in 1981, with the proportion of part-time employees who are female remaining stable at 83 per cent (Mallier and Rosser, 1987: 135). The growth in part-time work for women has continued in recent years and between 1981 and 1984 women's full-time jobs fell by 15,000, while women's part-time jobs rose by 77,000 (*Employment Gazette*, January 1987: 34).

Mallier and Rosser (1987: 135) also give the comparable figures for America. There voluntary part-time workers (that is those accepting a job they know to be part time) have stabilized since 1970 at about 14 per cent, with adult female employees working part time stable at about 20 per cent of the female labour-force. They make up 70 per cent of all part-time workers, as compared with over 80 per cent in the UK. The substantial difference in the proportion of women working part time may offer some explanation of greater involvement by UK husbands in child care; part-time hours may be selected according to the man's availability, allowing him to assume care of the children while his wife does paid work. The arrangement would not be possible if both members of a couple were employed full time.

Part-time employment in both Britain and America is more common among married than non-married women, and stood respectively at 51 per cent as against 15 per cent in 1981 in the UK, and 25 per cent as against 16.6 per cent in the US (Mallier and Rosser, 1987: 140). The numbers peak in both countries for the 35–44 age group and Mallier and Rosser (1987: 139) offer the following explanation:

> Part-time employment increases over the 25–34 age range, which contains many women with children, a feature which places a constraint on the time available for paid employment. Although the proportion of women with very young children is highest in the 25–34 age group, the percentage of this age group working part-time is lower than the 35–44 age group. This is because between the ages of 25 and 34 those women without children will usually work full-time, whereas those who have small children will often stop working completely.

Explaining the Patterns

At one level explanation must be sought in the existence of a section of the potential work-force prepared to accept, or even actively seeking, part-time employment. The statistical coincidence of marital and child care obligations with part-time working has been demonstrated above. Research on a smaller scale provides some insight into the decisions made by married women seeking work, and their perceptions of the options available to them. Morris has reported on such research in both South Wales and the north-east of England. She argues (1987b: 138) that given a well-established pattern of female responsibility for domestic and child care tasks, a woman's paid work must either take account of her domestic obligations, or those obligations must accommodate her employment. For many married women, then, entering paid work was found to be largely the result of exploiting informally acquired knowledge of 'suitable' work opportunities; suitability being defined as opportunities that did not interfere too severely with traditional patterns of domestic organization. Women explained their situation as follows: 'I've always done part-time with these [the children] still little. I want to be here when they get in [from school], and there's the dinner to get for him. He likes it as soon as he's through the door, you know what they're like' (Morris, 1987b: 136) or: 'When you have children and they're only little it puts you off working 'cos you feel you should be at home with them, and you try to manage without the money, then you start to look out for a little [i.e. part-time] job . . . it's a struggle but the money keeps you going' (Morris, 1987c: 96).

The constraints of married women's domestic circumstances are clearly some part of the explanation for their concentration in part-time working, but unless the sexual division of labour is substantially different in British and American households, which subsequent chapters will show is not the case, then additional factors must be operating. Although the recognition of child care obligations through tax allowances in the US will favour full-time employment for women, an explanation is still required for the greater *availability* of part-time employment in the UK.

Mallier and Rosser (1987: 141) discuss this question, noting firstly that there are several reasons for a growing demand for part-time workers in both countries. Part-time employment has always been more common in the service sector of the economy and as noted in chapter 1 this has been the area of employment expansion for the UK and the US. Thus an increase in demand for part-time work may in part be a reflection of changes in the industrial structure. World recession and an emphasis on efficiency, flexibility and competitiveness have also favoured part-time workers who are less likely to be unionized or to oppose management decisions, and have traditionally commonly been denied a number of job-related benefits such as holidays, pension rights, sickness benefit and so on.

This still leaves us to explain the difference between levels of part-time employment in the UK and the US. Dex and Shaw (1986: 12) and Mallier and Rosser (1987: 142–3) discuss this question in detail, but the major reason is summed up as follows:

> The British income tax and national insurance systems (NI) have . . . operated in such a way as to make part-timers relatively cheaper. Below a specified earnings level, which has fallen relative to the average full-time weekly wage . . . an employee does not have to pay income tax or make NI contributions. Thus employers will not have the expense of administering payments, or of making NI contributions for employees who fall in this category, most of whom will be part-time workers.　(Mallier and Rosser, 1987: 143)

Thus we have a configuration of circumstances that are found in both the UK and US whereby both married women and employers might find part-time employment convenient. However, the more advanced state recognition of child care needs in the US militate against a preference by women for part-time work, as does qualification for health insurance which goes with full-time employment. In contrast, state-regulated financial incentives to employers of part-time workers in the UK, together with constraining domestic circumstances for women, have encouraged their concentration in part-time jobs. A further point worth noting here is the existence in the US of another potential 'part-time population': those under 20 years of age who account for 24.5 per cent of American part-time workers (presumably paying their way through college) and only 1.4 per cent in Britain (Mallier and Rosser, 1986: 138).

Theoretical Debates

Walby (1986) has identified two approaches to women's employment that are rooted in women's place in the household: the human-capital approach (for example Becker, 1981; Mincer, 1962) and the reserve army of labour approach (for example Beechey, 1977; Braverman, 1974; McIntosh, 1978). The former school sees women, and particularly married women, as choosing between alternative forms of productive activity – domestic work and paid employment – and opting in and out of the labour market as conditions vary.

Women's time outside of paid employment is thus seen as voluntary, with their standing in the labour market determined solely in terms of the human capital they bring to it. One objection to this view of women's employment is that it ignores the inequality of power within the household that may determine the distribution of paid employment, domestic work and leisure. Some writers working within the perspective of human-capital (for example Matthaei, 1982) have, however, introduced an ideological dimension to the allocation of these roles through notions of appropriate gender behaviour, but the question of why women occupy a disadvantaged position in the labour market is not satisfactorily addressed.

In the reserve army of labour approach the home similarly features as a place to which women retreat from the labour market, to be drawn back in during times of expansion. The key point in relation to the household has been developed by Beechey (1977, 1978) who suggests that married women's disadvantaged position is to be explained by the fact that they are partially supported by their husband's earnings, and can therefore be paid an inferior wage. This argument, however, raises questions about how and why men and women come to occupy different kinds of jobs.

A missing dimension in both approaches concerns the structuring of the labour market (see Barron and Norris, 1976; Beechey and Perkins, 1987) and the sorts of opportunities available to women, which are largely inferior to those available to men. The question commonly raised in this context (see Beynon and Blackburn, 1972; Siltanen and Stanworth, 1984) is why women have not organized to protect their interests better, though Walby (1986) suggests that in fact men have organized *against* women in the labour market in order to protect their own position (see also Hartmann, 1979).

We are still left with the question of why this was possible, and the answer would seem to lie with the competing demands on the time and labour of married women through their traditionally established responsibility for child care and domestic work. Why these responsibilities should have devolved upon them rather than men is a question that has not yet been satisfactorily answered, and would ultimately require some insight into the household dynamics underlying the sexual division of labour that emerged in proto-industrial society. But whilst there is still considerable speculation and debate about the historical developments that led to the consignment of women to the domestic sphere (Brenner and Ramas, 1984), sociologists have seen in current circumstances of falling male employment and expanding female employment a new opportunity to study the dynamics of the sexual division of labour in the household.

Women Breadwinners?

The increased numbers of married women entering the labour-force, most notably over the last four decades, is a departure from previously established work patterns and associated ideas concerning 'natural' roles, and has been particularly remarked upon in recent years when male unemployment has also been rising. We noted earlier, however, that falling employment opportunities for men and dependence on a female breadwinner do not appear in either Britain or America to offer an explanation for the change in married women's employment figures.

The proportion of wives in employment is higher in both countries where the husband is also working. As we noted in chapter 2, in 1986 in the UK 24 per cent of wives of unemployed men were in work as compared to 67 per cent of the wives of employed men. In the US in 1983 the proportions were respectively 19.5 and 64.9 per cent, although the figure is rising in the US and falling in the UK. We are now in a position to speculate about the possible reasons for this unexpected outcome.

The first general point to make is that, as we have seen, married women's movement in and out of employment is quite complex, and strongly influenced by their child care responsibilities. We cannot *assume* that the availability of an unemployed husband will necessarily produce a marked change in this situation, a question we examine more closely in chapter 5. In the UK, for example, male unemployment is concentrated in homes with dependent children, which are also homes where the wife is least likely to be working prior to her husband's job loss.

An explanation for the relative scarcity of female principal earners in the UK is fairly straightforward. We have so far established a number of factors that conspire to produce in the UK a concentration of married women in part-time employment. We have only to understand the way in which this feature of the labour market interacts with benefit rulings to appreciate the complex of influences whose effects support a traditional sexual division of labour.

In Britain an unemployed man is likely to have entitlement, for a fixed period of six months or a year, to unemployment benefit. Thereafter, or if his benefit falls below a stated minimum for his household arrangements, he or his wife[6] must claim income support (previously Supplementary Benefit) on behalf of the household. When such a claim was made, up until April 1988, any additional income above £4 was deducted from the benefit. This constituted a strong disincentive to the woman to remain in or take up employment, unless it seemed likely that her husband would soon be resuming paid work. It was only if a woman's wage substantially exceeded the household benefit claim that her assumption of employment in place of her husband was in financial terms a logical outcome. This situation is unlikely to arise where women are offered only part-time work, yet their domestic responsibilities have traditionally been such that this is often the work they seek out, added to which the incentive to employers to create part-time jobs remains, as does a population of women whose husbands are still in employment. Hence the two earner/no earner tendency among married couples which we remarked upon in chapter 2.

A change in the operation of benefit rulings in April 1988 raised the general earnings disregard to £5 but ceased to exclude work-related expenses from this sum. More important was a special change for couples who had been unemployed long term, which proposed a higher level disregard of £15 per week for the couple. It remains to be seen whether the effect of this change will be a wider distribution of part-time work for married women, away from its concentration among those whose husbands are employed, hence breaking the two-earner/no-earner polarization. To date, the benefit rules have constituted a convincing explanation for the absence of role reversal among British married couples facing male unemployment.

There is no such clear explanation for the paucity of female sole earners among American couples, where the incidence is even lower than for the UK and where unemployment is highest among childless couples. As we noted above, only 19.5 per cent of the wives of unemployed men in the US were themselves in employment in 1983. Though this figure has risen from 17.8 per cent in 1970 the rise is nowhere near the rate of increase for wives of working men, which went up from 50.8 to 64.9 per cent over the same period.[7] Despite this fact there is much less part-time employment among married women in the US, and there is no automatic right to benefit for the

[6] Since November 1983 it has been possible for either member of a married couple to claim income support for the household, subject to the claimant satisfying certain conditions indicating recent contact with the labour market. The 1985 White Paper *Reform of Social Security* (1985: 26) proposed abandoning this condition.

[7] Figures taken from *Monthly Labour Review*, April 1980, vol. 103, no. 4, table 1, and *Monthly Labour Review*, December 1984, vol. 107, no. 12, table 3.

unemployed who are not eligible for contributory unemployment benefit. Mallier and Rosser (1987: 75) have observed that: 'in some cases social security payments to an unemployed husband may be cut if his wife works', but estimates indicate that only 45–50 per cent of the American unemployed are in receipt of benefit (Voydanoff, 1987: 101). There is no equivalent to UK income support for the unemployed in the US, and, as we noted in chapter 3, AFDC is paid to families of the unemployed in only 23 states. So why are wives not taking over as sole earners?

Discouraged Workers?

Much discussion of women's employment fluctuations in the US has attempted to test out two opposing hypotheses: the discouraged worker effect and the additional worker effect, both of which seem to apply to *married* women (Dex, 1985: 201). In times of recession the 'discouraged' worker, after difficulty in finding a job, will withdraw from the labour market, whilst the 'additional' worker makes a more concerted effort in order to maintain household income, possibly in response to her husband's unemployment. Mallier and Rosser (1987) make an interesting distinction, pointing out that the discouraged worker thesis implies it is the unemployment rate in the local area that is significant, whilst the additional worker thesis places emphasis on the employment status of the husband. Thus, whilst high local unemployment will reduce the probability of a wife's employment, her husband's unemployment may increase her incentive to seek paid work.

The idea of women as a homogeneous mass has long since been criticized (Dex, 1985: 201) and some writers have begun to argue (see Bowen and Finegan, 1969) that both hypotheses may apply, but to different women. Research by Francine Blau in 1978, whilst somewhat speculative, recorded some interesting distinctions within a sample of married women aged 34–48 in 1971, when unemployment in the US had reached a peak at 5.9 per cent. Of the married women who were in the labour-force in 1971, 10 per cent had left by 1972. Conversely, of those who were out of the labour-force in 1971, 13 per cent of the white women and 20 per cent of the black women had entered by 1972.

Blau interprets her findings as suggesting a predominance of the discouraged worker effect among the white women (an effect of unemployment *rates*), and a predominance of the additional worker effect among black women (an effect of husband's employment *status*). This distinction, she argues, is probably due to two factors: a higher incidence of unemployment among blacks than whites, and lower mean income and asset levels for black families (Blau, 1978: 268, table 1). A confirmation of the stronger presence of financial need among black women is that for them additional children tend to encourage participation in the labour-force, whilst for white women the opposite is true.[8]

We may be seeing here different aspects of a relationship between eligibility for benefit, duration and incidence of unemployment and the persistence of wives in labour market participation. We noted in chapter 2 that in the US unemployment is much more commonly short term than in the UK, although less so among black men than white. A man unemployed for a short period is more likely to be receiving contributory benefit, and if his wife is not already employed she may feel less need to seek work; her husband is in receipt of benefit and common experience leads her to believe that he will soon be back in employment. Where unemployment is long term, and this is more commonly the case among black workers, then the man will not be in receipt of benefit income, there will be less grounds for optimism about his future prospects and his wife will be more likely to persist in a search for employment.

In the UK the effects of unemployment duration are the converse of this. The short-term male unemployed are likely to be in receipt of contributory benefit with a higher disregard of wife's earnings and a greater probability of her working. As length of unemployment increases and the couple move onto means-tested income support, earnings disregards fall and the woman is less likely to remain in, or continue to seek employment.

Single Mothers

One further comment from Francine Blau (1978: 278) is of interest in this context:

> A change in marital status . . . to widowed, divorced or separated strongly increases the probability of labour force entry among whites, but no significant effect on entry is obtained for blacks. This may be due to the greater likelihood that black women will be eligible for welfare programs that reduce the incentive to participate in the labour force.

The question of welfare benefits and single parents is one we return to in chapter 9. We may remark for the present, however, the *possibility* at least that America's low incidence of a wife's employment in place of her husband could be related to the absence of state assistance for the long-term

---

[8] We should note here Mott's (1979) argument that in recent years general employment levels for black women have remained stable whilst for white women they have risen. These figures seem unlikely to apply to the wives of unemployed white men.

unemployed and the likelihood that the wife and children could fare better on welfare as a single-parent family.

There has been a startling increase in the incidence of single-parent households in the US, documented by Voydanoff (1987: 49). The number has doubled between 1970 and 1984, and although the incidence is much higher in the black population, the rate of growth has been similar for blacks and whites. The respective increases have been from 30 per cent to almost 50 per cent, and from 8 to 15 per cent. The percentage of such households maintained by women has remained relatively stable, 89 per cent in 1970 and 88 per cent in 1984, and whilst women in single-parent families were less likely to be in the labour-force than men maintaining families, their rate of participation is slightly higher than that of married women.

In the UK the reverse is the case, and the 1980 Women and Employment Survey (Martin and Roberts, 1984) found that, for women with children under 16, 49 per cent of lone mothers were employed as opposed to 53 per cent of married or cohabiting mothers. For the never-married women the employment rate was particularly low at 34 per cent. Martin and Roberts (1984: 109) explain the generally lower rate for single mothers by age of youngest child, but also present data that suggest a stronger financial motivation for working among single mothers, with 85 per cent working from 'financial necessity' as compared with 37 per cent of married women, and 78 per cent to earn money for 'essentials' as compared with 28 per cent of married women (Martin and Roberts, 1984: 110).

In chapter 6 we shall investigate the problematic nature of the notion of financial need in the context of household and gender dynamics, but for the present we should none the less note the higher vulnerability of lone mothers to feelings of financial stress:

> Almost half of the single mothers (48%) and 41% of the formerly married mothers came into a high financial stress category, compared with only 11% of married mothers. By contrast, over half the married mothers were in the low financial stress category, compared with only 18% of the lone mothers.   (Martin and Roberts, 1984: 111)

Voydanoff (1987: 50–1) has reviewed the literature on the impact of labour-force participation on family life of lone parents in the US, noting less time spent in household tasks, recreation and personal care, and in a middle-class sample finding fewer visits from friends, and lower social competence on the part of the children. She notes other studies considering the possibility of strain due to 'family work' in the absence of a husband and reports: 'Married and single mothers do not differ in child related job/ family management and role strain or number of child problems reported;

however, single mothers have higher levels of depression and lower life satisfaction' (Burden, 1986).

Ethnic Minority Women

Household structure and the differing incidence of female headship constitute one source of differentials between ethnic groups, and Cordelia Reimers (1984) has analysed these differences among Hispanics, blacks and white non-Hispanics in the US. Reading 'family' as household, which is what she appears to mean, we see that black household earnings are only 62 per cent of the average white household, with Hispanics at 72 per cent, though showing variety between groups of different origin. Among Hispanics, Puerto Ricans have the lowest earned incomes with only half as much from male 'heads' and 60 per cent as much from wives as white households. Among blacks and Puerto Ricans a high incidence of female 'headship' is given as a major reason for low average household income, but black households receive more earnings from wives and female 'heads' and less from male 'heads' than any other group 'Black wives and female heads contribute 14% more to family income than white women do, while black families get less than half as much income from male heads as do white families' (Reimers, 1984: 893).

Differences of female labour-force participation between minority groups is considerable, however, with Puerto Rican women lowest and black women highest, despite high rates of female 'headship' among both groups. As Reimers points out, such differences may be due to cultural attitudes to work and gender roles, or to employers' discrimination, or both.

In view of the findings above it is surprising to discover evidence presented by Mott (1979) to suggest 'a major racial convergence in work participation' among black and white women. 'As recently as 1960, black women 35 to 44 years of age were almost 50% more likely to be working than their white counterparts; by 1975, this racial gap had narrowed considerably' (Mott, 1979: 86).

In 1967 the rates were 70 and 46 per cent for black and white women respectively, whilst by 1972 the gap had narrowed to 62 and 54 per cent. Opposing trends have been at work for the two groups with both the absence of preschool children and marital separation or divorce increasing employment rates among white women, presumably in competition with black women. We noted earlier that an indication of low household income among blacks could be the propensity for women to stay in the labour-force as their families grew larger, and this is consistent with evidence that young white women are more likely to leave a job when they have their first child than are black women (Mott, 1979: 89).

The pattern of marital breakup is more difficult to explain. Between 1967 and 1972 there was a sharp rise in households receiving AFDC, principally in cases of separation and divorce (Mott, 1979: 94). This period was also marked by the withdrawal of low-paid black women workers aged between 35 and 44, the group most likely to have dependent children and therefore to be eligible for AFDC. Mott notes that for such workers one needs to raise the question of whether earnings from low-paying employment are sufficient to exceed the income available through welfare. He argues, however, that average annual welfare payments were so far below the wages of even low-skilled jobs that the explanation lies more in the dearth of appropriate jobs than in the disincentive effect of welfare.

UK data on differences in work and household patterns by ethnic identity show some similarity with the US. There is, for example, considerable variety between ethnic groups in both domestic life and the employment prospects and status of women. Stone (1983) notes unfortunately rather dated figures that show a much higher rate of employment for West Indian women (74 per cent in 1977) as compared with white and Asian women (45 and 43 per cent respectively in 1977), with Muslim Asian women showing a much lower involvement (17 per cent in 1977). She suggests that whilst a major factor in the employment decisions of ethnic minority wives is male disadvantage in the labour market and consequent need for more than one income, there are important cultural differences (p. 34).

Whilst Pakistani/Bangladeshi households would benefit particularly from a wife's wage, Muslim women are less likely than other women to be employed. Asian women in general were more likely to be of the opinion that men are naturally more capable outside the home and that women excel in the domestic sphere. West Indian women, in contrast, show no such rigid acceptance of the traditional sex role divisions. A majority of Stone's West Indian respondents (75 per cent) felt there was no natural basis for task orientation by gender.

Bruegel (1988) examines more recent data on black women generally (that is considering West Indian and Asian women together), finding that black women are more likely to be economically active and are less likely to work part time than white women. They are also more likely to work shifts, which is one way of accommodating child care needs. Bruegel raises the question of how black women deal with the 'double burden' of paid work and domestic/child care responsibilities, finding the link between child care and part-time work to be weaker in the black population. One suggested reason for the commitment to full-time employment is the particularly high rate of single parenthood.

By far the largest ethnic minority group in Britain is of West Indian origin and the rate of single parenthood for this group is much above the average, though as a result of delayed marriage rather than marital dissolution. Jackson (1982: 171) states: 'Many West Indian women bear and bring up their young children with no stable support from a man. They are three times as likely to have to go out to work [as white women].'

Whilst one in three of all West Indian origin homes with children are single-parent households the rates for white and Asian homes are respectively 10 and 5 per cent. However, since part-time work is almost as rare among Asian women as among West Indian women, single parenthood cannot be the sole explanation. Bruegel's argument is that the difference between black and white women is to be explained by different economic pressures in that black households rely more heavily on women's income, though as Stone (1983) has noted, cultural factors may override financial necessity.

Because of black male disadvantage in the market for labour and apart from any established cultural pattern within the black British and West Indian population, the low economic status of many men may have a disruptive effect on marital and domestic patterns, as has been argued for the black population in the US. A debate continues about the relative influence of culturally specific domestic styles, and financial and welfare constraints, both of which have been argued to favour single parenthood. There has more specifically been speculation about the effect of welfare provision for single parents, with particular emphasis on the availability of priority rights to public sector housing, and a degree of interest in their employment patterns (for example, Nixon, 1977, see chapter 9).

There are certainly differences in propensity to seek work between single mothers and married mothers in the black population. Though financial stress has been found to be greater among single mothers than married women (Martin and Roberts, 1984: 110) no clear conclusion immediately follows from this. Popay (1983) has argued that the complexity of the benefit system makes it difficult for a lone mother: 'To make a "rational" choice about whether to claim benefit, work full time, or combine receipt of benefit with part time work.'

Despite black women's generally high commitment to employment they are predominantly engaged in low-paid, low-skilled work, for long hours, and Bruegel suggests that as a result, their earnings are so low that where benefit is available (that is for single parents) it makes little sense for them to seek employment. A similar point has been made for the US (Mott, 1979). Where benefit is not available, as in most married or cohabiting couples, black women are more likely to seek paid work, and that work is likely to be full time. In contrast, Bruegel argues, the propensity for white married women to seek part-time work is in a sense because they can afford to do so. Whatever the constraints of child care that encourage part-time employment they are not absolutely determining: financial need and/or earning potential can override them.

Marital Disruption

Discussion of marital disruption is not confined to the possible effects of single-parent benefits noted above, but arises in the US in a more general body of literature concerned with the effects on marriage of wives' employment. This literature appears to have no direct parallel in research in the UK and is designed to investigate the hypotheses of economic theorists,[9] which suggest that: 'As economic opportunities for women expand, wives become less dependent on marriage for financial support. Increases in female employment and earnings have been thought to lessen the opportunity cost of divorce and to provide wives with the economic wherewithal to dissolve unhappy marriages' (South, 1985: 32).

This argument is closely related to the research mentioned in chapter 3, which suggests that male unemployment or unstable earnings will unsettle a marriage, and the two rather different emphases are in some ways related. Cherlin (1978) demonstrates this when he identifies the two effects that a wife's earnings can have on a marriage.

1 The income effect – in which a wife's earnings should decrease the probability of dissolution because higher income families are less likely to divorce.[10]
2 The independence effect – in which separation from a troubled marriage is more viable for a woman with an independent income, whilst her husband may also feel less reluctant to leave.

Examining data from the National Longitudinal Survey for 1967–71 on women in the 30–44 age group, Cherlin (1978: 166) found that the critical factor is the *relative* earnings level of the wife, such that: 'the greater the ratio of the wife's to the husband's expected wage in 1967, the greater the probability of dissolution by 1971'.

We should note, however, that other factors, such as the unreliability of the husband's earnings, can substantially affect this relationship, and also that the economic effect is greater for women in second marriages.

Booth et al. (1984) are also concerned with the different factors which might mediate marital responses to a wife's employment, pointing out that time spent together may be diminished, and domestic labour may have to be reorganized, and that these issues should be taken into account when considering the income or independence effects referred to above. Their findings are that both marital happiness and instability are affected by the number of hours the wife is employed. Employment increases instability, especially where the woman's job entails more than 40 hours per week, but

[9] See Becker (1981) and Becker et al. (1977).
[10] Cherlin sites Bernard (1966).

the process by which stability is eroded will also involve disagreement and low satisfaction, as well as the existence of an independent income for the woman.

Work in this area is extremely complex. For example, the degree of distress suffered by a husband because of his wife's employment may be mediated by the relative size of their two incomes, but the more prestigious and better paid the woman's job the more threatened the man may feel. Voydanoff and Kelly (1984) introduce additional factors such as role strain resulting from the competing time demands of employment and parenting, which must be set against the financial requirements of the household and its members.

In fact, the closer we get to a consideration of the effects of women's employment the more complex the questions become. For example, to what extent do domestic roles change with a wife's entry into paid employment? Is any subsequent marital stress a result of her dual role as unpaid domestic labourer and paid employee, or a result of her husband assuming new domestic duties? What are the extent and sources of variations in the internal organization of the household? Domestic labour is clearly a central component in household organization, but so too is the distribution of income. How far does an understanding of the effects of a wife's earnings depend on what we know about her access or lack of access to her husband's earnings?

What has so far been established is that Britain and America have in common a recent history of expansion in the married women's work-force, although the demographic background and employment outcomes show some contrasts. Most notable is the high proportion of British women in part-time jobs. Despite differences in detail, however, it is clear that in neither country does married women's employment commonly result in a female sole or principal earner. Even for single mothers this is not the majority case.

The phenomenon of married women's increased employment is predominantly to be understood, therefore, in the context of dual-earner couples, rather than role reversal, and this raises a number of questions about both the use and significance of women's earnings within the households and the sexual division of domestic labour. Ironically, one effect of women's increased assumption of employment has been a heightened awareness of the problems posed by women's unemployment. This topic will not, however, be broached until chapter 7. Any assessment of the impact of job loss for married women must first address questions concerning the domestic and financial implications of their employment. Such questions, as with our queries about the effects of male unemployment, require that we look much more closely at what goes on inside the black box of the household in terms of unpaid labour and the distribution of and access to what are notionally termed household resources. These topics will be the focus of the two chapters to follow.

5 The Division of Domestic Labour

The introductory chapter of this book briefly referred to a sexual division of labour that has here been termed 'traditional', and accords women a principally domestic role, and men the role of main earner. This arrangement was to be understood in terms of a process that separated the home from the work-place, and subsequent developments that brought a weakened labour market position for women, and consequently relegated them to the domestic sphere. This was roughly the situation in both the UK and US at the beginning of the 20th century.

Post-war developments, which have seen increased entry of married women into the labour force, and increased numbers of men suffering job loss and unemployment, might lead to doubt over the continuing validity of the traditional model. Yet chapter 2 has shown that such changes have not in any large numbers brought women's replacement of men as principal or sole earners in the nuclear family household. The question remains, however, of whether either women's growing employment in paid labour and/or men's experience of unemployment have brought a renegotiation of domestic roles and the organization of domestic labour.

The Study of Domestic Labour

Chapter 1 outlined a number of perspectives that have been concerned to elaborate the relationship between family or household and society or economic system, whilst complementary work has looked more closely at what happens inside the household. In doing so a number of writers have set about documenting the experience of being a domestic labourer, treating housework as an occupation and investigating the terms and conditions under which it is performed.

One example of such work is Lopata's study of American housewives (1971) in which the position of housewife is characterized as an occupational role, but one lacking a place in the general occupational structure, having no criteria of assessment or circle of referents who judge competence, and receiving no financial or status rewards. The position involves little or no formally acknowledged training, and the nature of the demands placed on the incumbent will vary according to the resources available, which are in turn dependent on the husband's income and disposal of income. Essentially it is a position lacking in both power and social recognition. Research in the UK has made many of the same points.

The best-known British study of domestic labour, which took what at the time was a step of remarkable innovation, was Oakley's study of housework (1974). Oakley treated the role of housewife as an occupational role and studied domestic labour as 'work', thus challenging the characterization of the housewife role in modern industrial society. The central features of this role she identified as follows (1974: 1):

1 Its exclusive allocation to women rather than adults of both sexes.
2 Its association with economic dependence, that is with the dependent role of the woman in modern marriage.
3 Its status as non-work – or its opposition to 'real', that is overtly economically productive, work.
4 Its primacy to women, that is its priority over other roles

The fact that the role is viewed as essentially feminine, Oakley argues, places tremendous pressure on women to identify with, and derive satisfaction from housework. Because the housewife receives no wage, her role is open to a view that sees privilege and freedom as its chief characteristics. Oakley's study, however, reveals housework as low status, monotonous, fragmented, isolated with inherent time limits, bringing no financial remuneration, performed to no externally established standards, and often receiving no recognition.

Luxton (1980), in her study of the domestic role among working-class women in a US industrial town, provides a detailed account of the housewife's tasks in terms similar to those of both Oakley and Lopata. She also gives data on the way in which the nature of the work has changed over time, becoming more isolating, and involving less creativity, socially acknowledged skills or intrinsic reward. This effect is attributed to the impact of new technology. Luxton's work stresses the multidimensional nature of the housewife role, with its social, emotional and psychological aspects, as well as those of manager of home and supplies, and organizer of the domestic budget.

Both Oakley and Luxton stress the woman's prevailing responsibility for housework: 'In only a small number of marriages is the husband notably domesticated, and even then home and children are the woman's primary responsibility' (Oakley, 1974); 'Husband and child typically supplement but do not replace the wife's efforts' (Luxton, 1980: 142).

Studies such as these provide us with first-hand material of the housewife's life and experience. It is only implicitly, however, that such studies give us insight into the *relationship* between husband and wife, and in characterizing the role of housewife as essentially female the question of how the roles and obligations within the household are distributed is left unasked.

Exchange Theory

This approach was developed with a view to examining family cohesion from the perspective of reciprocity and the exchange of rights and duties between husband and wife, drawing on the Parsonian notion of instrumental and expressive roles (Parsons, 1956). Scanzoni (1970) has developed a gender-based model of such exchange which sees marital satisfaction and expressive exchanges, that is companionship, empathy and affection, developing by virtue of the traditional instrumental exchange between economic provision and domestic labour. One problem with such an approach is that it fails to take account of differential power within marriage, and of social status outside the marriage, which might accrue to the (male) spouse, who has the provider role. As we noted in Komarovsky's work on male unemployment (1940) this role was a source of authority in many marriages, which was seen to be undermined by job loss.

An alternative view to that of complementarity and exchange, which amounts to a 'different but equal' model, is a view that sees the domestic (female) worker as exploited and oppressed. This view has its roots in the domestic labour debate, a literature that, as we have seen, sets out to analyse not simply the relationship between domestic labour and the capitalist system, but also queries the nature of the relationship between the paid worker and the domestic worker. If we accept a view that emphasizes the advantages accruing to the *individual* paid labourer, and see them as the beneficiaries of the unpaid domestic labour, then this implies a position of domination by the former over the latter. If rather we stress the gain to employers through holding the wage down then the beneficiary is capital.

We have already noted that the traditional association between women's role and domestic labour cannot be explained without stepping outside the theoretical framework to seek an account in historical terms. Having done so, however, it becomes possible to pose an additional theoretical question. Once we take the feminine nature of the domestic role as our starting point then the focus of analysis shifts from an exploration of the relationship between capitalism, waged labour and domestic labour, to a focus on the nature of the male–female relationship. This change of emphasis leads us inevitably towards the conclusion that the sources of women's oppression and domination as unpaid labourers is not capitalism but patriarchy; that is a system of values that asserts and maintains man's dominant position in society. As Hartman (1981: 386) puts it: 'Women of all classes are subject to patriarchal power in that they perform household labour for men.' For examples of this view see Mainardi (1970), Hartman (1981) and Barret (1980).

Resource Theory and its Influence

What the approaches mentioned so far lack is any means by which we might seek to understand the specific negotiations and decisions arrived at by individual couples in the organization of domestic life, and, specifically, the distribution of their labour. One framework that holds out some promise of how this might be achieved is resource theory, which Berk (1985: 10) argues can be located within a perspective more broadly concerned with conjugal power. Berk's brief critique of this predominantly American treatment of household labour within the conjugal power framework, however, suggests that it fails to deliver its promise in that task allocation is treated as the outcome, or at times the indicator of power, rather than as a process requiring study and documentation. The formula applied suggests that the more powerful spouses do least household labour, and that if the wife does most household labour it is because she wields least power.

Wolfe's resource theory of power (1959) applied the idea of differential control of valued resources, and Blood and Wolfe (1960: 73–4) elaborated its application to the organization of household labour:

> A few tasks . . . require skills which may not be distributed equally in the family nor easily learned. Hence they are best performed by whoever has the technical know-how. Some tasks . . . require muscular strength in which husbands usually surpass their wives. But most household tasks are humdrum and menial in nature; the chief resource they require is time. Usually the person with the most time is

the wife – provided she isn't working outside the home. If she does work the husband incurs a moral obligation to help her out in what would otherwise be her exclusive task areas.

They go on to argue, on the basis of some cross-cultural comparison,[1] that the husband's relatively low contribution to domestic labour is not ideologically based but a result of rational resource distribution. In other words, the man has strength in the labour market and the woman has time.

Berk (1985: 13) identifies the following issues to emerge from the wealth of research carried out under this rubric, all requiring more detailed attention:

1   A greater range of relevant resources and the perceived opportunity costs of alternatives.
2   The relation of resources to power.
3   The relation of resources to normative orientations in determining power outcomes.
4   The importance of unequal exchanges between partners.

The questions concerning power, inequality and the importance of access to resources have mainly been addressed in a body of literature exploring the management and control of household finances. This work will be the subject of the chapter to follow. There have, however, been recent advances in the specific area of the division of household labour that have built upon the resources approach, notably the new home economics (Becker, 1981) and the 'household strategies' approach (Pahl, 1984), which were discussed in chapter 1. Both view the household as a productive unit, not just the site of consumption, and offer a theory of the household based on the allocation of resources in time and labour.

This move was prompted by an increasing desire on the part of sociologists to understand the impact of recent economic change, and must therefore be measured against empirical evidence on who does what within the home, and how the division of domestic labour (inside the home) is related to the sexual division of labour in paid employment. We have already seen from chapter 2 that male unemployment is often followed by a resistance to the assumption of domestic tasks, but what of the effects of increasing labour market participation by women, and the rise to prominence of the dual earner couple?

Early Work on Domestic Labour

By the 1960s the received wisdom in family sociology was that a 'great

---

[1] This was achieved by a comparison of rural and urban, and Catholic and non-Catholic families, which showed little variation in domestic labour patterns.

transformation' had occurred (Young and Willmott, 1957); the lives of husband and wife were becoming increasingly shared in terms of both companionship and domestic labour. A review of developments in the UK literature at this time can be found in Harris (1983) and will be mentioned only briefly here. Harris identifies the work of Elizabeth Bott (1957) as the point of departure for debate about changing marital relations in modern Britain. Bott attempted to investigate variations in degrees of 'jointness' and 'segregation' between husbands' and wives' domestic and leisure activities, whilst accepting as given the traditional division of labour between the sexes.

Young and Willmott (1957) gave the differences identified by Bott a temporal dimension by arguing that there was emerging a 'new kind of companionship among men and women'. They developed their position more fully in *The Symmetrical Family* (1973), suggesting that the middle classes were at the forefront of a move towards symmetricality in marriage, by which they meant that husband and wife were increasingly sharing in the complementary, but hitherto largely segregated tasks of wage earning and domestic labour.

Doubt was cast on this optimistic interpretation by a number of other studies. The Pahls (1971) discuss the stress for middle-class wives when the *ideal* of sharing in marriage is contradicted by the primacy attached to the husband's paid work, which encourages a marked sexual division of labour, whilst the Rapoports (1971, 1976) highlight the difficulties experienced by dual-earner couples, and particularly the role conflict confronting the woman. Other evidence at around the same time (notably Oakley, 1974) seemed to point to the continuing primacy of the woman's domestic role, findings confirmed in a later work by Edgell (1980), who does, however, note some indication of change in the way that men and women think about their respective roles. He reports evidence of a growing flexibility in attitudes and behaviour, which have nevertheless left the established sexual division so far free from challenge.

The best-known American work of around this period is Blood and Wolfe's study *Husbands and Wives* (1960). Writing in 1960, the authors remarked on recent discussion about the American family's 'alleged abandonment' of a traditional sexual division of labour as more wives take jobs outside the home. They go on to state, however, that the idea of shared work is incompatible with efficiency, and document data on task division in 731 Detroit families that show a sex segregation of tasks to be largely intact. Outdoor tasks and tasks requiring 'mechanical aptitude' were found to be predominantly the duty of men, whilst indoor tasks tended to be performed by women. The least clear division was responsibility for 'administrative' duties, that is budgeting, which was the responsibility of women in 30 per cent of the homes, of men in 19 per cent and shared equally in 34 per cent.

This is a difficult topic that receives special attention in the following chapter. The overall finding of the study, which examined seven tasks, was that: 'The median family has a completely stereotyped allocation of five of the seven tasks, leaving only two for even marginal variation' (p. 51).

Much more contentious has been the reported finding that employment for the wife significantly influences the husband's domestic involvement. Blood and Wolfe report that under these circumstances the woman's increased burden leads to the man assuming more of the traditionally female domestic tasks, but in amounts subject to his own availability. The critical factor they found to be comparative availability, such that a household with a working wife and non-working husband shows a low task performance for women, and low adherence to female roles. Where both partners are available in the home, however, arrangements correspond more closely to the traditional pattern (1960: 62). More recent findings have called into question some of the conclusions of early research, as we shall see below.

Recent Empirical Findings

The early work on household gender roles was followed by a period of neglect for family sociology, and a general lack of interest in domestic labour. Recently, however, both the UK and US have seen an explosion of research into domestic responsibilities, and household studies in general, as a result of economic change and a growing interest in gender relations; specifically the effects of married women's employment and male unemployment.

A number of writers suggest that the allocation of husbands' and wives' labour to the market and household sphere will be determined by their relative productivity in each, but recent data suggest that the traditional allocation of domestic work to the woman holds firm. Geerken and Gove (1983: 90) report on interviews with members of married couples in the US as follows: 'The most striking result is the huge difference between the time the husband spends on housework, compared with the wife (even if the wife is employed); the drastic effect of the wife's employment status on her own level of housework; and the stability of the husband's housework time, whether the wife works or not.'

Similarly Berk (1985: 108) reports on 335 American couples that: 'Husbands' employment activities and the individual characteristics that establish husbands in the occupational sphere are the most critical determinants of total household market time . . . [whilst] . . . few married men engage in significant amounts of household labor and child care.' She also notes (p. 122) that when households require more labour time it is wives who meet the demand, thus: 'As the total productive capacity moved from "low" to "moderate", the wives' monthly tasks increased from 250 to 537, and with an increase to "high", 773 additional tasks were undertaken by the wife' (p. 142). She also found that the household labour efforts of mothers and daughters were linked more intimately than those of mothers and sons (p. 160), and that a husband's 'household-labour tastes' are positively correlated with amount of schooling (p. 150), which increases his household task involvement.

In the UK Pahl (1984: 275), using a typology of high, medium and low for sex segregation of domestic tasks, found that 96 per cent of homes with a male earner and full-time female housewife fell into the 'high' (that is segregated) category, as compared with 61 per cent of dual-earner couples. Gershuny (1982), reporting on findings from an inner-city survey, identifies a gender specialization of domestic tasks, which is also reported in analysis of time budget data from another survey (Gershuny et al., 1986). The research identifies a core of routine domestic tasks that are principally the responsibility of women, with men more likely to perform non-routine tasks. In the mid-1970s husbands performed less than one-quarter of all domestic work, and less than 10 per cent of routine domestic work (Gershuny, 1982).

Using data from a total of seven surveys,[2] Gershuny and Jones (1987) do, however, note a doubling of male routine domestic work between 1974–5 and 1983–4, albeit from a low base, during which time female involvement in non-routine tasks increased. This is not to say that gender specialization does not persist, but rather than there has been a blurring of the boundaries in the sexual division of domestic labour.

The more closely we look at the household, however, the less possible it becomes to generalize. We have so far explained the emergence of 'traditional' sex roles by the complementarity of market labour, usually performed by men, and domestic labour, usually performed by women. Harris (1983: 230) describes this arrangement as: 'an adaptation to the demands made upon the domestic group by the occupational system'.

The recent growth of married women's employment (as well as the release of many men from the rigours of the occupational system by unemployment) inevitably raises the question of whether a gendered responsibility for domestic labour will persist. The prediction of much of the theorizing about the sexual division of labour has been that men's contribution to domestic labour will increase if women's market labour time increases (see, for

[2] The seven surveys referred to are the 1983 Mass Observation collection, the 1961 BBC survey, the 1971 Symmetrical Family Survey, the 1974/5 BBC survey, the 1981 Scottish sample, and the 1983/4 ESRC and BBC surveys.

example, Becker, 1981). The results of empirical investigation, however, show the responses to women's employment to be extremely complex.

Domestic Labour and Married Women's Employment

UK studies

We have already noted that in the UK married women in employment tend to have husbands who also have a job, and the concentration of part-time employment among women suggests that they may be accommodating a traditional division of domestic labour – though of course full-time jobs may simply be unavailable. Martin and Roberts (1984: 64) report some findings on the competing demands of home and jobs for women: 34 per cent of full-time workers scored high on difficulty in coping with these demands, and only 22 per cent scored low, whereas for part-time workers the figures were 21 and 39 per cent respectively. Among both full- and part-time workers, the childless women generally found coping easier, whilst among full-time workers those with dependent children found greater difficulties than those with grown-up children, especially the non-married.

Such findings do suggest that employed women continue to carry their traditional responsibilities in the home, although the problem with this particular piece of research is that it gives no direct data on men. The use of both male and female respondents is, however, a considerable strength of Pahl's work in Sheppey (1984), and *Divisions of Labour* presents a complex account of the organization of domestic work, which finds the key variables to be stage in the domestic cycle and employment status.

The main argument is straightforward enough, and supports Edgell's notion of growing flexibility within the context of established gender roles. Though Pahl finds no evidence to suggest the complete overthrow of traditional divisions, he does report (1984: 275–6) that the more hours the female partner is in employment, then the less conventional is the organization of domestic labour. The same effect is found the fewer hours the male partner is employed, except in cases of male unemployment, where the association is reversed.

Pahl also makes the point that the woman's domestic burden is particularly high when she is not in gainful employment and there are young children in the home. This is interpreted as a life-cycle effect. When young women in such circumstances take on employment it will usually be part time, and their domestic duties remain high. Pahl (1984: 275) does, however, find a relationship between paid-work and domestic labour, such that the *more* hours the female is in employment, the less conventional is the domestic division of labour.

Against this observation we must set the findings of Laite and Halfpenny (1987: 220). They note, in a study of households in Macclesfield and Blackburn, that women in part-time employment perform more of the core 'female' tasks than either full-time or non-employed women. Their findings appear to be consistent with Gershuny et al.'s conclusion (1986: 33) that a disproportionate domestic burden on women employed part time is likely to stem from child care and related domestic work since, as we have noted, women with young children usually opt for part-time work.

Gershuny's earlier research (1982), which also addresses the question of household divisions of labour, reports that in general the unpaid work of employed wives does not decline in proportion to their increase in paid work, and that 'even in the most liberated, young, two-job household' the husband averages only 15 per cent of routine domestic work.

Time budget data from other research (Gershuny et al., 1986: 33) is helpful here. For couples with children and two full-time jobs, men's routine domestic work was found to be higher than in other couples, but this was only true for homes with very small children. In other two-earner homes women were found to bear a heavier 'dual burden' of paid and unpaid work. This finding is consistent with Pahl's argument that the more adults there are in the home the more likely it is that the woman will perform a 'traditional' female (that is domestic) role; though we should note that in his research the presence of young children seemed also to produce a highly segregated pattern of domestic labour and an increased burden for the woman.

Gershuny et al. (1986: 33) also found that in couples where the wife has no paid work, or is employed part time, the husband seems to reduce his domestic input and work longer in his paid job. This is interpreted as increased specialization within couples at a particular stage in the life-cycle. The general consensus of research findings seems to be that the burden falls hardest on women employed part time who have young children.

Gershuny (1982) interprets a general tendency for work to cumulate on employed wives not as a complete absence of adaptation but as a result of insufficient compensation for their increased share of market work. This view is consistent with Laite and Halfpenny's finding (1987: 229) that where men and women share the same employment status men do more of the domestic tasks than in other households. Indeed, for the period 1961–84 Gershuny and Jones (1987: 48) report that a 10 per cent reduction overall in men's paid work has been largely offset by an increase in unpaid domestic work, whilst both full-time and part-time employed women have experienced a 15 per cent decrease in domestic work. There is some comparable American data looking at change across time that produces similar results. Nickols and Metzen (1982: 211) examine the period 1968–73 and found that although traditional patterns predominate there has been some slight change. More husbands each year reported doing housework, which raised the mean score over a period when housewive's mean hours were being reduced. An increase in women's employment hours in this study also brought some small response from husbands in the form of domestic work.

The end result of such processes does not lead to an equal distribution, however. Evidence for the UK from the British Social Attitudes Survey (Jowell and Witherspoon, 1985) shows that the employment status of wives affects the extent to which they perform domestic tasks, and that working women are less likely than those not gainfully employed to carry the entire responsibility for housework. The study goes on to report, however:

> Not that women working full-time outside the home had an egalitarian division of domestic work: they were merely somewhat less unequal. And women with part-time jobs outside the home had a particularly unequal division of labour, partly reflecting the fact that many women who worked part-time also had young children. (p. 56)

It is interesting to counter this statistical data with a more qualitative piece of research on 62 married women in employment (Yeandle, 1984). One-third of the women acknowledged an important contribution by husbands to domestic work, but male readiness to co-operate was seen to depend on how significant the woman's earnings were judged to be for the household's standard of living – though this notion is itself problematic, as we see in the next chapter.

The general patterns from these varied studies can be summarized as follows:

1 Even in employment women continue to bear the main burden of domestic work.
2 Men have increased their participation, but not in amounts sufficient to offset women's increased market work.
3 Women in part-time employment seem to fare worst, and this seems to be a life-cycle effect, related to the extra work created by the presence of young children.
4 This does not preclude the possibility that men are more involved in domestic tasks at this stage of the cycle than at other stages.

How do these findings compare with work in the US?

American studies

An American work that focuses specifically on domestic labour in dual-earning couples is Pleck's *Working Wives, Working Husbands* (1985). As well as reporting on his own research, Pleck reviews a wealth of other data, and in doing so resolves some rather puzzling inconsistencies. Whilst Blood and Wolfe's (1960) influential study reported that when wives were employed husbands' domestic labour increased, a number of more recent studies have argued that it does not.

Pleck reports findings from three studies, Walker and Woods (1976), Robinson (1977) and Meissner et al. (1975), which consistently show that men do not participate more in housework and child care when their wives are employed. These studies respectively showed husbands' 'family' work stable at 1.6 hours per day regardless of wives' employment status, rising from 1.0 to 1.1 when the wife was employed, and stable at 0.6 whether or not she was employed. The daily 'family' work hours of non-employed and employed wives for the three studies were respectively 8.1 falling to 4.8; 7.6 falling to 4.0; and 4.6 falling to 2.3. In other words, the working wife may reduce her domestic labour time, but her husband is unlikely to increase his (1985: 31).

To square these findings with Blood and Wolfe's conclusion Peck points out that the latter study examined the relative proportions of total housework performed by both spouses, not the absolute amount. The three time-use studies referred to do indeed find that the *proportion* of the man's contribution rises with the wife's employment, but only because her own household labour time falls, not because his rises. These studies, however, report on data collected between 1965 and 1971. Pleck goes on to examine more recent data from two surveys conducted in the mid and late seventies to ask if there is any evidence of more recent change.

The two surveys produce somewhat different conclusions. One showed the wife's domestic labour time to be only negligibly higher than the husband's (only 0.2 hours per day more), whilst the other showed a substantial difference (2.2 hours a day more). The latter study, however, also showed husbands' domestic work to increase with wives' employment. The difference is accounted for by differing measures of child care, the latter study using a less restrictive definition. Pleck's conclusion is as follows:

> Employed wives continue to be overloaded relative to their husbands, but this overload derives from their spending more time being available to their children rather than extra time in housework and more direct kinds of childcare interaction. Husbands do respond to their wives' employment, but primarily in their time availability to their children, not housework or more narrowly defined childcare. (p. 50)

This argument seems consistent with some of the British findings that the woman's burden will be greatest when there are small children in the home (see Pahl, 1984: 273) but contrasts with Gershuny et al.'s finding that in working couples with very small children the husband's increased contribution to domestic work comes in the form of routine domestic tasks, not increased child care. We have nevertheless noted in chapter 3 that British fathers are more likely than American fathers to be involved in child care. A related point to note in comparing Britain and the US is the effect of a greater availability of part-time work for women. We have noted that women working part time seem to carry the greatest double burden since men are more likely to relieve their wives' domestic burden when they are employed full time. Part-time working, primarily to accommodate children's needs, is far more common in the UK than the US (see chapter 4), and American women are more likely to pay for child care. This as we saw was related to the availability of tax relief on such payments.

Pleck goes on to report a number of specific findings noting that the time-use survey for 1975–6 showed employed wives spending 40 per cent less time than non-employed wives in 'family' work, and non-employed wives showing markedly lower overall work loads than all other groups (husbands included). In seeking a general explanation for gender differences in work loads, however, Pleck finds that even when time in paid work is controlled for: 'sex accounts for substantial variance in total family work time – between 10 and 15 per cent' (1985: 71).

Pleck uses this finding to counter the argument that men are caught in a 'breadwinner trap' (Gronseth, 1971; Scanzoni, 1970). His argument is that although men's domestic contribution does vary in relation to their time in paid work (cf. Gershuny et al., 1986, on UK data) this cannot fully account for male–female differences. He does note that women have more room than their husbands to reduce their 'family' work with employment, and finds such reductions to be greatest among women with conservative attitudes towards sex roles. Their 'family' work was perhaps most likely to be high prior to employment.

Berk (1985) reports some interesting findings in this area. First she notes some generally established points about existing research into domestic labour:

1 The effects of employment on wives' household labour is through 'short-cuts' to reduce their time, not through reapportionment.
2 Aggregate estimates of husbands' household labour time amount to 10–15 per cent.
3 Husbands with employed wives and small children participate at higher levels than other husbands.
4 Overall husbands' participation in comparison to wives' is minimal.

She goes on to note some specific details from a sample of 335 couples, one-third childless, and 36 per cent with an employed wife (16 per cent part time and 20 per cent full time), noting the 'normalization of the double day' (p. 108) for wives, the absence of substantial change in the domestic work of employed wives, the absence of significant contributions from husbands, and the generally low market hours worked by women. She observes a negative relationship between hours in domestic work and hours in market work, and also states that an infant adds approximately ten days' worth of domestic tasks to the household, and a small child five days. It is, she argues, the experience of wives that explains the negative relation between household time and market time.

When total market commitment increases the husbands' household commitment remains small. Wives' household responsibilities therefore remain unchanged but the time dedicated to them may shrink. Any increase in household demands are met by the wife. Questioning the logic of comparative advantage, Berk points out that wives will make a contribution to market time in response to household need, but that there appears to be virtually no level of household work that prompts a substantial contribution from husbands. This arrangement, she says can only be explained by the operation of some normative structure. She adds that:

> Institutional and normative forces combine to limit severely the choices of all members of the household. [For example] the overwhelming demands of an infant child, the rigid organisation of employment, and the clear cultural message that only a mother can truly satisfy a child's psychological and emotional needs. (p. 199)

In searching for the forces that might overcome such constraints, Berk examines a subsample of 'outlier' husbands having a level equivalent to the mean household task or household time contribution of the sample of wives. They amounted to 10 per cent of all husbands, were slightly younger and poorer than the average, had greater numbers of small children and over half had employed wives. Thus it appears that there is an ultimate level of household need to which husbands will respond, but that level is rather high. It is not clear, however, whether the husband's age contributes to their flexibility, younger men perhaps being less bound by gender conventions, or whether the effect is simply imposed by the constraints of stage in the life-cycle.

Geerken and Gove (1983), in a study of 1225 married couples, set about an investigation of why it is that the recent rapid increase in women's' labour-force participation has not brought about a general equality in the allocation of household tasks. Measuring four components for each respondent – work, housework, relaxation and sleep – they single out the following striking results:

1 A huge difference between the time the husband spends on housework compared with the wife, even if she is employed.
2 The drastic effect of wife's work status on her own level of housework.
3 The stability of the husband's level of housework time whether the wife works or not.

They cite a number of studies that confirm their results (Geerken and Gove, 1983: 91), and summarize their own findings as follows:

> The picture that emerges . . . is one of traditional allocation of task responsibility even when the wife works. The shifts that do occur when she takes a job primarily tend to be an increase in helping behaviour by the husband and others (children primarily) rather than takeover of primary responsibility by other family members. The relatively small change in task responsibility introduced by the wife's entry into the labour force contrasts sharply with her drastic reduction in time spent on housework. Her time is cut in half but her responsibility score drops by only about 6%.

This study, like others we have mentioned, also discusses the effect of the presence of children and the expansion in domestic work that they create. An increase in the number of children can decrease the wife's household responsibility, by virtue of the children taking over some tasks, but this does not decrease the wife's housework time in general as children's work contribution is not equivalent to the amount of work they create. The presence of very young children increases both the wife's labour time and responsibility. The effect may be a withdrawal from, or non-entry into the labour market, whilst the husband's market time will remain stable, or possibly increase. There may, however, be some increased household responsibility on his part. These findings parallel those from the British research, reporting an increased gender specialization at this stage in the life-cycle, though without precluding the possibility of some (small) increase in husbands' household contribution.

Role Strain and Women's Employment

There appears to be general agreement about the dual role performed by employed mothers, and its effects have been commonly conceptualized in terms of 'role strain'. Role strain is manifest as a 'wide, distracting and sometimes conflicting array of role obligations' (Goode, 1960: 483). The accumulation of roles and their incompatibility are judged to be a source of strain (Burr et al., 1979); the incompatibility can flow from contradictory role expectations or from competing demands for time and attention. The result may be an overload of total demands on time and energy.

Pleck (1985: 97) has traced the debate which has grown up around the idea of role overload. The initial response, he argues, was that since wives' employment violates traditional roles it must have a negative effect on the women. An alternative view arose, however, which saw employment as offering positive social and psychological rewards that could counter the ill-effects of the housewife role on women's mental health (Bernard, 1972; Brown and Harris, 1978; Kessler and McRae, 1982). Pleck then notes a more recent view that sees employment for wives as a source of stress, and for him sits oddly with the argument that such work brings positive psychological rewards, although he concedes that there will inevitably be both demands and gratifications.

Reviewing the same topic, Voydanoff (1987) points out that research has revealed several types of relationship between women's employment and family roles, quality of family life, and mental and physical health. Thus whilst one study finds that employment role strain and marital role strain are associated with depression (Aneshensel, 1986), another reports that employment buffers the effects of marital strain on depression, whilst parenthood exacerbates the effects of occupational stress (Kandel et al., 1985). The best-known British study in this area is that by Brown and Harris (1979), which has demonstrated the effects of social contacts outside the home, and the role of employment in providing these contacts, as a counter to depression.

Clearly there will be a number of different variables involved in the relationship between home and work. Some are identified by Voydanoff as work hours, job involvement, job autonomy, time expectations at work, marital status and number and ages of children. Not least of these will be the motivation to seek employment at all, and the professional, personal or financial reasons for doing so. The circumstances of a mother of a large family in an unrewarding, poorly paid job, who has been driven to seek employment because of the insufficiency of her husband's wage, or his failure to supply adequate housekeeping money, will be different from the mother of one child whose husband provides well, but who is returning to rewarding employment to which she is professionally and personally committed.

The literature in this area, however, seems less sensitive than other work – notably Komarovsky's study of the effects of unemployment – to the importance of the pre-existing marital relationship. Komarovsky's argument is essentially that the way a new event (in her study, male unemployment) is received into the household and family relations will depend on the circumstances and nature of domestic life and marital relations prior to the event. This same must be true of employment for women, and Hiller and Philliber (1986) have argued that the extent to which role expectations of husbands differ will be critical to their ability to negotiate mutually accept-able roles, and ultimately to their marital stability.

What has been learnt from research into the organization of domestic labour is that there are strong cultural predispositions that may make adjustment to married women's employment difficult, not least for the women. The conclusion of a number of studies has been that the organiz-ation of time and labour resources in the home cannot be understood simply in terms of a model of rational decision making about the optimal distribution of these resources, but must take into account the cultural forces that support the idea of women's role as essentially domestic. Whilst to some extent accommodating women's entry into paid employment, gender ideology still proves a major disincentive against men assuming domestic obligations. Hiller and Philliber (1986: 192) found that even in 'modern, dual-earner families tradition endures and the husband's view of marital roles strongly influences behaviour' (cf. Gershuny, 1982).

Role Strain for Men

Less attention has been paid to role strain experienced by men with refer-ence to the competing demands of home and work, but there are some US data available. Clark et al. (1978) review some of the assumptions about men's work orientation that are common to sociological writing. These include the assertion that men are too preoccupied with work concerns, or too tired after a long day to assume any share of domestic responsibilities, whilst the satisfaction of wives with husbands' companionship is reckoned to be lower at the higher occupational levels. The underlying assumption they identify in the range of literature reviewed is that: 'Occupational roles were dominant for husbands and, therefore, the more husbands worked, the less their available time for all other roles' (p. 11).

The authors examine these assumptions for four roles: the housekeeper role, recreational role, sexual role and therapeutic (supportive) role. The findings that most interest us here are in the first of these areas. Men's work time was found to have no significant direct effect on housekeeping, but acted indirectly through level of income: 'Increases in husband's income directly reduced their sharing of the housekeeping role, and in-directly reduced it by diminishing wife's work time and housekeeping role expectations for husbands' (p. 15).

The possibility of greater resource power in avoiding the undesirable is noted as a possible explanation. Higher income was found to be positively related to sexual satisfaction, and the only direct negative effect of work time was on the husband's therapeutic role.

Lein (1979) takes up a similar approach, but detects rather more role conflict when she argues that: 'men's ambivalence to changes in the structure of home life reflects the multiple pressures on them as citizens, workers and concerned family members. . . . Effort expended in home life is often perceived as energy diverted from the primary effort of breadwinning' (p. 489).

One of the sources of stress for men faced with conflicting demands is the absence of any informal support system to encourage or enable them to meet the demands of family life, thus: 'Men, like women, are caught in the grip of family and societal forces which exert considerable pressure on them to maintain traditional standards for the organisation of family life' (p. 490).

Men, she argues, experience a set of inconsistent demands from family and from the wider society and she lists the following sources of difficulty:

1 Husbands perceive their paid work as their primary contribution to the family.
2 Both husbands and wives may have difficulty relinquishing responsibility for their primary roles in the family, respectively breadwinner and home-maker.
3 Men and women tend to experience community action and the reaction of the larger society as a pressure against change in the allocation of responsibility and tasks among family members.
4 Men experience very different social support networks than do women, and those networks tend to preserve traditional roles.
5 The allocation of tasks in the household reflects other aspects of the relationships among family members: the relative importance of earnings in the paid labour-force, the balance of decision-making power in the family, and the sense of self-image as a participating family member.

Her arguments are born out by research in a somewhat different context that examines the responses of the households of redundant male steel-workers (Morris, 1985b). Resistance to involvement in domestic tasks was found to be greatest where the man was involved in social contact with a single-sex peer group with some sense of collective identity. It is under these circumstances that rigid norms guiding sex role behaviour, and the means of sanctioning such behaviour, are likely to develop.

Variations in Domestic Labour

A number of the studies we have mentioned have used random samples of large populations and, as a result, whilst not providing detailed understanding of how particular sections of the population operate, they have been able to identify a number of apparent sources of difference. The most obvious of these has been the life-cycle, and we have seen that household labour needs are highest when there are young children present (Berk, 1985; Pahl, 1984; Pleck, 1985), a stage at which sexual specialization is likely to be accentuated. It also seems that there is more room for flexibility and a relaxation of sex roles as couples age (Pahl, 1984: 274), and especially once children have left home. Up until that point, as we have seen, their presence seems likely to continue to mean extra work for the woman.

The broader distinctions in the organization of domestic labour seem to be based on differences of class, race and education, and, perhaps related to these, the general orientation of the couples concerned. We referred in the previous section to research that has focused on the social network, and sources of mutual support, and their role in reinforcing gender roles. The starting point for such work was Elizabeth Bott's study (1957), which argued that there is a relationship between the division of labour between husband and wife and the type of social network in which they are embedded. Thus: 'The degree of segregation in the role relationship of husband and wife varies directly with the connectedness of the family's social network.'

Other research has tied social class into this analysis, and Ericksen et al. (1979: 303) have summarized the argument. They begin with Rainwater (1965) who sees the structure of the network to be tied to social class in that upper-middle-class husbands identify closely with their homes, whilst their wives expect to penetrate the world of their careers, thus producing closely connected networks and joint conjugal roles. The contrasting situation is that depicted in research on *particular kinds* of working-class life, such as Dennis et al.'s *Coal is our Life* (1956) and Komarovsky's *Blue Collar Marriage* (1957), which both depict highly sex-segregated societies, dominated by male employment in heavy industry with employment opportunities for women fairly scarce. In such circumstances men's and women's spheres of operation and interest are sharply segregated.

As Ericksen et al. point out, Bott emphasized mobility rather than class as the determining factor in network structure. This may to some extent be consistent with social class differences, however; middle-class couples are more likely to move for career reasons, whilst working-class couples who do so may actually enlist kin in the new area as a source of employment and arrive with ready-made networks. Nevertheless, Young and Willmott (1957) found that when working-class families moved away from close-knit networks this increased interdependency for the couple and brought more sharing of conjugal roles.

Edgell (1980) has challenged the association of middle-class status and 'jointness' in marriage on the basis of domestic variations within a sample of geographically mobile middle-class workers. His research shows no cases of joint conjugal roles except in relation to child care, though more couples fell into the 'intermediate' than into the 'segregated' category. His findings do not, however, refute the possibility that social norms and supportive services embodied in a close-knit social network can exert a significant influence over the nature and content of gender roles.

The division of labour as a reflection of power within the household has also been translated into class terms, and Goode (1964: 74–5) argues:

> Toward the lower strata, the husband is more likely to claim authority simply because he is male, but actually has to concede more authority to his wife. Towards the upper-strata men are less likely to assert the values of patriarchal authority, but in action manage to have more power anyway.

This perspective seems to neglect the force of normative constraints, which studies such as *Coal is our Life* demonstrate can be considerable. Nevertheless, there is some empirical support for Goode's view. Ericksen et al. (1979: 310), for example, find that: 'The best predictor of husband's assistance with housework is his success as an income provider. High income husbands are considerably less likely to do the housework than low income husbands.' Correspondingly: 'The higher the wife's status, relative to her husband, the more likely she is to work outside the home, and the more likely he is to perform tasks inside the home' (p. 311).

There is some echo of this status pattern in findings on education levels, with highly educated women more likely to receive help from husbands (Pleck, 1985), but highly educated husbands are also more likely to give help, and to hold egalitarian ideals (Farkas, 1976). These ideals may well come into conflict with the earning capacity of highly educated men, however. There is little work explicitly examining the effects of race, but Pleck (1985: 47) reports (on the basis of very small numbers) that black husbands seem to perform less household work than whites but to be more involved in child care.

Pahl's findings in the UK on class and status variations seem consistent with much of the American material. Whilst he detects very little variation across classes, he finds that males with lower-status partners or full-time housewives are less likely to be involved in domestic labour than where the reverse is the case. Thus a wife's status (measured by her own employment, with an additional category for full-time housewives) improves her chances of gaining her husband's participation in domestic tasks, whilst Pahl found generally that sharing of domestic labour increases lower down the social scale.

This latter finding is counter-intuitive in that the traditional sexual division of labour has usually been associated with male employment in heavy industry, producing a pattern commonly associated with working-class culture, and graphically described by Dennis et al. (1957). Some writers have even framed a 'subcultural hypothesis' on this basis (for example Farkas, 1976). But, as we have seen in the results of several studies, it may be level of husband's income, not hours in paid work or type and status of work, that determines domestic labour.

Specific studies of domestic labour have tended to focus either on couples where the man is out of work, and these we have examined in chapter 2, or on dual-career couples, often in professional or middle-ranking occupations. The possibility that male income, rather than hours in work, or type and status of occupation determines the division of domestic labour comes as something of a surprise to those of us who have associated the traditional sexual division of labour with traditional working-class culture where the sexual roles were segregated but complementary, though the man held the position of overt control.

Chapter 2 looked in detail at the existing studies of male unemployment, where findings appear to contradict the prediction that male employment status and earnings are negatively correlated with participation in domestic labour. In fact, although unemployment frees men from the constraints of paid work, and notionally makes them available for unpaid domestic labour, their assumption of domestic chores does not necessarily follow.

We might also expect that the authority of the man within the home, and his power to exercise his will would be damaged by unemployment (for example Komarovsky, 1940) and that this would be an additional reason for increased domestic labour. Research has shown the situation to be more complex than this, however, with men often resisting suggestions that they assume a greater involvement in domestic life. This is partly to be understood as a defence of their previous position in the household, which had been accorded by virtue of their 'breadwinner' status.

We also saw, however, that although some resistance to assuming a domestic role seemed virtually universal, there is considerable variation in degrees of resistance, and the amount of domestic labour which men will eventually take on. Nevertheless, there was little evidence of male unemployment leading to major responsibility for domestic work, nor even to their taking an equal share.

In fact there was some indication of resistance from women to such participation because of its disruptive effect on their own routine, and the possible lowering of standards. The power of gender ideologies about appropriate roles was seen to be the underlying influence in all these responses, although this seems to vary with the strength of peer-group norms supporting and enforcing traditional roles.

Conversely, as we saw earlier, studies such as the Pahls' *Managers and their Wives* (1971) and the Rapoports' *Dual Career Families* (1971) showed ideas about equality and sharing in marriage to be often frustrated by the demands of the husband's occupation, and the tendency for this to take precedence, usually because he was the highest earner. Edgell's study of middle-class couples (1980) similarly concluded: 'It is . . . the wife who tends to accommodate the husband who in turn has to accommodate to the occupational system.'

More recently Ostrander's US study of *Women of the Upper Class* (1984: 39) reports that women in the upper stratum of society: 'centered their lives around their husbands and their husbands' work and adapted themselves to the men's needs . . . showing solidarity, giving help, rewarding, agreeing, understanding and passively accepting.'

Yogev (1981) carried out a study specifically to examine the situation of a sample of 151 faculty women at Northwestern University in the US to enquire as to whether professional women have egalitarian marital relationships. Although there were relatively small differences in the number of hours worked (9.4 per week less for women with children, and 1.5 less for childless women), both sets of women did substantially more hours per week in household work (16.0 and 12.1 hours, respectively) Their interesting finding is that only a few women believed their husbands were not doing enough, and the majority did not want or expect their husbands to share household responsibilities equally.

Angrist et al. (1976) compare working American mothers in different socio-economic groups to find considerable differences in domestic and child care patterns. Professional women were more likely to purchase cleaning and child care services, whilst women in clerical-technical occupations are more likely to rely on kin and friends. This could be perceived as a network effect, but what is of interest is that neither group relied substantially on husbands.

Conclusion

Whilst a summary of the sources and significance of variations in domestic labour throws up a number of puzzles, gaps and inconsistencies, none of

the data seems to warrant any suggestion that the traditional female responsibility for household work has been substantially eroded, or that male
participation has substantially increased. This does not mean to say that it
has not *significantly* increased.

There are, however, a number of areas in the explanation of domestic
patterns that need further investigation. Of particular interest would be the
notion of power over household relations, what form it takes and the use to
which it is put. There is in some work an underlying assumption that men
wish to avoid domestic labour and will use their superior power within the
household to do so. The relationship between power, domestic roles,
personal ideals and cultural patterns is relatively unexplored, however.
Similarly, whilst male income level has been found to be a major determinant of household work (or rather its absence), we know little about the
way the potential for power embodied in high earning is exercised. Such
questions require a much closer look inside the household at the dynamics
of particular marital relationships, and the mechanisms of negotiation. One
area in which the power and authority conferred by earning capacity has
been more rigorously considered is the management of household finance,
our topic in the following chapter.

6 Household Finance

Our discussion so far has been largely concerned with the sexual division of labour in the household, and its implications for gender roles and identity. A closely related question is the distribution of financial resources – the fruits of labour – within the home. There are two senses in which we might wish to investigate this aspect of domestic organization with reference to labour market experience (see, for example, Morris with Ruane, 1989). On the one hand we might hypothesize that attitudes towards employment, and behaviour in the labour market, can only be fully understood with reference to access to, uses of, and benefit from earned income. Such a hypothesis leads us into questions about the motivation for earning and the balance of concern for self against concern for the household as a collectivity. On the other hand it is possible that the way in which a given household organizes its finances and the way in which its members set their spending priorities will be strongly influenced by their position and experience in the labour market.

Any concern with the generation and distribution of resources within the household must in some way address the question of to what extent the household may be viewed unproblematically as an economic unit. There are obvious practical reasons for why, in the collection of data, the household has been the focus of research (as for example in the British General Household Survey) but this begs certain questions. How rigorous is the sharing of resources within the home? To what extent do individual desires and priorities conflict with, and take precedence over, the interests of the collectivity? And who within the household defines what those interests might be? This was one of the limitations noted in a previous chapter with reference to the notion of a 'household strategy'. A full understanding of any such strategy must take account of the process by which it emerged, and here distribution of, and access to, resources within the home will be critical.

Resource Theory of Power

Perhaps the best-known sociological attempt to grapple with such questions took the form of a resource theory of power, developed by American writers Blood and Wolfe (1960) in their study of husbands and wives in Detroit and Michigan. We have discussed this work with reference to divisions of labour within the home, but the location of power in the home is also intimately linked to control of resources. Blood and Wolfe's 'pragmatic theory' (p. 29) suggests that: 'the balance of power in particular families and in whole categories of families is determined by the comparative resourcefulness of the two partners and by their life circumstances'.

Their measure of power is based on decision making in several critical areas of life, most of which involve income and/or expenditure. Perhaps unsurprisingly they find power to be closely related to occupational prestige, and, even more so, to levels of earnings. Highly paid husbands were found to be the most influential in marital decision making, but only where they were also *sole* earners. High-income husbands are most powerful if their wives contribute no income; where the wife also earns there is a corresponding diminution in the husband's power (p. 32). This finding suggests that power in the labour market translates into power within the home, but also suggests the possibility that a desire for greater influence could prompt entry into the labour market.

Blood and Wolfe derive a broader variable of 'social status' by aggregating income, occupation, education and ethnic identity, and find power to be directly related to this measure. This power was noted in operation in the home in three particular household areas: whether to buy life insurance, what house to purchase and whether the wife should be employed. Thus it would seem that any desire by the wife to increase her own power, and to generate independent income would first have to be negotiated with the husband.

The overall result of these associations seems to be that high-earning husbands become involved in decision making in areas that involve large amounts of expenditure. This is interpreted by Blood and Wolfe as a more active sharing of responsibility by high-status husbands than by low-status husbands, who often have no part in the decision-making process. The picture to emerge is one of more involvement by high-earning men in spending decisions requiring large amounts of money, and no such involvement by low-earning men, though probably because no such spending occurs. For the women this means greater responsibility, but also greater potential power, in the latter category of homes. Women are also found to be freer in such homes to make their own employment decisions.

Blood and Wolfe's account, however, is unclear on the interpretation of a number of these points. What began as an identification of differential power within the home which saw high-income husbands as more powerful, has in the course of analysis been translated into a higher degree of 'sharing' of marital responsibility in such homes. Confusion about precisely what constitutes 'sharing' and what reflects the power and interests of particular individuals is a recurrent problem in the study of household finance management. Blood and Wolfe's data provide some evidence of associations between earning levels, control over expenditure and labour market decisions, but in doing so introduce us to a complexity of interrelations that the study does not begin to unravel.

Gillespie (1972), drawing on the work of Safilios-Rothschild (1970), has criticized the measurement of power on which the Blood and Wolfe study is based. The argument is that: 'the conception and measurement of power is already biased in that it does not expose certain kinds of power which automatically accrue to the husband by virtue of his job, and . . . takes no account of the differential importance of . . . decisions in the power structure of the marriage' (p. 124).

Gillespie's judgement, then, is that Blood and Wolfe underestimate the power wielded by the husband through his earning role and occupational status, but nevertheless treat 'wife dominance' as a deviant case. A wife's power is gained unhappily, 'by default of her "no good" or incapacitated husband' (Blood and Wolfe, 1960: 45). This view is consistent with their discussion of employment decisions, which is based on the assumption that the wife's earnings are necessarily secondary. For example, Blood and Wolfe remark that the woman's job is seldom her major preoccupation, that her pay cheque is not indispensable to the family finances, and that the repercussions of a wife's employment on the husband is a significant consideration in the question of whether she should be in gainful employment at all. They argue in conclusion that: 'The work role is so much the responsibility of the husband in marriage that even the wife's work is but an adjunct of his instrumental leadership' (p. 22).

The data given by Blood and Wolfe about gender-differentiated decision making raise some interesting questions about on whose behalf expenditure is being incurred. For example, they note that two decisions are primarily the husband's province: his job and the car; and two the wife's: her work and the food, though with the former substantially influenced by the husband. This leaves only food spending predominantly in the wife's hands, an area of *household* consumption, in contrast to the husband's expenditure on a car to which he, of all household members, has by far the greatest access (pp. 20–1). What these data suggest is that any adequate understanding of household finance management involves more than a listing of individual spending decisions. The interpretation of such data becomes problematic once we concede that earning capacity, employment decisions, access to resources, power over expenditure, and benefit through consumption, all appear to be interrelated.

Central Questions

A number of writers have approached the study of household finance by the identification of distinctive patterns or procedures, which can be used to classify households and which differ in their implications for power over income, benefit from spending and motivation for earning. In the UK it was research concerned with the alleviation of poverty in the early post-war period that first raised the question of to what extent 'family' or rather household income could be used as a satisfactory indicator of the standard of living of a principal wage-earner's dependants. Thus Young (1952: 305) writes: 'The first task . . . is to discover the ways in which the total earnings of wage-earning members are divided up between different spenders of the family. The second . . . is to discover the distribution of actual goods and services between members of the family.'

In other words, we need to ask who decides how household income is to be divided, who spends it and who benefits from expenditure. These are questions that have been most fully addressed in a relatively recent, and predominantly British literature concerned to understand the variety of arrangements made by different households, and to specify their implications.

Jan Pahl (1983) has identified a hierarchy of financial responsibility, with three distinct levels:

'Control' is primarily concerned with the way in which money is allocated within the household, and involves decisions about the distribution of income and of responsibilities for different areas of expenditure.

'Management' refers to the process whereby control decisions are actually put into operation, primarily in the management of designated areas of expenditure of household income.

'Budgeting' is the process of spending within particular expenditure categories, and the use of the resources to achieve minimal consumption requirements.

Pahl here is identifying functions in the management of money that each carry different implications for power within the household. Ultimate power lies with the controller whose decisions are administered by the manager, both of whom are concerned with the whole pool of resources available, leaving the budgeter with discretion only within strictly defined limits.

A further useful distinction has been made by Morris (1984a: 494) who questions the implications of the notion of a 'household income' in contrast to what she terms 'domestic income':

> 'Household income' refers to the total amount of money received by the various members of the household from whatever source.
>
> 'Domestic income' refers to the total income available for spending on the collective needs of the household, i.e. food, fuel and accommodation.

This distinction highlights the potential power of the controller of earned income who always has available the option of withholding all or a portion of earnings from the domestic purse.

Does Money Equal Power?

Much of the American literature concerned with household finances follows in the Blood and Wolfe tradition with a general concern on the overall locus of power, rather than on the detail of how finances are organized. The basic premise behind such work is summarized by Komarovsky (1962: 224): 'There were good reasons to suspect that the better providers, the more skilled, and the better educated men would enjoy more power in marriage than the men of lower socio-economic status. The good providers can use money as a means of control.'

In fact, Komarovsky's findings, in agreement with those of Blood and Wolfe (1960: 31, 33), found no such simple correlation, but instead suggest: 'a curvilinear relationship between occupation and social status, on the one hand, and husband's power, on the other'.

Thus where low earnings and low skill are accompanied by low education there is an uncritical acceptance of the idea of masculine dominance in marriage. At higher educational (and therefore occupational) levels this view is less firmly adhered to, although male authority rises again at the highest earning levels. There is further confirmation of this finding in Rubin's work (1976), which reports a shift from female to male finance management at higher income levels. Kandel and Lesser (1972) list a number of other US studies that have confirmed the curvilinear relationship (Kandel and Lesser, 1969; Rodman, 1970; Safilios-Rothschild, 1970), and argue that such evidence disproves any naïve argument relating financial resources to power within the household.

The work of Hiller and Philliber (1986: 194) reports little evidence of differential power over finances, finding 69 per cent of couples in their study in agreement with the idea that the management of money should be shared. There are three points to be made here, however. Firstly, two-thirds of their sample were dual-earner couples, which might offer support to the resources theory of power; secondly, as Rubin (1976) notes, there is a common tendency to subscribe to an ideology of sharing where in fact the man has power of veto; and thirdly, management may be notionally shared but still reflect a hierarchy of decision making. We have seen this in operation in Blood and Wolfe's (1960) findings, and Rubin reports a similar variant in which the man makes major decisions at higher income levels, but leaves the woman to administer them. A British study of middle-class couples (Edgell, 1980: 59) provides further data on this question, finding larger items of expenditure to require the man's decision: 'The husband decided the overall allocation of financial resources and had most say in the case of decisions involving large sums of money, whereas the wife in every research family tended to make all the "minor" decisions.'

The woman's powerlessness in homes where the man is the sole earner has been remarked upon at a variety of socio-economic levels. Ostrander (1984) in a study of upper-class American women found they had more influence in marriage when they had an independent income, whilst Luxton's study of working-class couples (1980: 166, 168) and Blumstein and Schwartz's more general study of American couples (1983: 58) notes a belief that it is ultimately the earner who has rights of disposal over the wage. The same sentiment is expressed by both men and women in Hunt's UK study of working-class couples (1980). And yet the power equation does not seem to operate in both directions.

Hertz (1986) found in a study of US dual-earner couples that the mere fact of women earning an independent income did not necessarily mean a revolutionary change in authority relations between husbands and wives. Stamp (1985) comes to a similar conclusion in her UK study of female main earners. And yet joint management of finance has been argued to occur more commonly where the wife earns (Gray, 1979; Pahl, 1983), and Pahl has argued more generally, citing a number of writers (Bahr, 1979; Blood and Wolfe, 1960; Kandel and Lesser, 1972; Lupri, 1969; Michel, 1967), that women's independent income increases their power. Morris (1984a) suggests, however, that we need to distinguish between types of job and levels of earning for women, and where a low female income is used to augment inadequate funds from the man it can have the effect of simply freeing his resources without implying any substantial shift in the wife's influence over the financial system as a whole.

Classification of Finance Types

To get any further in an understanding of how finance systems operate requires more detail than the locus-of-power approach provides. A number of writers have attempted to draw up schematic outlines of the different possible arrangements for household finance management. There are considerable problems involved in doing so (see Morris with Ruane, 1989) but four basic models have emerged (cf. Pahl, 1983), which may be briefly characterized as follows:

1 The whole-wage system In this system one partner is responsible for managing all household income, and responsible for all expenditures. Examples are to be found in studies from both the UK (Gray, 1979; McIntosh, 1981; Morris, 1984a; Pahl, 1980; Stamp, 1985) and the US (Blumstein and Schwartz, 1983; Luxton, 1980). In some writing (for example Luxton, 1980: 165; Pahl, 1980: 319) we find cases where the man makes a small retention from the wage in homes classified as 'whole-wage' households, although strictly speaking they represent one variant of a different system which is allowance based.

2 The allowance system Here the main earner hands over a set amount for housekeeping and uses the remainder for his/her own designated areas of expenditure. Again examples are to be found in both UK studies (Gray, 1979; Land, 1969; Morris, 1984a; Pahl, 1983) and US research (Blumstein and Schwartz, 1983; Luxton, 1982). Somewhat unusually, Rubin (1976: 83) notes an arrangement in which the earner hands over two allowances, one for household expenditures and the other for personal spending.

3 Joint management system Both partners have access to all household income, and are jointly responsible for management of, and expenditure from a common pool. UK examples include Gray (1979), Morris (1984a), Pahl (1983) and Stamp (1985) and US examples are found in Luxton (1980) and Ostrander (1984).

4 Independent management This system is characterized by the absence of access to all household income by either partner. Each has a separate income and specifically designated areas of responsibility for expenditure. Such an arrangement seems relatively rare but is discussed by Stamp (1985) and Pahl (1983) in UK studies, and cited by Blumstein and Schwartz (1983) with reference to American cohabiting and/or homosexual couples.

The power implications of each model are very different. In the whole-wage system ultimate power lies with the recipient of the wage, but once a decision has been taken to hand it over intact then power of disposal is also, notionally, handed over, although there is still room for ambiguity here, as we see in cases where the earner expects money back on request (for example Homer et al., 1985; Morris, 1984a; Pahl, 1980). In the allowance system the wage earner sets the allowance, but with the implication at least that once this has been handed over the recipient will be free from inter-ference in its management. These problems are ostensibly disposed of with a joint management system in that both partners have an equal call on the pool of funds, which is notionally accessible to both, although again there may be some deviation from the theory in the operation of this system. Finally, independent management leaves personal discretion over personal incomes intact, being based on exchange rather than commonality and involving less potential for the exercise or abuse of power.

Explanatory Factors

One way in which labour market status interacts with finance management is by influencing the system to be adopted in any given household. We noted earlier Pahl's distinction between control, management and budget-ing. Logically control will lie with the direct recipient of income for he or she will have power of disposal from the point at which money enters the household economy. It is still the case in both Britain and America that this person is more likely to be a man than a woman, whilst the traditional association of women with activity in the domestic sphere, which we remarked on in chapter 5, seems likely to lead to female involvement in management and budgeting, rather than control.

Whole wage

This association between women and the domestic sphere seems to have led to a particular pattern of finance management in the case of low-income households. The whole wage in its commonest form, that is the man hand-ing over his full wage to the woman, seems to occur both where income is low and position in the labour market weak, and in areas of traditional working-class culture. UK examples are to be found in Dennis et al. (1956), Kerr (1958) and Land (1969), and for the US in Luxton (1980) and Blood and Wolfe (1960). Land (1969) in her study of large families in London notes: 'The primary responsibility for managing the household finances shifted from the father in higher income families, to the mother in low income families.' Similarly, Blood and Wolfe (1960) note the absence of involvement in spending decisions on the part of low-income men: 'leaving the wife saddled with the burden of making family decisions unaided'.

British research also points to the conclusion that source of income is an important additional factor, with unemployment, or more precisely benefit dependence, consistently reported as leading to a whole-wage system (Land, 1969; Morris, 1984a; Pahl, 1983). Comparison with the US on this point is difficult since long-term benefit dependence is less common for married couples. This is partly because unemployment is of generally shorter duration in the US and there is anyway no universally available benefit once contributory benefit has been exhausted. AFDC is available in cases of male unemployment in 23 out of 50 states, but by far the commonest recipients are single mothers. There has been some speculation about whether this household form is associated with male unemployment in that welfare payments offer a more reliable source of income than marriage. Similar arguments have been made in research on battered wives in the UK (Homer et al., 1985; Pahl, 1980).

The tendency for female management of a whole-wage system in cases of low income has been explained by the general pattern of responsibility for day-to-day expenditure (Land, 1969), and the significance of this category of spending in poorer homes. Blood and Wolfe explain the lack of male spending involvement in such homes with reference to the absence of high-cost decisions on expenditure, which conversely account for the participation of high earning males. Morris (1984a) has argued on the basis of research in South Wales that there is a greater need for close surveillance of spending where income is low, and as a result there is a high probability of unitary control. The woman's traditional association with the domestic sphere, and the priority commonly attached to food, fuel and accommodation, make her the most likely candidate. A similar point is implicit in Rubin's work in the US (1976: 107), where we are told that at income levels that allow 'substantial discretionary spending' (that is where income is higher) there will be a shift from female to male management.

Allowance system

This system seems also to be adopted in traditional British working-class communities but at higher income levels than are found with the whole wage (see Dennis et al., 1956; Pahl, 1980: 333), and we have evidence from the US that notes more involvement by men in financial management as income rises (Blood and Wolfe, 1960; Rubin, 1970). How this shift should be interpreted, however, is not clear. Is the woman being relieved of some of the more arduous demands of managing implied by the whole-wage system, or is she losing power to her husband as soon as discretionary spending increases? Certainly in this system the woman never sees the unopened wage-packet, and may not even know how much her husband earns (see Gray, 1979: 199 for a discussion of secrecy). Thus on the one hand the allowance system limits the wife's access to her husband's earned income whilst securing and protecting his retention from the wage; but on the other hand the shift to an allowance system as income rises facilitates male assumption of responsibility for some aspects of collective expenditure.

Much of the discussion of this system of finance management in British literature has revolved around the distinction between personal and collective (or household) spending, with key considerations hinging on the structure and methods of payment of male earnings. Gray (1979) sets out the main argument, stating that where the allowance is kept low the man secures greater choice about how many hours a week to work. This device may be used to protect the allowance against fluctuating earnings (see Dennis et al., 1956; Kerr, 1958), or alternatively the allowance may fluctuate with the wage (see Woodward et al., 1954). It may also serve to secure a larger amount of the wage for disposal by the man by holding the allowance steady when earnings rise. A regular allowance means that the rewards of additional effort exerted at work can be kept by the man for his personal use *if he so chooses*. Tunstall (1962) gives an example, whilst Zweig (1961) found overtime earnings to be shared with the wife.

Gray notes a distinction regarding male orientation within the allowance type which makes some sense of the tendency to classify small retentions by the man as a whole-wage variant. This pattern was found to be associated with a sexual division of labour and low skill levels, and an emphasis on male personal spending. Such a complex could possibly be equated with features Komarovsky noted in patriarchal marriages (1967). Cases of larger retentions were found with higher skill, higher income and greater home centredness, though in the more egalitarian marriages the tendency was for retentions to be used for items of collective expenditure. Any attempt to explain the allowance system by reference to male spending priorities must take account of the variety implied by these differing orientations within the system.

Joint management

This system differs from the other two discussed so far in that there is no privileged position of power, and no designation of individual responsibilities. Instead it is a model based on equal access and joint responsibility. Because of this it depends on a high level of trust and agreement about priorities for spending. Pahl (1983) has argued that pooling systems are characteristic of a relatively high income, and specific UK studies have shown this to be so. Land (1969) in a study of large London families found 'jointness' increasing as income rose, whilst Morris (1984a) in South Wales found joint management to be associated with higher *disposable* income and higher occupational grades. We must, however, exercise caution in the interpretation of the data for, as we have seen, Blood and Wolfe (1960) seem to view increased male involvement in spending decisions, and arguably increased male *power*, as an indication of increased sharing.

Luxton's US study of working-class couples provides a clear description of joint management defined by equal access to funds, shared responsibility for the payment of bills, and discussions about items of collective and personal expenditure. There is no reference to levels of income but joint management is found to be more common in younger couples, occurring in respectively 25 and 23 per cent of the second- and third-generation couples interviewed, but completely absent from the first generation. We might speculate that income would be higher for younger couples, though of course there will be considerable variation in demands on income, notably according to numbers of children. Other writers have introduced the idea of stage in the life-cycle as a determining factor, though as Morris (1984a) notes, there will also be an association with patterns of female employment. The general effect is summarized by Pahl (1980: 330):

> The pooling system may be characteristic of the newly married couple who are both earning; this may change to the allowance system when the wife leaves paid employment to look after young children, and change again to a modified pooling system with two earners, or where teenage children may be contributing to the household economy.

Kandel and Lesser (1972), in a comparative study of decision making in American and Danish urban couples, have made similar observations about stage in the life-cycle and women's labour market position, whilst Gray (1979) finds decreasing jointness as family size increases – and presumably disposable income decreases.

Most evidence does seem to support the suggestion that pooling and higher income are in some way associated and the most obvious reason for this is the converse of the 'unitary control' aspect of the whole-wage system (Morris with Ruane, 1989). The higher disposable income is, then the less need for tight control of spending and the more viable a joint system. The assumption here is that control of expenditure is necessarily more difficult if two people have free and independent access to money than if only one does. The argument becomes more complex, however, when we introduce questions of sources of income, the effect of women's employment and ideological/cultural factors. Both Pahl (1983) and Gray (1979) have argued that joint management is most likely when wives are employed, and Pahl (1980) has also argued that cultural factors shaped by the nature of the labour market may have some influence here. Thus a tradition of secure employment for women is argued to have the opposite effect of a rigid sexual division of labour associated with a whole-wage or allowance system and the gendered separation of spheres, such that a pooling system is more likely to be adopted.

We have already noted the more general observation from a number of writers (Blumstein and Schwartz, 1983; Ostrander, 1984; Rubin, 1976) that women's influence increases when they have an independent income. This should not be interpreted as necessarily producing 'jointness' however. A US study by Blumstein and Schwartz, for example, does not identify a joint management system in the discussion of finance management types but rather emphasizes an increased potential for conflict: 'Because the wife now earns her own money, she expects to exercise more control, and her husband's attempts to compel her (as the buyer) to spend her money in ways he sees fit may meet with greater resistance.'

Independent management

It may be that the tensions identified by Blumstein and Schwartz will lead a household to adopt an independent management system. Certainly their discussion of cohabiting and homosexual couples suggests that such a system is adopted as a means of minimizing the potential for disagreement. What lies behind this tendency is the wish to avoid any established pattern of dependence, thus 'cohabitors believe strongly in each partner's contributing his or her equal share' (p. 61). The authors go on to suggest, however, that the ideology of marriage can serve to permit a greater degree of conflict than alternative arrangements where commitment may not be so explicit. Independent financial accounting in such relationships lessens commitment, makes dissolution of the partnership easier and hence, argue the authors, more likely.

The connection between separate accounting systems, independence and equal authority within marriage has been made by Hertz's (1986) study of professional dual earners. In her study it is not employment for the woman *per se* that is likely to challenge the traditional relations of authority: 'The existence of two incomes itself does not make the crucial difference; rather the mechanisms devised to deal with this income should provide the focal point.'

The fact that pooling is more likely at lower levels of earning for the wife suggest that there may be a critical level at which the claim to independence will be made and incorporated into the household finance system. Thus: 'Having two high and secure incomes increases the likelihood that couples will distinguish between individual and communal resources.'

Whilst independent management may require two incomes as a basic condition, it will not necessarily be adopted simply *because* there are two incomes. Much the rarest reported system, possibly as a result of a tendency for research to focus on the lower levels of the socio-economic scale, it is absent entirely from several of the studies concerned with household finance to which we have referred so far (for example Gray, 1979; Luxton, 1982; Morris, 1984a; Rubin, 1976). Whilst such a system can form the basis of a claim to self-reliance for both partners it does not necessarily operate in this way. For example, husband and wife may carry very unequal financial responsibility. One of the important features of the system, however, is that it makes spending visible, a particularly important point for women, many of whom augment an inadequate housekeeping allowance often without their husbands' acknowledgement (see, for example, Morris, 1987c).

The Influence of Finance Systems

Our argument so far has been that the arrangement adopted for the management of household finance is partly to be understood with reference to the labour market position of household members – notably with reference to who earns, how much and in what form. The question may be posed in reverse, however, to ask in what way finance systems can influence *behaviour* in the labour market, either through the attitudes and practice of employees at their place of work, or by acting upon the incentive to take on employment. These issues prompt some consideration of personal spending requirements, individual commitment to 'collective' (household) expenditure, and individual access to and power of disposal over total 'household' income. In other words, they raise questions about the motivation for earning.

Assumptions about these issues have crept into an employment-related literature, often without being fully investigated. Shimmin (1962), for example, notes three different studies, all of which purport to show that hours of work increase with family responsibility (which is read off from family size), citing Walker (1961), Buck and Shimmin (1959) and Robertson (1960). But can we assume that the additional earnings of men with large families are spent on those families, and that this is necessarily their main motivation for earning? It would be equally possible to argue that the large families are driving the men out of the house, or that longer hours in paid employment are a means of evading family responsibilities. The point is that without looking inside the household to examine the allocation of resources and patterns of expenditure we are in no position to distinguish between the varied possibilities.

Dennis et al. (1956), in a detailed account of work, home and community in a mining village, have documented the tension between an accepted ideology of the male role which places great emphasis on the responsibility to cater for household needs, as against the pull on funds which derives from the wish, supported by strong peer-group norms, to have adequate resources for personal spending. Such spending maintains membership of the peer group which in turn re-emphasizes its importance. Tunstall (1962) reports a similar set of associations in a fishing community, where a rise in basic pay was seen to be less valuable than a rise in bonus payments since the bonus was defined as the man's personal spending money. A bonus serves in this case as a more effective incentive to work effort because of its immediate personal benefits. Similarly, the motivation to work overtime may be greater where an allowance system of household finance operates – the allowance may remain fixed despite the increased earnings in a particular week.

We cannot, of course, generalize about such findings from small and distinctive populations. Male involvement in household organization, and in collective expenditures can vary by class, culture, income levels, personal orientation, and even method of salary transfer. Todd and Jones (1972) found men paid by non-cash transfers, for example, were more likely to be responsible for mortgage repayments than those receiving cash through the pay-packet. Such variation has been noted in a number of studies of the different operations of the allowance system in relation to overtime earning (Gray, 1979; Zweig, 1961).

Zweig's work, somewhat confusingly, contains both a detailed outline of the nature of the association between overtime and home-centred spending, but nevertheless contains the statement: 'There is one factor of a traditional nature which must be taken into account, that is, the distinction between housekeeping money and pocket money which is usually made. In the large majority of cases overtime is not used for housekeeping money.'

Gray's study (1979) makes some sense of such apparent contradiction. She divides her sample of male workers into those who worked at least ten hours overtime per week, and those who worked less, finding two contrasting tendencies. Within the group of skilled workers, male responsibility for significant amounts of 'collective' expenditure was associated with longer hours. Among the unskilled workers the trend was the opposite, and longer hours were associated with minimal male involvement in collective spending. In the former case overtime working will be prompted by consumer ambitions focusing on the home, and in the latter case additional earnings will be used to finance male social activities away from the home. This fits well with Gray's findings that overtime working was associated both with separate acquaintance sets for husband and wife, and conversely with heavy commitments to home-based expenditure – and presumably a home-based social life.

Women's Labour Supply

In contrast to the predominantly work-place literature on men's labour market behaviour documented above, women's incentive to work seems to have been addressed largely in terms of the decision to enter employment, rather than on behaviour at work. I have argued elsewhere (Morris with Ruane, 1989) that implicit in the asking of the question 'why work?' is the assumption that for married women at least some alternative means of support is available. A full appreciation of the decision to enter employment therefore requires a consideration of the use of the married woman's wage, and of her access to her husband's wage, both of which may be shaped by the way in which the household manages financial matters.

The orthodox approach to labour supply economics has focused on individual decisions and strengths and weaknesses in the market for labour. In the case of married women there has usually been some allowance for the effect of the husband's wage, and in more recent thinking an income effect which may operate in either direction is incorporated. If such models are based on the assumption of perfect information then they will clearly have severe limitations, for individuals will not always know how much their spouses earn (see Young, 1952; Marsh, 1979). Nor can we assume that a high income for one partner necessarily benefits the living standards of the other. In other words, models that attempt to explain and predict joint labour supply decisions cannot ignore what happens to earnings after they enter the household.

In the US the 'new household economics' advanced by Gary Becker uses the household as the unit of analysis in an attempt to represent the relationship between husband and wife's labour supply and consumption decisions. He does take account of the possibility of 'shirking, cheating, pilfering and other malfeasance' in task performance, which he notes will be more likely where there is a marked task separation. This move concedes the possibility of inequity in the actual operation of household dynamics, but Becker's discussion of the problem revolves around the concepts of selfishness and altruism, which he seems to argue are sanctioned by 'invasion of privacy'. The great failing of this perspective is that it nowhere addresses the problem of control. As Ben-Porath (1982) has argued, the model is based on an assumption of consensus, with no acknowledgement of the possibility of distributional conflict. A wish to escape from such conflicts, together with a desire for control over income and an escape from dependency drives many women to seek employment, and this response is not necessarily determined by the husband's level of earning.

The Woman's Wage

We have already found that the increasing participation of married women in paid employment is not to be explained by the fall of employment opportunities for men, since role reversal occurs in both the UK and US in only a minority of cases of male unemployment. The tendency in existing literature has accordingly been to concentrate attention on the effects of women's employment in dual-earner couples.

A good deal of discussion on this topic has been centrally concerned with the question of how important is the woman's wage to the maintenance of the household standard of living. This question has arisen as a counter to the argument that women's earnings are typically for personal spending on luxury items or are somehow not central to domestic budgeting. One example of this view is Rainwater's comments (1984) on a study of American wives contributions to household income:

> For a great many families in which the mother is a labour force participant, her earnings have a special role in the family economy and in no sense function to keep the family consumption up to a particular level. . . . Much of the way in which families seem to use the income that wives contribute suggests the primacy of non-pecuniary motives. (pp. 81–2)

Such a claim raises a number of key questions:

1 In what way does women's employment relate to levels of overall household income?
2 What are the major factors motivating married women to seek employment?
3 Are there distinctive patterns in the use to which women's income is put?

Rainwater et al. (1986: 65) report that the wife's median financial contribution to household income levels averages 21 per cent in the US and 15 per cent in the UK, and that contrary to much economic theory there is no strong relationship between spouse's income and propensity to work. In the US wives were slightly less likely to be employed the higher their husband's income, but the general picture, according to Rainwater

(1984: 79) is one in which: 'Wives' decisions to work are not heavily influenced by their husband's economic circumstances, but rather are related to
the woman's own goals and interests'.

In the UK Cragg and Dawson (1984) attempted to investigate the
relationship between wives' employment and husbands' earnings but found
that the lack of knowledge about husband's earnings on the part of the wife
made this impossible, whilst Martin and Roberts (1984) found little difference between husband's earnings for employed and unemployed women.
As with the US data, evidence for a strong effect of the husband's wage is
weak: 'The gross earnings of the husbands of non-working women were
somewhat higher . . . but the difference is very small in relation to the
average earnings of the working women.'

As Rainwater points out, however, there is considerable variation in
household arrangements. The higher the household income the more likely
it is that the wife will be employed, partly of course because her income
contributes to this ranking. In the US 40 per cent of wives in the lowest
income third are labour-force participants, 50 per cent in the middle
income third and 60 per cent in the highest income third. In the UK the
corresponding figures are 45, 65 and 72 per cent, suggesting that the wife's
income is less important in establishing a difference between the middle
and upper group than in the US. One factor affecting these differences in
household income and employment structure could be the operation of
different household dynamics in different socio-economic classes. Thus,
argues Rainwater, traditional role definitions play a stronger role in working-class homes, discouraging female labour-force participation. For
middle-class couples, Rainwater argues, the husband's preferences and
demands are less determining, and where the woman is employed it is a
reflection of her psychological and social gain from employment.

One possible reading of these comments is that since working-class
women are more likely to face male opposition to their employment their
entry into the labour-force is likely to be where financial constraints are
such as to override any objection. There is substantial evidence available
for both the US and UK to suggest that economic pressure is a primary
motive in the employment of many married women. Blood and Wolfe
(1960), for example, found 31 per cent of black wives in Detroit to be
employed, as compared with 22 per cent of white wives. This they attribute
to the inadequacies of the husband's income. They add that 25 per cent of
employed black wives put in more than 40 hours a week, compared with
only 17 per cent of white wives, a reflection of the poor occupational status
of both black men and women. Shaw (1985) has also noted the greater significance of the wife's earnings for black couples as compared with white.

Bruegel (1988) has reported on similar findings in the UK where black women are more likely to be economically active, and less likely to work part time than white women. Expressed as a proportion of employment by ethnic group, part-time work makes up 45 per cent of white female employment, but only 16 per cent among black women (West Indian and Asian). Although these figures are not broken down by marital status, Bruegel's interpretation suggests that poor earnings for black men, and the significance of the wife's wage, are major contributors to this pattern.

A considerable literature has grown up in the UK which is concerned to emphasize more generally the importance of wives' earnings in keeping many households out of poverty, and it has been calculated that the number of households in poverty would increase threefold without this contribution (Rimmer, 1981). Given that proportions of wives working in the lowest third of household incomes is similar for both the UK and US, it seems fair to assume a similar figure would apply in the States. Martin and Roberts (1984) present some useful data for the UK that address the question of the significance of the woman's wage. Contrary to expectations, they found that women contributing over 30 per cent of gross household earnings were less likely to say that they could manage financially without these earnings. In contrast, among wives contributing less than 20 per cent of joint earnings, a quarter did not feel that they could 'get by alright' without.

Such data call into question Rainwater's interpretation of statistics on wives' contribution to household income. Women's contribution to earnings in the US and UK are averaged at 22 and 18 per cent, respectively (Hamill, 1978, estimates 25 per cent for UK women), but the general thrust of her argument is that wives' earnings are not critical to the household. This kind of judgement ultimately requires some data on the use to which women's earnings are put, and on the degree of access they have to the husband's wage.

Use of the Woman's Wage

We noted earlier in this chapter several works from both the US and UK that cited women's feelings that an independent income gave them more authority within the home, feelings which were related to the desire for a degree of financial independence. We have also found evidence of an acceptance of the earner's rights of disposal over the wage. Given the gendered nature of household responsibilities, it becomes difficult to make a clear distinction between earning for financial necessity and the wish for financial independence. Cragg and Dawson (1984), for example, note the possibility of minor discord within marriage over the size of the housekeeping allowance, hence remarks such as: 'If I had a wage I wouldn't have to ask him to pay for shoes for the kids. I could just go out and get them.'

Cragg and Dawson also note that many women have difficulty in regarding their husband's income as their own, even when encouraged to do so, a difficulty noted by a number of other writers in this country and the US (see Blumstein and Schwartz, 1983; Hunt, 1978, 1980). This fact is reflected in research in the north-east of England (Morris, 1987c), which found 'borrowing' from a husband when housekeeping ran short to be a common notion, and often related to a woman's desire for paid employment. A common sentiment expressing the need for personal earnings was expressed as follows: 'More or less to get by with the housekeeping. I hate borrowing off him. I'll borrow to get to the end of the week then I get behind' (p. 92).

For the husbands, the problem was often perceived as a need to control their wives' spending: 'It's not that I can't manage on what I bring home. It's just that I'm trying to make her manage on what I give her. That way we might get a bit behind us like' (p. 92).

Luxton (1980: 164) reports a disagreement between a working-class husband and wife in the US that highlights similar problems. The woman's remarks include the following statements: 'I'd like to work then I wouldn't have to spend your money, I could spend my own . . . you do your own goddam shopping from now on. . . . All your precious money would be gone in no time.' Whilst the man states his position as follows: 'I help you when I give you my money that you use to buy that lot [groceries]. Your job is spending it and just see to it that you spend it carefully.'

In cases of this kind, where the household operates an allowance system paid from the husband's wage, the motivation for women's employment is often to augment an inadequate allocation for housekeeping. In such cases the woman's contribution to the household maintenance is often invisible, and the man's breadwinner role remains unchallenged. The argument that women's earnings increase their power in the household is not convincing in such cases, and, as we have noted some writers suggest that the effect is simply to reduce demands on the man's wage, possibly freeing funds to be used at his discretion (Jephcott et al., 1962; Morris, 1984a). This is not to argue that men are therefore necessarily profligate spenders and neglectful of collective needs. Rather that their concerns are to secure the long-term well-being of the household, whilst the woman, because of her housekeeping role, is more concerned with immediate needs, hence the tension over housekeeping money and the common desire for women to seek employment.

In other cases, however, the woman's earnings clearly do enhance her status within the household, and this seems most likely to be the case where there is a strong career attachment on the part of women, where finances are handled jointly, and where the woman's wage covers clearly visible items of collective expenditure, as for example in the case of mortgage repayments or regular payment of large bills. Some American writers have found the employment of wives to reduce husband's job commitment and/or to lower their hours of work. In a study of clerical, technical, professional and administrative personnel, Gould and Werbel (1983) found that lower work involvement among workers in dual-wage households was related to enhanced financial security, whilst Hayghe (1981) reports not only that men in dual-wage couples earned less than sole-earner males, but in some instances worked fewer hours. This is interpreted as evidence against financial necessity as a motive for the wives' employment, an argument Hayghe supports by the finding that relatively more of the income in such homes is spent on convenience items. None the less, if women's employment is relaxing the work commitment of some men, and lowering their earnings, as Hayghe suggests, then the effective and overt substitution of the woman's earnings for her husband's implied seems likely to enhance her influence over household finance.

There is clearly considerable room for variation in the use of the woman's wage and in perceptions of its significance. In allowance or whole-wage households, which are predominantly working-class arrangements and correspondingly found at relatively low income levels, the employment of a wife seems often to be to supplement domestic spending, and its significance is likely to be underestimated. In joint or independent management homes the woman's wage will be more visible, but in these predominantly middle-class couples the woman's motivation seems more likely to be related to career commitment, social contact and/or identity, rather than pressing financial need. This point has been made in general terms for American couples by Kenkel (1969: 147), whilst Land (1969) has shown that in the UK the percentage of women whose earnings are spent predominantly on housekeeping is inversely related to class position (69 per cent in the unskilled manual class and 50 per cent in the managerial professional class). Thus, ironically, the lower the woman's earnings the more critical they are likely to be for household survival, and this is a point to be recognized in discussion of the effects of women's unemployment, our topic in the following chapter.

7 Women's Unemployment

With the growth of jobs for women, the increased presence of married women in the labour force and the consequent significance of their additional income in maintaining the household there has been a growing awareness of the possibility that joblessness for women constitutes a problem, rather than simply reflecting their natural role. There are difficulties in the elaboration of this problem that will differ according to the marital status of the women concerned. For married women these difficulties concern both definition and quantification, as well as the assessment of personal and household hardship attendant on unemployment.

Most early work on unemployment dates back to the depression years and is largely concerned with the effects of unemployment for the married male. Where women feature at all it is in the consideration of the implications of male unemployment for wives and families. There are exceptions to this pattern in both British and American literature, however. In the US Pruette and Peters (1934) examined directly the economic and psychological losses suffered by women as a result of their own unemployment, though the focus was exclusively on professional women. Kempers and Rayman (1987) note that as a result the research tended to downplay family connections and to present a sketch of women workers as professional, autonomous, white and single. These authors do, however, draw attention to the work of the Women's Bureau Pamphlets (nos. 113, 1933; 92, 1932; 108, 1936; 139, 1936; 172, 1939) on unemployment fluctuations, unemployed women seeking relief, the effects of the Depression on female wage-earners' families and the situation of women earners.

The work of the Pilgrim Trust (1938) on the depression in the UK also includes a consideration of women's unemployment. The report distinguishes between the 'meanwhile' occupation of girls who enter employment only as a prelude to marriage, their ultimate objective and the event

of their permanent withdrawal from the labour-force, and of women who
enter employment for life, and for whom the home is not their primary
focus of interest. This distinction is largely one of regional difference, the
report states, being fashioned by the kinds of jobs available in a given area
which in turn relates to its industrial structure.

The report goes on to state that: 'The problem of the unemployed
woman cannot be separated from the question of the function of the woman
in national life' (p. 232), and makes a number of points about the effects of
female unemployment. The woman may be healthier and happier in being
released from the dual burden of domestic work and paid work, she is less
likely to be destitute than is the man without work, and a more 'genuinely
civilized' standard of home maintenance is kept up. On the other hand,
there is the question of the significance of her income for the running of the
home, the importance of her earnings in offering a safety net for the
husband's unemployment, as well as the personal independence which
accrues from her paid employment. Hence:

> Do we consider that by making it possible for a woman to devote
> herself to her home, society is securing for itself a paramount advan-
> tage in the maintenance of a high standard of home life? Or do we
> believe that this view is out of date; that the modern woman can both
> work and keep house, and that by doing so she gains a status of which
> her predecessors have always been unjustly deprived?

These sentiments still underlie much of the debate and discussion of
women's unemployment today, though we should note the telling assumption that even employed women remain responsible for the running of the
home.

Theories of Female Unemployment

It is because of the assumed availability of an alternative status and identity
for married women rooted in their domestic role that the conceptualization
of female unemployment has been seen as problematic. The arguments
have been summarized admirably by Walby (1983), drawing on both UK
and US literature. She identifies two main approaches to the explanation of
women's unemployment, corresponding to attempts to theorise women's
employment. The first relies essentially on women's place in the household –
and is therefore an explanation of *married* women's unemployment – and
argues that their option of returning to the home in the status of full-time
housewife makes it easy for employers to shed women's labour in times of
recession. One variant on this position is expounded by Mincer (1962,

1966) who argues that women are in a position to choose when to enter and withdraw from the labour market, according to the pay and conditions on offer, withdrawing in periods of economic downturn. For Walby this defines women's unemployment out of existence by the implication that their labour market withdrawal is voluntary. Whilst the emphasis in the 'reserve army of labour' literature differs (see, for example, Beechey, 1978), the central thesis is the same; because of women's place in the home they may be paid less than the value of their labour power and easily dismissed from employment. Husband's earnings subsidize basic maintenance when wives are working, and provide a safety net when they are not. Walby argues that if this were true women would be employed by capital all the time, but her argument would hold only while alternative support through the male wage remains. The *replacement* of men by women would disrupt the arrangement.

Walby's more general argument against the family-based explanation of women's unemployment is that it fails to take account of what she terms 'patriarchal relations in the labour market'. The second main approach to women's unemployment she identifies examines the structure of the labour market and explains women's unemployment by the nature of the jobs they hold (Barron and Norris, 1986; Bergman, 1980; Bruegel, 1979; Milkman, 1976). In this vein Milkman (1976), for example, has suggested that women in the American Depression of the 1930s were protected from the worst of recession by their concentration in service employment, though as Walby points out, their rates of unemployment were lower than men's in all occupations, but lowest of all in services. Bruegel's (1979) argument for Britain in the mid-seventies recession is similar but more complex. Whilst women's concentration in services offered some protection from unemployment in aggregate, *individually* women were found to be more vulnerable to redundancy than men. This is largely because of their concentration in part-time, and therefore easily disposable, jobs which usually lack employment protection. This of course brings us back ultimately to a household-based explanation, since it is women's domestic and child care obligations that often lead to a preference for part-time employment, though less so in the US than the UK. More generally, we are posed with the question of why women occupy jobs that are inferior to men's.

Walby makes a different point on the basis of these arguments, however. If women are protected by a concentration in service employment, then this suggests a substitution of male for female workers does not occur. The logical corollary of this is that rigid sex-typing of occupations also prevents women's substitution for male workers. Thus, the reserve army thesis does not hold, but, equally, women's employment cannot in any simple manner be held to be responsible for male unemployment. Nor will the sex-typing of occupations always work in women's favour in terms of employment opportunities, as Bergman argues for the US, where in recent years women's unemployment has exceeded that of men. Women are confined to a narrow spectrum of occupations, and as women's demands for employment grow then these occupations become overcrowded and female unemployment is the result.

Niemi (1980) has examined the question of women's consistently high unemployment rates in the US, suggesting three further explanatory factors:

1 A high level of frictional unemployment because of movement in and out of the labour force (usually to give birth).
2 A relative lack of training and consequent vulnerability to lay-offs.
3 Occupational and geographic immobility (the latter often because of priority given to spouse's job).

Whilst all of these factors would be as applicable in the UK as in the US, women's unemployment in the former country has tended to hover below the male rate, largely because of the way the figures are collected. Walby, however, produces EEC figures that show a *higher* rate for women than for men in the UK (1.3 times the male rate in 1979). But why should definition be problematic?

Quantification

Whilst the reasons for women's unemployment are similar in both Britain and America, comparison between the two countries is extremely difficult. Mallier and Rosser (1986), however, do a good job in explaining why and drawing such comparisons as the data permit, accounting in the process for apparently disparate rates; the male/female unemployment ratio in the UK for the years 1975 and 1981 respectively was 0.41 and 0.59, whilst for the US the figures were 1.2 and 1.1.

Until October 1982 the official figures on unemployment in the UK were a statement of numbers registered with the Employment Services. Since then they have recorded numbers claiming benefit and indeed the *principal* reason for registering, though not the *only* one, was to make such a claim. Two benefits are available for the unemployed – unemployment benefit, which is contributory and lasts for up to 12 months after job loss, and income support (previously supplementary benefit), which is non-contributory with indefinite eligibility. There are a number of points about eligibility for benefit and the incentive to register as unemployed that affect the count for women:

1 Until 1977 it was possible for married women to opt out of paying a full national insurance contribution and hence to lose the right to unemployment benefit; an option that reflected the assumption that married women had alternative means of support, notably their husbands. This meant that many women did not register as unemployed and hence were represented in the figures.

2 Whilst this option is no longer available, women earning less than £43 a week are exempt from national insurance contributions and therefore not eligible for benefit and less likely to register. They are, however, particularly vulnerable to redundancy and therefore unemployment.

3 With income support one member of a couple claims for the household and there is no obvious incentive for both to register as unemployed.

4 Since October 1982 the figures on unemployment have simply reflected the numbers of claimants. Although from November 1983 it has been possible for women to claim on behalf of a married couple, the previous ruling that men made the claim is likely to have become an established tradition, especially when supported by an ideology which sees the man as the principal earner, and 'natural' breadwinner.

US unemployment statistics, being survey based, are less likely to exclude married women who are actively seeking work from the count than are UK statistics, and Hughes and Perlman (1984: 187) have noted rates consistently higher for women than for men, at least until 1982 when the female rate fell just below the male rate. UK figures on women's unemployment are not comparable and substantially underestimate the rate, which has been consistently lower than the male rate (Hughes and Perlman, 1984: 183). Walby (1983), however, cites an EEC figure for the British male/female ratio of 1.3 in 1979, the same as the American ratio for that year, in contrast to the *official* UK ratio of 0.64. This is by no means to argue that the situation in the two countries is in fact the same, and Mallier and Rosser (1986) have reviewed the differences.

The number of unemployed women in Britain from 1950 was stable for over two decades but began to rise in 1975 and by 1983 was nine times its 1974 level (Mallier and Rosser, 1986: 145). This rise in unemployment was accompanied by a fall in full-time female employees from 1974 to 1983 although the same period saw a rise in part-time jobs for women by 500,000 with a parallel growth of 700,000 in the female labour-force (Mallier and Rosser, 1986: 151). Mallier and Rosser point out that the fall in full-time jobs could account for three-quarters of the growth in female unemployment to 800,000 which was most strongly felt by young single women, whilst the growth in the female labour-force was accounted for by married women taking up part-time employment.

The US shows consistent growth in female employment from 1962 to 1982, but the number of women in the labour-force has grown at a faster pace, thus accounting for the rise in women's unemployment. As we have noted, part-time employment is not so significant or so much dominated by married women in the US as in the UK, but the concentration of unemployment among the young is common to both countries, though more severely felt in Britain than America. An understanding of women's unemployment requires that we make the distinction between young, single women about to embark on family formation, and married women who may be replacing but are more probably supplementing a husband's income. The concern here is with the latter group, whose marital status has further complicated the question of defining and assessing the impact of female unemployment.

Definitional Problems

A survey of women's employment in the UK, completed in 1980 (Martin and Roberts, 1984), took up the problem of classifying women's employment status. Of the 35 per cent of a total sample of 5,588 women who were identified as 'non-working', 15 per cent (5 per cent of the total sample) were classed as unemployed as follows on the basis of their reasons for having no paid job: (a) waiting to take up a job already obtained; (b) looking for work; (c) prevented from looking by temporary sickness or injury.

The other reasons offered make it clear that a large majority of non-working women (75 per cent) were economically inactive for domestic reasons, that is looking after children or other relatives or keeping house (Martin and Roberts, 1984: table 7.1, p. 81), but probing about hopes or intentions for employment raised the unemployed group by 3 per cent to 18 per cent. On the basis of further questioning about employment position and intentions, Martin and Roberts produced a continuum made up of five categories that together covered all non-working women in the sample. These were as follows:

1 Unemployed – as defined above.
2 Others looking for work – not working for domestic or other reasons but looking for work or found a job.
3 Planning to start work in the next year – not currently looking but expecting to start work in the next year.
4 Planning to start work in a year or more – not currently looking.
5 Will not/may not work again.

Those officially registered as unemployed cut across these categories and totalled 10 per cent of non-working women, but there were other discrep-ancies. Only 54 per cent of the unemployed group thought of themselves as unemployed, whilst as many as 13 per cent of the least active group (group 5) adopted the label. Nor were those who thought of themselves as un-employed necessarily registered as such, and even among the most narrowly defined unemployed only 36 per cent had registered. This raises some points specific to the UK about the way in which unemployment figures are compiled, but has more general implications for any classifi-cation of women's employment status, even by survey. As Martin and Roberts state: 'For a sizeable majority being unemployed meant having nothing to do which was manifestly not the case for them . . . two thirds of these women saw working in the home as a full-time job' (p. 84).

Other reasons for rejecting the label 'unemployed' were not being officially registered, not currently looking for work and not having been recently employed. The currently unemployed category was disproportion-ately represented in the 16–19 age group, which contained 30 per cent single women, and was more likely than the other categories to contain childless women. In fact, 80 per cent of all non-working women gave domestic duties, notably child care, as their main reason for not working, though this was not the case for the unemployed women, 74 per cent of whom gave non-domestic reasons for not working. This does not necessarily mean that should work become available the necessary domestic or child care support would not be found to free the woman to take up the oppor-tunity. Morris and Harris (1986) and Morris (1987c) have shown how informal networks can operate to channel women into part-time work deemed appropriate to their situation, as the following case demonstrates:

Mostly you'll rely on friends. My first job when I got back was through my auntie. She knew I'd be looking for something. It was afternoons in the pub, and a friend from the next street had offered to have the baby if I wanted to go back. (1987c: 96)

Domestic pressures do figure prominently, however, in women's with-drawal from employment, and the highest percentage of non-domestic reasons (69 per cent) occurred in the most tightly defined unemployed category (group 1). As always there is some ambiguity involved, however, since 19 per cent of non-working women left their job for non-domestic reasons, but stayed out of employment for domestic reasons. The influence of home life on women's propensity to seek employment, or ability to sustain it, has not only made it difficult to define categorically those women who are unemployed. It has also influenced attempts to assess the impact of married women's unemployment.

The Question of Identity

The traditional sexual division of labour that associates women with domestic and child care tasks, as well as the commonly espoused view that this is woman's primary and natural role, has fostered a belief that unemployment is unproblematic for women because they have available both an alternative means of support – through the male breadwinner – and an alternative source of identity – through housewifery and motherhood. An instance of this view of the nature and locus of women's identity is given in Mumford and Banks's assertion that: 'Women . . . accept routine jobs that are unlikely to lead anywhere. For most of them matrimony is their principal objective or interest and work is regarded as temporary or incidental, rather than as central in their lives' (1967: 21).

Such a view will, of course, carry implications for perceptions of female unemployment. In the US Kempers and Rayman (1987: 139) quote a report from the Office of Economic and Community Development (1975) that cites a sentiment similar to that expressed above, and echoes some of the definitional points made by Martin and Roberts: 'Because the alternative of staying at home full-time is socially acceptable for women, and not for men, very likely many "unemployed" women may appear in the statistics as housewives engaged in work in the home' (Darling, 1975: 111).

We noted in chapter 5 the nature of this alternative identity as portrayed by writers such as Oakley (1974), Lopata (1971) and Luxton (1980). These writers render accounts of the housewife role as socially isolating, based on work but lacking any place in the occupational structure, having no external criteria of assessment, no referents of competence, and receiving no financial or status reward. The incumbent lacks power, financial remuneration and social recognition. What is the nature of the identity to emerge from this complex of characteristics?

An early study by the Pahls (1971) of managers and their wives illustrated how unsatisfactory the result can be: 'Many wives are in an ambiguous position in that the relationship which is most salient to them is one in which they are the less powerful partner.'

It is in the context of this argument that Harris isolates the source of the housewife's dilemma as: 'resulting from a combination of adult responsibility without the correlative degree of autonomy' (1983: 230). Oakley does, however, give an account of housework that illustrates the way in which a work role seen in largely negative terms can nevertheless provide a basis for identity, by one of two approaches (p. 98): the 'traditional' which: 'tends to be characteristic of working class communities where the accent is on sex-segregation and the restriction of women's non-domestic opportunities', and the 'instrumental', which tends: 'to be performed for ulterior goals, in which a self-conscious commitment to motherhood and a belief in companionate marriage are all-important.'

We need therefore to ask whether married women who assume paid employment ever subscribed to such a view of themselves, have relinquished domestic sources of identity, derive their central identity from occupation, maintain both areas of activity as constituting equally important aspects of their self-image, or maintain their paid work role out of necessity, seeing it as an unwelcome competitor to their central domestic/mothering role. This is essentially what we need to know to begin to assess the personal significance of female unemployment.

Women's Responses

It will be apparent from Oakley's distinction above, and also from much of the discussion in this book so far, that there are a number of different responses to women's experience of job loss. Kempers and Rayman (1987) note: 'The range and complexity of women's roles suggests that women as a group cope with the realities of unemployment in a variety of ways.'

They note that whilst for men unemployment means the loss of activity, for women it can increase domestic activity and responsibility. This argument has been expressed by both British and American writers (see, for example, Milkman, 1976; Morris, 1984a) and the point being made is that where income falls the household's standard of living may be buoyed up by an intensification of domestic labour; creative budgeting, making and mending, economical food preparation and so on. This argument is most likely to apply in low-income homes where the wife's wage was essential in keeping the household out of poverty.

In considering the locus of identity, however, there is another dimension to be taken into account. Work in both the US and UK suggests, at least by implication, that women's feelings about unemployment should not be separated from their generally inferior position and prospects in the labour market. In a study of a plant shut-down in Pennsylvania, Snyder and Nowak (1984: 94) noted that fewer women than men had found their way back into work two years after the closure (83 per cent were still unemployed compared to 64 per cent of the men), fewer had regained jobs as crafts-workers (15 per cent as compared to 47 per cent), and more held only part-time work (38 per cent as compared with 15 per cent). In the UK Barron and Norris have argued that social values operate to define women as having a weaker claim on job opportunities than do men, so how do women feel when they lose their jobs?

An American study of a plant closure (Perucci et al., 1985) found men to be more depressed than women as a result of their job loss, and there is certainly substantial evidence that women easily found alternative activities when faced with unemployment. In another US study Rosen (1987) reports expressions of contentment at the opportunity to spend time with children, take care of the home and lie in late. One such comment was: 'It didn't make any difference to me because I was collecting enough [unemployment insurance] and I was home with my kids' (p. 126), suggesting that apart from the financial loss the loss of the job itself was immaterial. This early reaction to unemployment as relief from tedious obligations and the opportunity for a holiday is, however, a common early reaction to job loss among men as well as women (see Kelvin and Jarret, 1985, for review) and should not be taken to indicate a lack of attachment to employment for its own sake among women, or as evidence of their primary attachment to the home. More convincing here is Rosen's finding that: 'married women regardless of their age or cultural background, are happier than single women to have time to stay at home and look after their families' (p. 128).

She also notes a finding by Snyder and Nowak (1983) that unemployed women who do not live with spouses tend to be more demoralized than unemployed men, and the feeling continues after re-employment. This is partly explained by the greater likelihood that women's new jobs will be of inferior status. Rosen does not, however, accept any simplistic interpretation of these findings. She cites the work of Sheppard and Belitsky (1964), which concluded that married women who lost jobs did not wish to return to work: 'About 70% of the women not employed at the time they were interviewed gave the reason that they preferred to stay at home' (quoted in Rosen, 1987: 135).

Her own argument on blue collar women's unemployment is not so straightforward: 'The ambivalence they feel about losing their jobs reflects the fact that displacement and unemployment reduce their earnings but also free them temporarily from the double burden of working full-time and taking care of their families' (p. 131).

Wood's (1981) study of British women made redundant from computer punching supports this approach. He points out that the women did not hold an either/or view of their lives as suggested by a marriage versus work orientation. Although women gave their marriage and children primacy, this did not mean that work was not an important part of their identity. They took pride in their skills and the ability to get a job anywhere in their trade. Martin and Roberts (1984) point out the difficulties of separating attitudes towards the pull of paid employment from attitudes towards the pull of home. Thus: 'Women with positive attitudes towards staying at home and little financial need to work may choose not to work, but equally women who see little prospect of being able to find a job may as a consequence adopt a positive attitude to staying at home' (p. 93).

In so far as this is true then the argument about alternative, socially acceptable sources of identity seems to have some force.

Cragg and Dawson (1984) take a closer look at the unemployed women from the Martin and Roberts study. They found that in general the main motivation to get a job was 'company and diversion from a household routine which had become tedious' (p. 21). Many of the unemployed women expressed dissatisfaction with unemployment which had its roots in boredom. In such cases: 'It was clear that they were bored not only because they did not have enough to do but also because they felt what they did do was intrinsically boring' (p. 24).

The tedium in some cases related to the demands of young children, as indicated by remarks such as: 'From their birth to the age of 5 a woman has no life of her own'; 'It's amazing being away for the day, how it's refreshing'; 'Being a housewife is very, very narrow' (p. 25).

Again, however, this study rejected the either/or version of women's identity. Despite the dissatisfactions and frustrations expressed with the housewife/mother role, employment was looked to as a source of relief, another dimension to life, but only in rare cases was it seen as offering the primary meaning and direction.

Social Contact

The references from Cragg and Dawson's study correspond much more closely to the account of housework as monotonous and isolating than do the comments quoted by Rosen. It should be stressed, however, that the majority of women in the latter study were strongly attached to the labour market and viewed their unemployment as a temporary condition. They became increasingly demoralized where there appeared to be little prospect of re-employment. What both these studies and many others have in common is the finding that work is an important source of social contact, and as a result a confirmation of identity, which counteracts the isolation associated with an exclusively domestic role.

Domesticity may mean for many tedium and isolation, but this should not blind us to the fact that there lies in this some sense of security. Snyder and Nowak (1983) found that the most demoralized of the unemployed women in their study were those living alone, and those whose circle of friends had changed most since shut-down. Whilst they do cite cases of married women who are regretful of the loss of the social circle work provided, the emphasis seems to be on single women. They make the additional point that the workers in their study travelled to work from rural locations of considerable social isolation.

Other studies have distinguished more explicitly between different marital statuses, and Cragg and Dawson's UK study of unemployed women (1984) found that social contact was important not only to single women. Many mothers were described as 'lonely' and feeling an 'urgent need' for companionship. Many also expressed the need to work in terms of a wish for access to a world of non-domestic concerns and interests which, by implication, can add an extra dimension to identity. As one woman puts it: 'so I could perhaps come home and say "Oh yes, I've had a good day at work today" – instead of him coming in and me saying "Oh yes, I've had a good day, she's been very quiet"' (p. 25), or: 'Although I enjoy being in my own home there are times when I'd pay a fortune for me to just turn round and say "Oh, so-and-so". But I've got nothing to say.'

More explicitly, one woman states: 'Working – well it gives you an identity doesn't it? There's a lot to be said for being able to earn money. You're trying to reinforce yourself all the time that being at home, looking after children is a very worthwhile thing but absolutely nothing except yourself tells you that' (p. 27).

Cragg and Dawson also illustrate the psychological stress caused by unemployment for some women, with such statements as: 'It disturbs me badly that I'm dependent, lonely, depressed. It all stems from the fact that I can't find work. There seems to be no reason to carry on' (p. 23); though they concede that although some women did derive enjoyment and satisfaction from housework and/or child care, the 'overwhelming majority' (p. 26) experienced deep frustration.

The importance of the social dimension to employment is demonstrated by Martin and Wallace (1984) in their linked study of female unemployment. This work found that most women filled the hours left free by unemployment by expanding their existing role as housewife, which was generally considered to be less interesting than paid employment. Whilst as with the Rosen study (1987) there was some appreciation of a lessening of the 'double burden', few women saw more of their immediate family as a result – a contrast with the common experience of unemployment for men.

This study usefully distinguishes between occupational statuses, finding that although work had been a source of friendship to the majority of women, whether or not they made most of their friends at work was inversely correlated with occupational status. High- and low-status women were, however, equally likely to think that unemployment caused loneliness. The study also distinguishes clearly between marital statuses, to find that: 'the large majority of married women and women over 35 . . . said they had less social contact on becoming unemployed. Married women were also the most likely to say they felt more isolated: 55% of married women said they felt more isolated as compared with only 27% of single women' (p. 255).

The importance of social contact for mental health has been discussed in work by Brown and Harris (1978) on clinically depressed women in south London. Working class women with children at home were found to be particularly vulnerable to depression, though generally vulnerability was lessened where women had a confiding relationship in their lives. Even without such a relationship, however, employment was found to halve the risk of depression (p. 279).

In several studies there is evidence of a running together of enjoyment of 'working' with a desire for the company it brings. Thus Nowak and Snyder (1983) state that, as with Rosen (1982), individuals who missed their friends at work most when laid off were also most likely to report that they missed doing their job. Cragg and Dawson (1984) cite similar instances: 'I really enjoy going out to work. . . . [I enjoy] the people. Feeling you're doing something worthwhile', though conversely they cite a case of a woman refusing promotion, because it was more important to her to maintain friendships without a position of responsibility.

Wood's interviews with women made redundant after the relocation of an engineering firm from London showed a similar conflation of job satisfaction and social satisfaction. One of the things the women most look for in a job was having a good time. This did not mean, however, that they failed to recognize that the job was not particularly interesting or pleasant (p. 668), but they valued the opportunity to form bonds with other women and were tied to the job by social and psychological needs. On closure 'the focus of the women's concern was what they would miss, and particularly each other' (p. 669).

Financial Considerations

Quite apart from the social and psychological benefits married women derive from paid employment, and the general dissatisfaction with an exclusively domestic role, there remains the question of the financial motivation to work. As we pointed out in the previous chapter, this is a complicated issue that cannot be dissociated either from the level of household income, or from the manner in which that income is controlled and distributed between competing demands. With regard to female unemployment then, we need to know not only, or even principally, what proportion of household income is made up by the women's wage, but how crucial it is to household maintenance.

Popay has argued that UK households with two earners made up 54 per cent of all couples of working age in 1973, peaked at 58 per cent in 1979 and fell to 53 per cent in 1982 as a result of increased unemployment. Pleck (1985) gives a US figure for 1981 that is only slightly lower at 51.8 per cent. Questions must therefore be posed about the significance of personal earnings for a woman's sense of independence, her power within the home and for gender identity more generally. If established views of gender roles see the man as principal breadwinner, does this image endure in the face of dependence, however partial, on a wife's wage?

Wives' earnings seem to be a somewhat lower proportion of husbands' earnings in the UK, at 25.2 per cent as compared to a US figure of 30.9 per cent (Rainwater et al., 1986: 65), and correspondingly the wife's median contribution to income is 21 per cent in the US but only 15 per cent in the UK, a difference that may be explained by the concentration of British women in part-time work. There must, however, be a larger proportion of earning wives in Britain since calculations about the total amount the wives contribute to household income are similar for both countries, amounting to 10 per cent of the total for all married couples in the UK and 11 per cent in America (see Rainwater et al., 1986: 65).

Whilst there are strong arguments about the role of the wife's wage in keeping households out of poverty, the figures also demonstrate the significant role of wives' earnings in explaining variance between households to a greater extent in the UK than in the US. Thus for homes with children present:

> In Britain 29% of the lowest sextiles mothers work, rising to 67% and then leveling off at 63% in the highest sextile. In the U.S., in contrast, there is not such a tight association. We find 32% of mothers working in the lowest sextile, rising to 62% in the fifth sextile, and dropping off to 52% in the top sextile. (Rainwater et al., 1986: 66)

One interpretation of these findings is that households with an employed wife fall into the lowest income band. The same source also tells us that in the US husbands' income accounts for 80 per cent of household variance, and in the UK only 65 per cent. This means, however, that wives' earnings produce a greater proportional improvement in income at lower levels because women's earnings across different household income levels are fairly stable.

Unemployment and Financial Strain

Little can be said about the motivation for wives' earning from data of this kind, however, as there is little correlation between wives' employment and husbands' level of earnings, and we would anyway need to know how that income was distributed before any inferences could be made. From the data available we might suggest that at low overall levels of income financial need is a major factor in motivating women to take up employment, whilst at higher overall income levels other factors will be to the fore.

As regards women's unemployment we are in a position to show on the basis of figures above that the impact on overall household income of job loss for the woman will be greater in the US than in the UK; that households with low overall income levels will suffer more from the loss of a wife's income because of being closer to poverty, and also because the range of income levels is much wider for men than for women. This latter point is more true for the US than the UK. It may be less appropriate to view women's unemployment at higher income levels in terms of absolute financial loss for the household than in terms of the significance of income for the woman concerned. In the US there is a stronger negative correlation between husband's income and wife's employment, with the proportions of mothers who work declining as income increases. In the UK the relationship is not so straightforward with a slight tendency for the proportion to rise with husband's income, and to drop off only where husbands are rich (Rainwater et al., 1986).

A number of writers in both the US and UK have been concerned to make the point that in many homes it is only the presence of the woman's wage that keeps the household out of poverty. The argument here is that however small the wage, and however minimal a *proportion* of household income it makes up, it is nevertheless critical for household maintenance. Although we have shown that wives' earnings contribute more to household income in the US than in the UK, there are grounds for arguing that women's earnings at lower levels are more critical for British households. Seventy-three per cent of potentially poor households are moved out of poverty by British working mothers, as compared with 64 per cent in the US. Combining poor and near poor, the percentages are 73 per cent moved to a higher level by wives' earnings in Britain and only 52 per cent in the US (Rainwater et al., 1986: 75). The previous chapter cited data that suggested that at this level a high proportion of wives' income was spent on household essentials, and under these circumstances unemployment for the women would cause substantial hardship.

Significance of Wives' Income

It is not only in cases of near poverty, however, that the financial benefit of women's earnings is felt to be significant. Coyle's study of redundant, female factory-workers notes (1984: 106): 'On the whole it was not a case of destitution, but of nagging worry. . . . Married women with children were confronted with what they always knew. A man's wage is not enough to live on.'

Martin and Roberts (1984) provide systematic data on this matter. Whilst a large minority of their sample of women (46 per cent) felt they could 'get by alright' without working, 60 per cent of working wives anticipated 'having to give up a lot' without their job (47 per cent full time and 33 per cent part time), whilst 14 per cent said they would not be able to manage at all. The higher the *proportion* of joint earnings contributed by the wife the less likely she was to say that they could manage financially without her working, but even wives contributing 25 per cent of gross earnings contained 25 per cent who did not feel they could get by alright without working.

Rosen's study (1987) of married, unemployed blue-collar women in the US is enlightening in that it is a study of women many of whom would be married to skilled craft-workers with reasonable levels of pay. Nevertheless, the overwhelming impression in this study is of substantial anxiety over household finance. This, however, was a group of women who when working earned almost half (45 per cent) of the household income. Thus the standard of living they had achieved was very closely tied to their own earning level, and there was a feeling that with unemployment for the woman 'everything could tumble'. The major worry was found to be concern about meeting the needs of a growing family.

Need or Independence?

Cragg and Dawson (1984) present material that confirms the significant contributions to household living standards made by the woman's income, but they nevertheless draw a distinction between simple financial need and women's desire to assert independence by earning their own income. When we look closely at use of that income and the implications of its loss, then we find that the distinction is not so clear. Whilst many women had been motivated to take up employment by fear over declining living standards, the importance of 'independent' earnings was stressed. Cragg and Dawson pay particular attention to the situation in homes that employed an allowance system of finance management (generally the system most commonly applied). They state: 'The most common complaint . . . in this sizable group of households where the husband had practical or emotional control over money, concerned the dependent, supplicatory role in which the wife was placed' (p. 53).

The tension was felt over the husband's failure to appreciate the costs of routine purchases and women's consequent wish for an independent income to supplement these purchases. The strain felt by unemployed women was that they had been deprived of a source of income over which they had discretion. Morris (1987c) gives a similar account that emphasizes the possibility of the husband's true ignorance of the process at work. Hence one man's response to his wife's employment was: 'It's not that we needed the money, it's just that it helps her a bit with the housekeeping' (p. 93).

A man's need to control his wife's expenditure on housekeeping was expressed in the same study as follows: 'It's not that I can't manage on what I bring home. It's just that I'm trying to make her manage on what I give her. That way we might get a bit behind us like' (p. 92).

Coyle's work quotes a strongly felt reaction in response to this apparently common male attitude: 'No woman works for pin money. I mean the men, none of them are over generous with their money are they? Let's face it. I mean not like a woman. She goes to work and she brings all her wage packet home and most of it goes on the house or on the kids' (p. 117).

Rosen's work reports a revealing case of a couple who ostensibly ran the household finances jointly, a perceived advantage for the woman as a substantial contributor to the income. The examples of failure to consult in spending, however, were in marked contrast; on his part a drinking outing with his friends, and on her part the purchase of rugs at sale price. Unemployment can mean the loss of the independent capacity to make even these spending decisions, as well as a loss of the more nebulous feeling of demonstrating worth by earning.

The Breadwinner Image

There is evidence of protection of the husband's ego and breadwinner status by women in employment, so that even in among the women studied by Rosen who were providing almost half of household income the idea of the husband's primacy as breadwinner was sustained: 'Despite the fact that couples know they have come to depend on the wife's paycheck . . . women continue to define their work as "helping" husbands; they define their earnings as supplementary' (1987: 107).

According to Rosen this fiction eases tension and is also a means of reinforcing a continuing willingness and obligation to provide on the part of the husband. Hence: 'There is a shared belief that he is the one whose income "really supports the family." The husband's income is for "essentials"; it goes into the bank to pay the mortgage and the other inevitable monthly bills . . . the wife merely works for "extras" like gas [petrol], groceries, things for the children, or savings' (p. 103).

This view echoes some of the statements quoted above from Morris's work (1987c) in north-east England, which suggest a failure on the part of the men to appreciate the significance of wives' earnings. On the question of what constituted 'essential' income, one man whose wife had previously had employment but who was no longer in paid work explained the dilemma: 'We've had this argument time and again. My wage is low so she went out cleaning for extra. So we had extra but it's not extra because you've raised your standard and you're still short. I'm trying to get her used to managing on what I give her.'

Cragg and Dawson's work reports more generally on adherence to a 'domestic bargain', a model whereby the husband goes out and earns the money to support his family whilst the wife looks after the home and children. A clear majority of husbands in this study were opposed to their wife's employment. In Rosen's study (1987: 102) 30 per cent of the women told interviewers that their husbands were not happy with them working, whilst another 34 per cent made somewhat ambivalent statements – and these were women contributing 45 per cent of household income.

There are two points to be made about the possible consequences for the experience of unemployment for women. On the one hand there may be a lessening of tension in marriage where the woman's employment did not have the support of the man, and an increase in *his* feelings of status deriving from being the principle breadwinner. It also seems likely, however, that men may fail to acknowledge the problems for women – whether financial or personal – in facing job loss. If the significance of their employment is not appreciated there can be little understanding of the effects of its loss.

Sources of Variation

Occupational status

The focus of much existing research, as in studies of male unemployment, has been on working-class occupations. In such cases work of itself is unlikely to be fulfilling or to become the focal point of life, and it is not surprising that evidence to support a family orientation among women in such occupations is not difficult to find. It also means that the attitude towards unemployment may well be ambivalent.

We might expect rather different findings to emerge from the study of the middle-class/professional woman, where career is much more likely to be the central source of identity and ambition. Such women are also likely to remain unmarried and childless until much later in life than those with less career interest or opportunity. When they do marry their expectations and assumptions may be rather different from those of working-class women. We have already noted that money does not necessarily translate into marital power and authority for women, but that it is more likely to do so in middle-class homes. We have also cited evidence that suggests non-financial motives for earning such as personal fulfilment, career commitment, are likely to be more common for middle-class women. Hertz's (1986) study of dual-career couples in the US refers to a new marital bond which is not based on gendered responsibilities. Women's unemployment in these cases may be more undermining than in a working-class home with a more traditional arrangement in that the woman's identity will be more closely linked to career, and the marriage may well be built around such an identity with notions of equality which are shaken by a disruption of career status. Whilst the dual-earning, professional couple has become a focus for research attention, the impact of unemployment on professional women has not yet been examined. As with the study of male unemployment the middle classes have been somewhat neglected.

Marital status

A variant obviously affecting the impact of female unemployment is household structure and marital status. The position of young, unmarried women in the parental home will be discussed in the next chapter. We have yet to consider in this chapter the position of women without a man in the 'breadwinner' role. Many of the assumptions that have been made about the role of employment in women's lives are also applied to single women prior to marriage in that they are often held to give primacy to marital prospects, and to plan a 'career' in familial rather than occupational terms. It is in this context that the Pilgrim Trust referred to the 'meanwhile' occupations of young girls.

In this vein Wood's (1981) report on female redundancy in a computer centre states that: 'Ultimately women saw security as achieved through marriage. The single ones were oriented towards getting married, some being already engaged, whilst the married ones viewed the home and family as their basic source of security. In this sense work was placed in a subordinate position to the family' (p. 657).

These women did not, however, see marriage and work as either/or options, or expect to work only between school and marriage, despite the assumption that the birth of children would mean a temporary withdrawal from employment.

As we noted above, this seems likely to be a complex of expectations characteristic of working-class women that could be less relevant for professionally trained women, who may place importance on marriage but would continue to derive identity and status from work. It may be that their profession becomes the means of meeting and attracting a spouse so that unemployment could well cut them off from the social channels that facilitate pairing. Unemployment for single women who have staked their future on a career could well be devastating. Having foregone, or substantially delayed, what is commonly perceived to be woman's 'natural' role only to lose their alternative must be a difficult situation to accommodate both emotionally and financially.

Snyder and Nowak stress the vulnerability of single women, especially those who live alone. Their feelings of economic insecurity are described as intense, and it was found that living with others who provided a degree of emotional and financial support alleviated anxiety. It is also this category of women who were most in need of the social networks provided by their jobs. Those living alone experienced higher levels of demoralization after job loss. A single woman living with an elderly mother in need of full-time care described how she felt as follows: 'Alone, lost. Depressed. Like someone just knocked the props out. It's like a death in the family, no one can know how you hurt' (p. 40).

Whilst women are thought to have available the alternative source of support and identity supplied by marriage, those who do not may well suffer more psychologically than any other group.

Ethnic identity

The studies mentioned in this chapter have been predominantly of white working-class women in conventional household arrangements. One variant on the way in which women's employment and unemployment is perceived will be cultural, and Rosen (1987) attempts to provide an example through a consideration of the Portuguese women in her sample. The culture of Portuguese family life is described by Rosen (1987: 112) as 'patriarchal and authoritarian', and so it is some surprise to learn that the men place considerable emphasis on their wives' employment. Hence, in contrast to the white working-class culture that underlies the traditional sexual division of labour referred to above, for the Portuguese: 'Masculine authority is not defined by the ability to support one's family alone and men are not reluctant to have their wives work' (p. 117).

This does not mean, however, that there is any sharing of women's work in the home. The only escape from the 'double burden' of paid and domestic work for these women then comes with unemployment. In Rosen's account, holding paid employment is simply an additional component in the obligations of wife and mother; it helps secure the well-being of the family. This argument seems to be contradicted when we are told that among younger women the percentage of husbands unhappy with their wife's working is *higher* among the Portuguese, although unrelated to the size of the man's income, in contrast to the American couples. This may be a generational effect connected with the assimilation of American values, but remains unexplained in the study.

A more common argument for black and ethnic minority populations has been that the disadvantaged position of men in the labour market has meant that employment for women assumes great significance. The low wages available for either gender have meant that household maintenance requires a composite income. There is, however, considerable variation between ethnic groupings, as Reimers' (1984) detailed analysis shows. Puerto Rican families have the lowest earned income of any Hispanic groups. They get only half as much income from male heads as white non-Hispanics do and only 60 per cent as much from wives and female heads. Total family income is only 58 per cent of that of white non-Hispanics, whilst the total income of Mexican families is 65 per cent of white non-Hispanics.

Cuban and Central and South American families actually get more earnings from wives and female 'heads' and from other family members than do white, non-Hispanics, but still fall far below them in total family income due to the low earnings per family of male 'heads'. Black American families get more earnings from wives and female 'heads', and less from male 'heads', than any other group. Black families get 14 per cent more income from wives and female 'heads' but only half as much from male 'heads' as do white families (Reimers, 1984: 893). One major factor is the differential rates of presence of a male 'head', and another is differential rates of female labour-force participation – Central and South American, black and Cuban women all spending more weeks in the labour-force than white non-Hispanic women. Mexican and Puerto Rican women are an exception here, spending respectively 90 per cent and two-thirds as much time in the labour-force as white non-Hispanic women. Reimers (1984) summarizes the findings as follows:

> The short-fall in Puerto Rican income from female heads is due mostly to lower labour force participation and higher unemployment rates. For Mexicans, however, the gap stems mainly from lower average hourly earnings. Blacks, Cubans and Central and South

Americans, the groups that have higher earnings from wives and female heads than non-white Hispanics, have them despite higher unemployment and lower wage rates, by dint of higher female labour force participation and longer weekly hours. (p. 897)

Evidence such as this certainly constitutes a powerful argument for the assertion that female unemployment is a greater blow to financial well-being for ethnic-minority and black households, particularly since in both the UK and US unemployment rates for men and women are higher in these groups.

The situation of ethnic minority women in the UK to a great extent repeats the US pattern. Bruegel (1988) notes that black women work generally longer hours than white women, whether in full-time or part-time employment, and do not show the same concentration in part-time employment that white women do. Despite what appears to be a stronger commitment to paid employment in terms of hours, however, black women are more vulnerable to unemployment than are white women. Bruegel has noted that the concentration of black women in manufacturing and the recent decline of this sector necessarily increases the likelihood of their becoming unemployed. Statistics for 1984–6 from the EEC Labour Force Survey showed 10 per cent unemployment for white women, 19 per cent for West Indians, 18 per cent for Indians and 38 per cent for Pakistani/Bangladeshi women. The impact of unemployment is likely to be particularly damaging for black women generally, because of the enhanced significance of their earnings, which we have noted was sufficiently strong in many households to override the effects of child birth and child care in disrupting paid work.

Single Parents

Such findings are all the more significant since ethnic minority status has been associated with single parenthood, and there is indeed a disproportionately high presence of black and ethnic minority women in this role. In the US in 1984 54 per cent of all black families were maintained by women, and 17 per cent of white families (Bergman, 1986: 227). Single mothers are a group deserving particular attention in relation to unemployment; as women with dependent children and no one to perform the 'breadwinner' role of the traditional, nuclear family model, they must depend either on their own capacity to earn a wage or on the state for their maintenance. The question of whether this group suffers more from the effects of female unemployment than any other is a difficult one, since one explanation of single parenthood has been that low male wages mean the wife/mother fares better on benefit and in the man's absence. As we have seen from US figures, the absence of a male head can explain the high overall contribution of wives and female heads to household income, but we cannot necessarily assume that it is the single parent women who are doing the earning. Nor is the pattern consistent in all ethnic groups.

Nevertheless, Bradbury et al. (1979) have shown for the US that women with husbands work less than women without husbands, and women with children work less than women without children. This is perceived as a conflict between needs for income and for child care among single mothers but is less the case for women living as 'sub-heads' within a wider family, since their child care is likely to be provided by kin. Unemployment thus figures in two ways: single mothers in the US are more likely to be members of ethnic minority groups, which suffer higher rates of male and female unemployment, whilst child care problems add to their difficulties in sustaining employment.

The situation in the UK is in some ways similar, with single parenthood more common in the West Indian population than in the white population. In 1982 West Indian single-mother households with children under 16 made up 16 per cent of all households and 31 per cent of households with dependent children. The corresponding figures for the white population were 3 and 10 per cent, respectively, and for Asians 1 and 5 per cent (Brown, 1984). Whilst single parents generally seem less likely to be employed than other mothers they show a slightly greater propensity to work full time as opposed to part time (*GHS*, table 6.6, p. 64), the usual preference of married women with young children. Overall, however, single parents are less likely to be in employment at all than mothers in two-parent families (Popay et al., 1983). One could therefore argue that, in aggregate, single mothers, depending less on employment are less likely to suffer from unemployment, though this argument is somewhat outweighed by both their over-representation in full-time work, and the high presence of West Indian women who suffer disproportionately from unemployment.

The stress experienced by those lone mothers who do depend on their wage is illustrated by figures from Martin and Roberts (1984). Confirming the above findings, now somewhat dated, they show that lone mothers are less likely to be working than other mothers (34 per cent compared to just over half), but more likely to work full time (21 per cent as to 16 per cent) and less likely to work part time (13 per cent as to 37 per cent). When age of youngest child is taken into account there is, however, no difference in economic activity rates but proportionately fewer were actually working as a result of very high rates of unemployment (14 per cent). Given this finding the reasons for working are particularly significant. Overwhelmingly the lone mothers work from financial necessity (85 per cent as compared to 35 per cent of married mothers). In giving their main reason for working, 78 per cent stated working for essentials as compared to 28 per cent of married mothers. Findings on stress are therefore unsurprising: 'Almost half of the single mothers (48%) and 41% of the formerly married mothers came into a high financial stress category, compared with only 11% of married mothers. By contrast, over half the married mothers were in the low financial stress category, compared with only 18% of lone mothers' (p. 111).

Single mothers are therefore more likely to suffer from unemployment than other mothers, and more likely to be stressed by it when they do.

Conclusion

In sum, it seems that the assessment of the effects of female unemployment poses more problems for generalization than the effects of male unemployment. This is largely because of the influence of women's domestic role, and the question of the degree to which it provides them with a satisfactory alternative source of identity. The other major variant is the importance of women's income, and this we have found not simply to differ by virtue of level of total household income, but to be affected by the manner in which different households distribute and dispose of that income. Thus it would seem that for women, much more than for men, the experience of unemployment is bound up with their domestic role and the nature of the internal organization of the household.

8 *Young People and the Household*

Earlier chapters in this book have questioned the validity of viewing the household unproblematically as a unit, and in this context have discussed the significance for individuals of access to and control over independent income. The question is a now familiar one in the consideration of married women's earnings and the significance of the woman's wage, but these same questions have been raised often with regard to young people in the household.

Rainwater et al. (1986) provide some useful data on the size and nature of young people's contributions to the household fund for both the UK and US, classifying contributions to household income from earnings as follows:

1 Traditional breadwinner:
   (a) husbands;
   (b) single women;
   (c) single men.
2 Wives.
3 Other earners.

It is this last category of other earners that is of interest to us here, totalling 8.5 and 5.3 per cent of aggregate 'family' income from earnings in the UK and US, respectively (for family here read household). On the basis of PSID data (Panel Study of Income Dynamics) in the US, Rainwater et al. suggest that: 'Most other earners, particularly when their earnings loomed fairly large as a proportion of total family income, turn out to be late adolescent/early adult sons and daughters of poor and working-class families who for a few years, perhaps only two or three, remain in their parents' household' (p. 44).

They report slightly more households in the US than the UK in which there are 'other earners' present – 28.3 per cent as compared with 22.2 per cent – but note that this group makes a higher contribution in the UK both to the receiving household's income and to aggregate household income. Other earners in the US, we are told (p. 43), typically contribute 12 per cent of their household's total income (18 per cent of the average person's total household income), whilst in the UK they contribute 28 per cent (or 38 per cent of the average person's household income). One explanation for the difference between the two countries could be the fact that a far higher proportion of young people enter further education in the US system, and may therefore be more likely to expect and receive some subsidy from their parents over a longer period than would otherwise be the case.

The questions to be asked of multiple-income households have been defined by Coleman (1986: 101) as follows: 'What basic standard of living has been established by the male head's income? Who are the other earners? What are their motives? The variety of stories is almost infinite.'

Finance Management and Contributions by Young People

The extent to which young earners should be regarded as an independent spending unit, rather than being included in calculations concerning household income, is a difficult question that touches not only on the contributions they may make to the household, but also on the degree of support and indulgence they may extract. In the management of household finance, the means adopted for handling young people's contributions correspond closely to arrangements identified in chapter 6 as the whole-wage and allowance systems. The young earner will either hand over their whole wage and receive an amount back for spending, or may pay an agreed amount to one or other parent, most commonly the mother since this contribution is reckoned to cover basic board. The rest of the wage will be retained for personal use.

Millward (1968) has reported on the situation of young working women in four British northern towns. His research suggests that a shift from handing over the whole wage to paying an allowance for board tended to occur at a particular age as a mark of independence, and is to be explained by reference to local norms. A move to the allowance or 'board' system was not to be understood purely in cultural terms, however, but was rather found to coincide with improvements in earnings. I have elsewhere noted the parallel with the marital move to an allowance system when the wage rises. One of the most interesting aspects of this finding was that incentive payments through the wage-packet were found to be ineffective unless the worker personally benefited. This will only be the case, as with overtime earnings, if the money being handed over for the household purse is a fixed amount.

More generally speaking, however, it seems that the board system usually works to the benefit of young people in that parents seem often to require fairly minimal contributions, which may even be outweighed by the value of indulgences above and beyond bed and board flowing back to them. This tendency has been described by Leonard (1980) as a system of 'spoiling and keeping close'. She found in her study of courtship and marriage in South Wales that young people living in the parental home paid well below cost for their board and lodging. This does not mean, however, that the money received by their mothers was insignificant, although where it simply served to reduce the amount of housekeeping required then it is the husband who is likely to be the main beneficiary. Nor does the nominal nature of contributions appear to detract from the status accruing to a wage-earner. As Leonard puts it: 'a source of friction is removed, a step towards adult status is taken' (p. 46).

Like Millward, Leonard notes cases of movement from 'giving-in' to 'board' as earnings rise, though generally speaking it seemed that handing over the whole wage was a rare occurrence (1972: 581). This may reflect a trend away from the giving-in system over time, and a recent study by Allatt and Yeandle (1985) of 40 households in the north-east of England, all with young people present, found no instance of its use. This is very much the picture painted by Coleman in his discussion of US data. One suggestion is that since young people are not expected to stay in the parental home for very long after becoming wage-earners their income is not considered by parents in deciding on their standard of living. Young people may derive food and shelter from their parents but operate as partially independent spending units.

The US situation as described by Coleman is rather more extreme than that in the UK: 'Grown children remaining at home seldom pay rent or contribute food money to their parents when they become full-time earners. . . . It is only when their parents' financial situation suddenly becomes desperate that grown children are expected to hand over any of their earnings to the household treasury' (p. 100).

Contributions will not necessarily take the form of money handed over directly to parents, however. Nor is the issue necessarily confined to adult children. Some insight into the use of earnings by American schoolboys is given by Strauss (1962). Although farm boys were found to work more and have less income at their disposal than city boys, over 50 per cent in each group contributed money to a savings account and to the purchase of school supplies, although the highest spending category was recreation. In the UK the Low Pay Unit's pamphlet *Working Children* (MacLennan et al., 1985) has argued that children may work to cover their own expenses where parents cannot afford to meet them, and may thus be indirectly subsidizing household income by paying for items parents would otherwise be required to fund.

This brings us back to the point made above by Coleman; financial constraints on parents may produce pressure on children and young people, and high rates of adult unemployment are particularly significant in this respect. More generally it would seem that the patterns of indulgence remarked upon by Barker and Coleman could well break down in cases of parental hardship, and may have implications for the labour market behaviour and choice of residence of young people.

Domestic Labour

As with household finance, the domestic labour performed by young people (or not) within the home has not been the focus of particular attention, and such data as we have available seem to be presented in passing, as a side issue in the discussion of the sexual division of labour between spouses. White and Brinkerhoff (1981) make this point in their assessment of the conceptualization of children's household work. The major focus on children's labour has been through the psychologists' interest in the developmental role of household chores for children, and this approach seems also to be reflected in the view taken by parents of children's contributions. White and Brinkerhoff, in their study in Nebraska, found that most parents explained their children's household chores in terms of child development, though in some cases the need for their contribution was an element added into the account. We will see later that financial contributions from the young have also been seen in this light.

Where there are practical reasons for the child's involvement in domestic chores then they are more likely to work longer hours and to be paid for the work, and some studies have found that it is child labour rather than participation by the husband that is used to lighten the burden of employed wives (Hedges and Barnett, 1972; Thrall, 1978). In White and Brinkerhoff's work the labour of children begins with responsibility for themselves very early, though by age nine or ten it has extended to more general tasks. At this age it is interesting to note that sons seem more likely to have chores than daughters, though the evidence is slight.

Berk (1985) has distinguished between households rather in terms of whether or not they use children's labour at all. If they did, then all children of an appropriate age were called upon. Berk goes on to note that it is prior to their own labour market involvement, between the ages of 11 and 15, that children's labour is most available: 'This age represents the optimal time to "collect" on children's ability to labour. Children have yet to expend their energies on work outside the home and do not roam far for very long, it is at this age that household chores are easily defined as character builders' (p. 155).

There are, of course, young children from disadvantaged backgrounds who roam very far indeed from the parental home, though as a general statement Berk's argument can perhaps stand.

It is interesting that gender differences do creep in as the children get older. Berk's quantitative data on domestic labour found that older daughters added more tasks to the household than did sons. Berk suggests, however, that the daughters may have provided more labour, hence adding to the overall number of tasks in the household. In support of this suggestion she found that daughters were more likely to be subject to the mother's orientation to housework than were the sons, and that where mother's assessment of task importance was high this decreased the number of tasks done by the son. In addition to this, it was only daughters whose household tasks actually substituted for a portion of the mother's tasks.

Aspects of Berk's conclusions are also to be found in Pahl's study of Sheppey in the UK (1984), which shows that the amount of domestic work increases with the number of adults in the home, but in contrast to Berk's findings it seems that the burden of this extra work falls on the wives. Hence for any task, increasing the number of adults in the home increases the probability that the wife performs the task. This outcome is not suggestive of any assumption of domestic work by young people, and serves to confirm the conclusions of Leonard's work in South Wales (1980). Her study found that in the absence of the wife, or in cases of illness, an adult daughter was the first to be called upon, but in general neither daughter nor sons made much contribution to domestic work. In some large families help was required of the daughter, but even then it was a fairly minimal amount, and indeed 'many of the young people were waited on by their mothers'.

Unemployment and Domestic Labour

The kinds of question that have been asked of male unemployment and its effects on the domestic division of labour, household tensions and changing role content have only recently begun to be posed in cases of unemployed young people. The reason for this seems to be, from the evidence available, that they do so little.

Hutson and Jenkins (1987) carried out a study of young people and the

household in South Wales, at a time of high unemployment. Their conclusion was that little had changed since Leonard's study in 1960: 'The wife
or mother continues to bear the brunt of housework in most families. The
children, be they male or female, typically infringe only in a small way
upon their mother's sphere of responsibility, and only assume a small share
of her burden' (p. 98).

As with studies of male unemployment, it was also found that domestic
tension could be increased by the effective confinement of young people to
the domestic sphere, although this appeared to be eased in cases where the
young person assumed some domestic responsibility. Nevertheless, it seems
that relatively small contributions to domestic labour can be used as part of
a bargaining process, or conversely be the source of major conflicts. In a
process of 'domestic bargaining' it was found that good behaviour, which
often involved domestic labour, was exchanged for a measure of greater
independence, hence: 'Willingness to help in the house . . . was often seen
as symbolic of "right" behaviour and "right" attitudes in a wider sphere
than the household' (p. 97).

In the final analysis, however, Hutson and Jenkins argue that spoiling is
the predominant pattern, and one that exists in order to hold young people
to the home, and, especially in cases of youth unemployment, to keep them
'safe'.

Another UK study places rather more emphasis on gender differences,
however. On the Isle of Sheppey, Wallace (1987) notes that domestic
services were among the things that held young unemployed males at
home: 'Where else could they have their clothes washed and ironed and
food provided for between £10 and £15 a week?' (p. 158).

With young women, however, Wallace found that they organized their
lives around domestic work, and that for many of them this became the
incentive to set up home independently since under these circumstances
domestic work would be more fulfilling than in the parental home. The
demands made of them gave more of a reason for leaving. There has been
some speculation about the 'value' of girls' domestic contribution (Morris
with Ruane, 1989) and the possibility that it justifies smaller financial
contributions in some cases. This seems most likely to occur where there
are differential male and female pay rates, however, rather than in cases of
youth unemployment.

Paying their Way

A number of British studies, largely qualitative in approach, have focused
on inter-generational dynamics within the household in the context of

financial contributions. As we saw from Leonard's findings, entry into employment, and with it the capacity to earn a living, has the effect of lessening friction between parents and children, and constitutes an important transitional stage in the achievement of adult status. The potential for friction remains, however, if members of the younger generation are unable to make this transition.

Allatt and Yeandle (1986) have reported on a study of 40 households in the north-east of England, all with young people aged 18–20, who had entered the labour market in times of economic recession. All young people in the study were expected to contribute to household expenses, whether from their wage or from their benefit, and the authors cite a larger-scale project (Ashton and Maguire, 1986) which found that 97 per cent of young men and 93 per cent of young women make such a contribution. Confirming Leonard's findings, Allatt and Yeandle note that in no case did the contribution of the young person cover their full economic costs. They also point out that *net* contributions vary with household circumstances. Some young people received back more than they gave, and unemployed boys were sometimes paid for household tasks as well as retaining spending money from their benefit.

The contrasting circumstance is that of the parent who observes 'You can't keep dishing out money if you're unemployed'. In such cases of parental unemployment the contribution of a young person, even if themselves unemployed, can be critical to household viability, and indeed the highest contribution recorded in the Allatt and Yeandle study (albeit low in absolute terms) was from an unemployed young man. This particular boy remarked that he would not leave home until his mother had paid off her debts. The significance of this finding is heightened by data for the UK that suggests that unemployment tends to be concentrated within family households (Payne, 1987). Other sources of variation are differing ideas about fairness, some homes operating a flat-rate system of contributions regardless of income, with all children paying the same amount of board money, others adopting a system of relativities, with contributions reflecting resources.

The questions of independence, obligation and mutual assistance also arise between siblings. Again there is considerable variety and Allatt and Yeandle report contrasting cases of mutual help with siblings in turn providing spending money when the other was unemployed. In another home, however, parental expectations to this effect were resented and clearly the length of time out of work, and whether or not others had also experienced unemployment, would be significant variables. In one home power accrued to an employed sister over an unemployed brother in the choice of television programme; she was perceived to have paid for her choice. In other homes resentment is caused by parental attempts to buffer a child from the deprivations imposed by unemployment.

The more general point to be made in this report is that in economic transactions it is not just money that is being transferred, but cultural values of, on the one hand independence and responsibility, and on the other of love and concern. The authors draw attention to the fine line to be drawn between practices arising from love and conducive to young people's personal development, and the costs incurred by over-indulgence or 'spoiling'. These ideas were also taken up in the study by Hutson and Jenkins, which examines the household position of young people in South Wales. Like Allatt and Yeandle, they argue that financial arrangements in the home, and specifically the giving of 'keep' is about 'the learning of values and the practice of right behaviour'.

Their argument is that in the absence of employment as a marker of entry into the adult world, young people can assume responsibility and gain parental respect and approval in the way they manage their benefit. Three reasons are given for the importance attached to the ability to 'manage':

1 It shows a recognition of economic constraints.
2 It demonstrates coping with the outside world.
3 It is a mark of independence from parents.

Again we find echoes of the north-eastern study in the conflict between: 'The desire to cushion unemployed children from hardship, on the one hand, and "keeping them hungry", on the other' (p. 98). Thus we see a strategy whereby the parents take 'keep' money, which is returned through various purchases such as cigarettes and clothing; alongside both fear and resentment if children appear to be learning to live with unemployment.

Youth Unemployment

Joblessness for young people has attracted attention for a number of reasons. As we see from the case studies above, the absence of independent earnings for young people have in some way to be 'managed' by the households of which they are members. The manner in which this is achieved will vary with the economic circumstances of parents and the moral position they adopt. One aspect of concern with the effects of youth unemployment has therefore been the potential for disruption to the parental household, and the problems it poses for the socialization of the next generation into values of personal and financial responsibility, as well as the work ethic.

The significance of these questions is, however, heightened by the fact that in both the UK and US unemployment is disproportionately represented within the younger generation. The problems of joblessness are therefore concentrated in a group facing the critical transition of school-leaving, mating, household formation and child-rearing. Lacking skills and experience the young may seem a poor choice to employers if older experienced workers are available on poor terms and conditions and for low pay. Thus in the US youth unemployment (under 25) rose from 11.2 per cent in 1960 to 17.8 per cent in 1982 as against overall rates of 5.5 and 9.7 per cent. The UK adjusted figures for youth unemployment were 2.4 per cent (1960) and 23.7 per cent (1982) as against 1.9 and 11.9 per cent overall. Since September 1982 young people on government training schemes in the UK have been excluded from the numbers and no realistic current figure is available.

There are contrasts between Britain and America, and also between different groups within the young population, but youth unemployment is recognized as a problem in both countries. Ashton (1986: 106) reports that in 1979 youth formed only one-quarter of the US labour-force but accounted for almost half of all unemployment, whilst in Britain youth constituted one-fifth of the labour-force but two-fifths of the unemployed. He attributes part of the youth unemployment problem in the States to the large numbers of young people who move in and out of the labour-force according to the college terms. This represents a much higher proportion of the population than in the UK because of the greater uptake of higher education, and the greater need in the US for self-finance throughout. The 'working' student is also a significant contributor to unemployment figures in the States and is described by Ashton as 'very much an American phenomenon'.

The other category of unemployed youth, however, is made up of those seeking full-time work in the secondary sector of the labour market, which represents a larger proportion of the total labour market than in the UK and is characterized by unstable jobs. Thus Freeman and Wise (1982) note that unemployment is largely concentrated among a small number of youths who lack unemployment for extended periods of time. Ashton suggests that blacks are disproportionately represented in this group, and are also disproportionately affected by any deterioration in job opportunities.

Until the early seventies the British rate of youth unemployment was low in comparison with the States. Ironically, although concentrations of youth unemployment in the States appear to be explained by the relegation of many young people to the secondary sector of the labour market, Ashton explains high levels of youth unemployment in the UK by the relatively small size of this sector and its consequent inability to absorb to any significant degree the unqualified school-leavers on the labour market for the first time. This suggests that youth unemployment in the States may be less long term than in the UK, and thus reflects the general unemployment pattern for the two countries.

Household Formation

We have suggested that one reason for concern about youth unemployment is simply the scale of the problem; the overwhelming concentration of unemployment in both the UK and US within the next generation of potential workers. If the transition from school to work, and hence to adulthood is now under question for many, the perhaps more significant transition out of the parental home and into an independent household seems likely also to be affected.

Kiernan (1985) presents data to show that a substantial number of young people in employment live with their parents in the UK. Over 80 per cent of employed teenagers and half of the 20–24 age group who are working do so. Kiernan states that the pace of leaving home is relatively slow in the UK, beginning gradually during the teens, and increasing during the 20s, but only reaching majority by age 25. At the age of 21, 43 per cent of women and 63 per cent of men are still living with their parents, and even in the late 20s 49 per cent of unmarried, employed men and 33 per cent of women are still living with their parents (Kiernan, 1986).

In the US the rate of leaving home is much faster in the teenage years, peaking the year or so after finishing high school and for many going to college, and changing more slowly thereafter. Ellwood and Wise (1980) found that 95 per cent of young people living in the parental home were unmarried, but by the age of 24 only one-quarter of white men and 16 per cent of white women are left at home, and one-third of black men and one-fifth of black women. By this age, however, employment has become a critical factor, such that lack of a job may prevent exit from the parental home, and this could account for the higher proportion of young black people still at home by age 24 (see below).

In Britain a substantial proportion of young adults transfer directly from the parental home to set up a new household with a spouse (Kiernan, 1985: 14), whilst in the US many make the initial break from home in the year following graduation from high school. The relatively low proportion of young people in the UK who go on to higher education could explain this difference. Kiernan gives figures of respectively 23.6 and 13.9 per cent for men and women, in contrast to US figures of 63.5 and 52.7 per cent. Thus, whilst marriage marks the transition from the parental home in a majority of British cases, US data reveal two broad groups: those who expect to make the break with home on leaving school, often when they go on to college, and those who follow the British pattern and leave on marriage.

The Effects of Youth Unemployment

It is not easy to identify clear-cut, general patterns relating to youth unemployment and parental dependence. At one level we have seen that parental indulgence in the way of subsidies may act to deter young people from leaving because financially this is the best situation they can hope for. Hutson and Jenkins (1986) certainly found cases in which the parents consciously used this strategy as a means of keeping the child in the home where at least they had some knowledge of and control over their movements and behaviour. We did note, however, that a parental dependence on contributions from the child can also serve to tie them to their home of origin, although we do find cases of conflict that eventually drive young people away from the parental home.

Available data are somewhat contradictory. For the UK Kiernan (1986: 8) notes that unemployed young people in their late teens and early 20s are less likely to be living with parents than their employed contemporaries. We have seen that the common reason for leaving home in the UK was to marry, and yet qualitative data suggest unemployment will inhibit such a move. Allatt and Yeandle, for example, note the disruptions of the masculine role caused by unemployment: 'Well, I mean . . . it's always been – that's been the role of a boy . . . that's what they function for. . . . They leave school, they get a job, they get married, they look after a family. I mean that's their whole purpose in life, is work' (p. 104).

In the US leaving home was less likely to be tied to marriage, but Burchinal (1965: 245) has noted that historically marriage rates have risen with prosperity and fallen in economic recession. More specifically he notes that unemployment among young men is not conducive to marriage, and that for young men aged between 16 and 24 unemployment rates were twice the average for workers of all ages. We noted earlier more recent figures that confirm these disproportionately high levels of youth unemployment.

Wallace's study in the UK on the Isle of Sheppey (1987) addresses the question of the extent to which youth unemployment challenges established ideas both about employment careers and also domestic and marital careers, following a sample of 44 young men and 40 young women from the age of 16 to 21. She divides the sample into four categories (1987: 9): dependent single persons (32 per cent), independent single persons (26 per cent), independent couples (34 per cent) and dependent couples (6 per cent). Those who remained single but left home were far more likely to be employed than unemployed (nine regularly employed, three long-term unemployed), though this finding is contradicted by Kiernan's quantitative data. Both Wallace and Kiernan found, however, that young women were more likely to leave home when single than young men. The reason suggested by Wallace is that girls' behaviour comes in for more parental scrutiny when at home, and they were expected to contribute to domestic work in a way that boys were not. Wallace also found, in agreement with other studies, that young unemployed people (but particularly boys) will be tied to the home by parental subsidies, though Kiernan's data would suggest that other constraints will override this effect.

Among those young people who formed couples in Wallace's study, marriage was associated with employment, and cohabiting with unemployment. Three reasons were given (p. 160):

1 Young people wished to marry in style, which meant expense.
2 Many parents disapproved of daughters marrying an unemployed man, and discouraged them from doing so.
3 There was general acceptance of the fact that to be a married head of household a man must also be a breadwinner.

Some of these findings are echoed in American writing. Ellwood and Wise (1980) comment on the relative ease of living in the parental home, rather than setting up an independent household, and note: 'Even out-of-school youths living with families in poverty or near poverty provide on average only 10% of family income. Some teenagers may face serious financial hardship when they are unemployed, but most probably do not' (pp. 80–1).

They provide some useful statistics on differential employment rates, though these date back to 1976. Representing a high unemployment year, however, they are perhaps worth quoting. For male 18 year olds in the US employment rates among those still in the parental home and those independent and single were much the same *within* both the black and white population, though there were differences *between* the ethnic groups (72 and 70 per cent for dependent and independent whites, and 42 and 39 per cent for dependent and independent blacks). The employment rates are highest in this age group (96 per cent) for whites who are married with no children, suggesting employment may be a prerequisite of marriage. At 24 the single independents have a higher employment rate than single dependents, 87 per cent as compared to 77 per cent for whites with an even more marked difference of 91 per cent as compared to 56 per cent among blacks. At this age employment rates of those married and living independently average out at 93 per cent for whites and 85 per cent for blacks.

The general message seems to be that unemployment is higher among *dependent* males in their 20s than any other group of that age, and particularly so for blacks. Comparable data for women are similar, with the exception of black women in their 20s who seem more likely to remain in the parental home when employed. As in the States, UK data show a concentration of unemployment among those young men in their 20s but still in the parental home, suggesting that this perhaps is the group in both countries whose wishes for independence are most frustrated (Murphy and Sullivan, 1986: 214).

In the UK, however, in contrast to the US, the availability of benefit has allowed young people to leave home even if unemployed, though we should note that since September 1988 benefit for 16 and 17 year olds has been tied to government training. In the US without eligibility for unemployment benefit there is no state-provided income and we might therefore expect the single unemployed in the UK to be more likely than their American counterparts to establish an independent home. There are, however, other factors to consider, most notably access to housing.

Young People and Housing

The sharpest contrast between US and UK housing stock is the relative importance in the UK of public sector housing. In 1983 64.7 per cent of occupied households in the US were in owner occupation, 34.9 per cent rented privately and only 2.5 per cent were in public housing (*US Census Bureau Statistical Abstracts*, p. 688). In the UK the percentages for 1985 were 62, 5 and 26 per cent (*GHS*, 1986, p. 48), and the critical difference for young people is the absence of any substantial private rented sector. The most immediate consequence of this is to make the achievement of independence for the young, single and unemployed a difficult transition.

Clearly home purchase is dependent on a regular income and mortgages will be available only to those who can demonstrate a reliable earning capacity. Not surprisingly, Wallace reports a clear association between having a regular job and becoming an owner-occupier in the couples in her sample. Whilst couples might begin married (or cohabiting) life in the private rented sector, it was more common to save for a home whilst living with parents, and this is one reason often given for parental subsidy to children at home (see Allatt and Yeandle, 1987; Leonard, 1980). In cases of unwed motherhood, remaining in the parental home increases the propensity to work, presumably because of child care support, and the effect is particularly marked among black single mothers.

The British social security system has so far made it possible for young unemployed people to obtain accommodation independently of parents by covering rent payments, but there are increasing problems of access to housing for young people wanting to establish themselves away from the parental home for the first time. Wallace's figures on housing suggest a high level of dependence by the young unemployed on the private rented sector. In her sample 14 out of the 22 independent singles were in private rented accommodation, in comparison with 7 of the 29 independent couples. Fifteen of the latter group were in fact in owner occupation, but as we noted above this is a tenure that requires a regular income, and is therefore not available to the young unemployed seeking independence or wishing to establish a nuclear family household.

It has been common in the past for young people, employed or otherwise, to start their housing careers in private rented accommodation and the role of the private sector has thus been an important launching pad for housing careers in other tenures. In 1980 38 per cent of household heads under 25 were living in private rented accommodation in contrast to 9 per cent in the 30–44 age group (Willis, 1984). The availability of housing in this sector has, however, been in decline throughout this century and in 1985 stood at only 7 per cent. The dearth of accessible rented accommodation is a contributing cause of homelessness among the young unemployed, who may be driven from the parental home by internal conflicts to drift towards the big cities, notably London (Willis, 1984).

The other alternative for those unable to command a mortgage is local authority rental, though competition for such accommodation is fierce. Malpass (1984) notes that the waiting list in England at the time of writing was 1,200,000 whilst recorded homelessness had risen every year since 1979. Young single people have no chance of being housed in local authority homes, except in rare cases of hard-to-let accommodation or short-life housing. Patterns of housing tenure by employment status do, however, demonstrate a high dependence by the unemployed on local authority housing, because of the difficulties of raising a mortgage. The usual route into public sector housing then is either by rehousing from substandard private lets, or from overcrowding in the parental home. In both cases the probability of rehousing in local authority accommodation is enormously enhanced if there are young children involved. For many the best means of access to housing by the local authority has been through the production of children in overcrowded conditions, though we should note recent criticism of policies deemed conducive to single parenthood.

Wallace found that unmarried motherhood was considered an acceptable option among unemployed couples, and could serve (by virtue of the benefit system) to provide both adult status and a claim to state housing. For the young women concerned 'Motherhood seemed to offer more status than either a low status job or unemployment, but less status than a "good" job. It would appear that marriage, motherhood and domesticity often caught up with girls rather than being an actively espoused status' (p. 164).

In practice, couples with irregular employment careers were as likely as the regularly employed to have children, and also likely to marry once this step had been taken.

A pattern of polarization by housing tenure has been documented by Murphy and Sullivan (1986) who found high concentrations of unemployed, married men with young children in local authority housing, in contrast to a pattern of young dual-income childless couples in owner occupation. This pattern is due to two tendencies:

1 The enhanced possibility of public sector housing when there are dependent children present.
2 The high proportion of income taken up in mortgage repayments in the initial years, which will often depend on two incomes and discourage early child-bearing.

A number of writers (Malpass, 1984; Willis, 1984) have expressed concern about the effects of government policy to increase yet further the proportion of owner-occupiers in the UK. Murphy and Sullivan (1986: 219) refer to a government aim of 80 per cent owner occupation, and point out the improbability of such an achievement given that 25 per cent of the population in their 20s are unemployed. Thus for the UK there seems to be a gap in the housing market that will make *household formation* (that is separation off from the parental home) increasingly difficult without *family formation* (that is the birth of children). Without a private rented sector there will be no exit route for the young unemployed, and without children there will be no possibility of accommodation by the local authority, whose stocks are anyway likely to be in decline. Homeless youth unemployment then seems likely to become an increasingly familiar phenomenon, although the problem may eventually solve itself as the population curve changes and the young come to make up a smaller proportion of the total. Between 1987 and 1994 the number of people in the 16–19 age group is expected to fall by 26 per cent (Finn, 1988: 7).

Youth and Household Structure in the US

There are a number of aspects of the US situation which differ from that in the UK. Firstly, there is no equivalent to income support (previously supplementary benefit) and so if a young person has no eligibility for unemployment benefit, or has exhausted that eligibility, then there is no automatic system of financial support available, though if they are members of a household eligible for food stamps a claim may be made on their behalf, thus providing subsistence. The structure of employment in the US means that unemployment is generally of shorter duration than in the UK, but we have noted the overwhelming concentration among black youth, who do experience long periods without work.

It is interesting then, that Ellwood and Wise (1980) found a marked difference in employment rates between black males aged 24 in the parental home and those who remain single but live independently (56 per cent as compared with 91 per cent). This suggests a pattern whereby unemployed black youths remain tied to the parental home but move out on finding employment. Since their employment is likely to be insecure there may be a pattern of movement in and out of the home for, in contrast to the situation in the UK, there is a fairly substantial private rented sector. We have else-where noted a pattern of single motherhood, particularly marked amongst blacks, and apparently associated with male unemployment, which seems consistent with such a pattern. The women concerned would either live alone claiming AFDC, which will not always be paid if an unemployed man is present, or will live with their parents and possibly find employment. Ellwood and Wise (1980) note:

> The living situation of unwed mothers sharply influences the likeli-hood of their working. A mother living with her parents is much more likely to work than one who is married or living singly. For black teenagers the effect is particularly pronounced. An unwed teenage black is four times as likely to work as an unwed mother living alone. (pp. 82–3)

These authors have made a number of more general points about employ-ment and household structure that should perhaps be mentioned here. They note that 85 per cent of white teenagers live in two-parent households, whilst nearly half of blacks (45 per cent) live with one parent. Employment and schooling patterns also correspond to these differences such that teen-agers from poor and single-parent families are less likely to enrol in school, and also less likely to find employment. Hence: 'For both races and sexes coming from a single parent family substantially diminishes the likelihood that a youngster out of school will be working. Some 40–45 percent of out-of-school blacks of either sex in two-parent families are employed; roughly 30 percent of those from single parent families are employed' (pp. 88–9).

Ellwood and Wise put forward a number of speculative explanations:

1 Less access to networks or contacts and information.
2 Less likely to have working role models.
3 More likely to be rejected when they apply.

4 Disincentive in welfare rules.

5 Work in the black economy (that is, the informal sector of the economy).

However, even if family structure and income levels were identical for black and white the overall employment rate for black teenagers living at home would rise only from 21 to 27 per cent, whilst the overall rate for whites was 48 per cent (p. 91). In other words the differential prospects of blacks and whites must be a major factor in explaining relative employment rates, over and above any other influences deriving from family background.

Patterns of Disadvantage in Young Marriages

Ineichen (1981) has documented a complex of characteristics that are found among marriages of young people from low occupational status in the UK. These include early marriage, early and pre-marital pregnancy, and a high incidence of residential dependence. These marriages also tend to be unstable. Early marriage and disadvantaged family background have also been reported in the US (Michael and Tuma, 1985), and one explanation that has been proposed is that unpleasant family circumstances are likely to be associated with early marriage, which is taken as indicative of a wish to escape. This view seems rather naïve in that those who are disadvantaged may in fact be least likely to be in a position to exercise this wish. Other writers have noted, for example, high residential dependence among the young, married, unemployed in the US (Goldscheider and Da Vanzo, 1985), as well as high unemployment rates among the single young blacks who remain residentially dependent.

Michael and Tuma have noted other factors that do not appear to fit easily into the schema of discontent and early marriage, notably ethnic variations in youthful entry into marriage that run counter to the hypothesis. Whilst on the basis of the above argument we might expect to find high rates of early marriage in the black population, in fact the proportion married by their 20th birthday is highest for Hispanics, followed by whites and finally, in third place, blacks. When we look at first birth figures, however, we find that the proportion with a first birth by age 18 is highest among blacks, with Hispanics second and whites third. It would seem then that the black population has established a different pattern of response to disadvantage than has the Hispanic, and that for the former group single motherhood is culturally more acceptable.

Youthful marriage has also been argued to be related to the availability of parental resources and of female alternatives to the wife role and the costs of assuming it. This was a finding from Waite and Spitze's (1981) US research. It has been suggested that as (and if) male and female labour market differentials decrease then there will be less incentive to women to enter into marriage, but the same must also be true if unemployment means that the man has no advantage to offer the woman.

The availability of alternative roles seems to have been one factor in pre-marital pregnancy, and certainly pregnancy in the face of unemployment, according to Wallace's interpretation of her UK material. Not only was unemployment a discouragement to marriage but it was an incentive to motherhood in so far as it offered some means of access to adult status and also to state benefit and housing. This is a pattern that seems to correspond to the black American pattern, although black/white differences can also be detected in the UK. It seems, for example, that marriage follows pregnancy more rapidly for whites than for blacks in either country and certainly single parenthood has a higher rate in the British black population than the white.

It may be, however, that we will witness the emergence of a pattern of single parenthood among white unemployed youth in the UK that parallels the pattern so far largely associated with the black US population. Thus it is no coincidence that the highest illegitimacy rates in mainland Britain coincide with the highest economic deprivation of Merseyside and Cleveland (*The Independent*, 13 June 1988). In such areas, the nuclear family household with a male breadwinner may no longer offer a viable model for sections of the young population. Their household and family formation prospects will be intimately associated with their labour market potential.

9 *The Household in Social Context*

This book has so far discussed the interrelationship between various aspects of domestic life and the position or behaviour of different household members in the labour market. Particular attention has been paid to the effects of recent change in labour market conditions, and especially their implications for the sexual division of labour and for gender roles. Reference was made in chapter 1 to attempts to understand such change through ideas of 'comparative advantage' (Becker, 1981) and 'household strategies' (Pahl, 1984), but a full understanding of the household–labour market connection implies a somewhat broader frame of reference. What is required is an approach that would identify and detail the social influences through which this connection is mediated; that would, in other words, place the household in its social context.

In the course of previous chapters a number of points have arisen that give some indication of how this line of thought could be developed, and of principal importance has been the role of state provisions in shaping or maintaining particular household structures and domestic relations. Whilst a comprehensive review of welfare and social security systems in the UK and US is beyond the scope of this chapter, and inappropriate to the focus of this book, it seems necessary here to return to some of our previous references to specific aspects of state policy and provision to give some explicit account of their household and labour effects in the two countries.

Provision for Unemployment

Since a principal concern of this book has been to trace the impact of changes in the structure of employment and their gender implications, then high levels of male unemployment have received particular attention. There are, however, significant differences with far-reaching effects between the provisions made in the US and those made in the UK for support for the unemployed. Both countries have established contributory social security systems in which payments are made through the wage to insure the worker against periods of time without work. In both countries the unemployed worker can claim benefits on the basis of payments made in employment, with a maximum duration of 26 weeks in the US and 12 months in the UK. It is what happens after this period that distinguishes the two countries in their treatment of the unemployed.

One of the distinctive features of the British system is that unemployment insurance is commonly supplemented by a means-tested benefit, and when a worker has exhausted his or her unemployment benefit then this 'supplementary benefit', which was replaced in April 1988 by 'income support', will continue to be paid, usually in larger amounts. In other words, there is a guaranteed minimum income available to those who are involuntarily without employment. Concern about the effects of this benefit on household structure and employment patterns have mostly been directed to the question of the effects on the motivation to earn of other household members. This was found to be one factor reducing the likelihood of 'role reversal' between husband and wife, an argument to be examined later in this chapter.

The largest means-tested benefit in the US is Aid to Families with Dependent Children (AFDC), which has tended to operate as a system of support for single mothers. In 1961, however, Congress authorized the payment of aid to families of unemployed men (AFDC-U), but only 50 per cent of states incorporated this possibility into their system (Rainwater et al., 1986). It has been argued that even where the provision exists the eligibility requirements are so stringent that only a small proportion of families actually benefit. Moen (1983) has provided figures on benefit recipients for 1975, a high unemployment year, and found that nearly half (48.1 per cent) of the families with an unemployed breadwinner in 1975 received no income from either AFDC or unemployment benefits. Fewer than 1 per cent of the families received both welfare and unemployment benefits, and while nearly half (46.5 per cent) received some unemployment compensation, less than 5 per cent received AFDC payments. There is considerable variation between states in terms of the non-federal programmes for support of the unemployed. Some offer 'work-fare' provision, where assistance is offered in exchange for work on state projects. In some states minimal means-tested benefits are also available. Nevertheless, it remains true that many of the long-term unemployed, having exhausted their eligibility for unemployment benefit, have no financial means of support.

Welfare and Marital Stability in the US

Because of the concentration of single mothers in receipt of AFDC research attention has been focused on the threat posed by welfare to marital stability. In the US there has been a dramatic rise in the incidence of sole female headship (Rodgers, 1986). Between 1959 and 1984 the number of female-headed households with children increased by 168 per cent whilst the number of male-headed households increased by only 7 per cent. By 1984 1 in every 5 households with children under 18 was headed by a woman: 16 per cent of all white households, 25 per cent of all Spanish origin households and 52 per cent of all black households, whereas in 1959 only 1 in 11 households with children was headed by a woman.

The main recipients of welfare in the US are single mothers, and in those states in which two-parent households do qualify for such benefit the amount is less than that available to a one-parent household (Bahr, 1979: 553). Scheirer (1983: 763) notes that in 1977 two-parent households in receipt of AFDC constituted 14.4 per cent of total welfare households, in contrast to mother-and-child households, which constituted 60.7 per cent. This raises questions about the possible effect on household structure and marital stability. Thus, as Bahr argues: 'For low-income families, AFDC increases the economic rewards of an alternative to the existing marriage. It follows that AFDC might increase the rate of marital dissolution among low-income families' (p. 553).

The argument here is that, firstly, the availability of a source of income alternative to dependence on a male wage creates conditions that make separation a viable option for women with children. Secondly, there is the possibility that in the specific case of households with an unemployed husband, separation becomes financially attractive to the woman; this proposition has been supported by Sawhill et al. (1975). Whilst these hypotheses appear to have a self-evident logic, analysis of data on welfare and family structure is complex and inconclusive. Some of the varied findings have been reviewed by MacDonald and Sawhill (1978).

Honig (1974), for example, found a positive relationship between average payments to AFDC families and the proportion of adult females who 'headed' families with children. For 1960 she found that a 10 per cent increase in average state AFDC payments increased the proportion of households 'headed' by women by 3 or 4 per cent, although the relationship was less strong for 1970 and for whites than for blacks. Using 1970 data MacDonald et al. (unpublished) found virtually no support for Honig's main conclusion, but Ross and Sawhill's (1975) treatment of 1970 data was consistent with Honig's findings, showing that a 10 per cent rise in benefit levels raised the proportion of *non-white* women 'heading' families by 7 per cent.

The Case of Black Female Headship

Bahr (1979) has argued that the ethnic differences noted above could be explained by attitudes to welfare, such that economic disadvantage in the black population over a long period of time has made welfare a legitimate source of income, whilst in the white population it carries stigma and disgrace. Darity and Myers (1984) focus specifically on the case of black female 'headship' but disagree with the view that AFDC payments are a direct cause of female 'headship' in the black population. They find the evidence of a causal relationship to be weak, though not entirely without foundation, but go on to develop a more complex argument to the effect that: 'the statistically significant determinants of black family structure are the female age distribution, the non-white male mortality rate, and the female–male ratio' (p. 773).

Whilst these demographic factors are seen as the major explanation of female 'headship' among blacks, however, the authors nevertheless point out that this does not mean that the existence of a social welfare system is irrelevant to the process leading to female 'headship'. Over time, as this form becomes established, there is a growing lack of familiarity with other arrangements, which is accentuated by the absence of marriageable men. The latter phenomenon is attributed to incarceration, military conscription, high black male mortality, alcoholism and drug abuse, with the result that motherhood on welfare is, for some, the only available option. This argument is consistent with the evidence referred to earlier (Reimers, 1984), which suggests that apart from other influences there are cultural differences between racial groups that affect the propensity for female 'headship'.

The interest in female 'headship' in the States has grown in part because of evidence that suggests the pattern may be self-perpetuating. We have seen one such argument above to suggest that, once established, a particular household form is likely to become part of the outlook and expectations, and in that sense part of the 'culture' of particular groups, although this suggestion has been discredited by the criticisms of the culture of poverty thesis. The latter argument, briefly put, was that part of this culture was a lack of the motivation to achieve, and the acceptance of an alternative system of values. These arguments, however, do not have to be conceded simply to acknowledge that particular household forms are more likely to recur when they have a high incidence and acceptability within specific sections of the population.

More recent accounts of the self-perpetuation of the 'female-headed', single-parent household have focused on the poor educational and economic attainment of the offspring. McLanahan (1985) quotes a wealth of research to indicate that those who grow up in one-parent families complete fewer years of schooling than those who spend most of their lives in two-parent households, a finding that is also related to low occupational status and marital instability. The key question is whether the effects are due to absence of a parent or to family economic status.

The distinction being made is between the effects of low income and poor prospects for an ill-educated, black population that is disadvantaged in the labour market, and the effects of decreased motivation for attainment and poor socialization resulting from the absence of a father.[1] McLanahan's conclusion is that although something more than the stress of low socio-economic status is affecting the attainment of the offspring of one-parent households, the major influence is the fact that children in these homes are less likely to complete high school education, and this itself may be related to pressure to earn and/or to assume child care responsibilities. If they are unable to find employment and have no eligibility for benefit, but are living in low-income homes, however, the household can claim food stamps on their behalf, and thus accommodate them at relatively low cost. We may find in this pattern an explanation of the high incidence of black male adults still in the parental home.

Unemployment and Benefits in the UK

Unemployment benefit and income support which are available in the UK have markedly different household effects than the US welfare system. This is because the safety net benefit of income support (previously supplementary benefit) can be claimed as of right by an unemployed man or by his wife, on behalf of the couple and any dependent children. Although rates for single parents will be somewhat higher, there is no strong incentive for women to establish themselves independently of the father of their child/children. This will only be the case, however, if a couple are already established in an independent household when the man becomes unemployed, for, as was noted in chapter 8, single-parenthood can strengthen a claim for state housing.

Where a young couple have not been able to establish a home because of unemployment, then the benefit system makes it easier for a woman, if she has children, to do so alone. It is also the case that some young couples take advantage of the preferential benefit rates available to single parents by registering two claims: one for the mother and child, and one by the father from his own parental home, whilst nevertheless operating as a cohabiting couple.

The major research concern of the household impact of the benefit

---

[1] Cf. the cycle of deprivation, which argues that inadequate socialization may produce the generational transmission of disadvantage (see MacGregor, 1981).

system, however, has centred on the disincentive effect for the wife. An unemployed man can claim unemployment benefit for 12 months, assuming he has made sufficient contributions, although the amount of income support he receives in addition to this benefit will vary with the number of dependents and on whether or not his wife is employed. The end result, however, is that a fairly substantial portion of the wife's wage is 'disregarded' in calculating the benefit due. The amount of 'disregard' falls considerably, however, once the household becomes dependent on income support.

In November 1983 it became possible for either the man or the woman to make a claim on behalf of the household provided the claimant could satisfy certain conditions that indicate recent contact with the labour market. These conditions have now been eliminated, but nevertheless the general pattern that remains in the case of male unemployment is for the man to claim rather than the woman. If the wife of a claimant is in paid employment, then a substantial portion of her earnings is deducted from the claim (all earnings over £5). The result has become known as the disincentive effect, and is partly responsible for the tendency in the UK for a polarization between two-earner/no-earner households.

Daniel and Stilgoe (1977), in a longitudinal analysis of a DHSS cohort study, found that where married men in the 24–44 age group had full-time working wives they had themselves been employed for a majority of the three-year period covered (1976–9), whilst in cases where the wife had no paid job the men had been out of work most of the time. Over the period of the study 10 per cent of employed wives left employment and 5 per cent took up jobs, in contrast to 20 and 6 per cent, respectively, in a later study (1978–9) reported by Moylan et al. (1984).

Although Daniel (1981) found only 2 per cent of wives moved from being economically active to being inactive within a month of their husband's registering as unemployed, one might expect a shift to occur when eligibility for unemployment benefit runs out, and/or when the man's employment starts to look long term. Moylan et al., for example, report that wives of men receiving unemployment benefit, with its more generous disregards, were less likely to give up paid work than the wives of men receiving supplementary benefit. Although they note a number of factors that operate independently of this effect, including a weaker tendency to be unemployed before the husband's job loss, they nevertheless conclude that: 'Some of the changes in the wives' employment status seem to be systematically related to the type of benefit the family was receiving in respect of the man's unemployment. The main result is the high proportion of wives in the families receiving supplementary allowance who left employment' (pp. 131–2).

The result has been a major disincentive against role reversal as a means of dealing with male unemployment. We should not, however, attach too much causal weight to this effect, for, as we saw in chapter 2, the wives of unemployed men in the US are even less likely than in the UK to have gainful employment. Joshi (1984: 25) runs through a number of reasons that, in addition to any benefit disincentive, could produce an association of unemployment between husband and wife. For women these reasons may include an increased domestic load as a result of the husband's presence at home, a wish to share time together or a reluctance to usurp the breadwinner role. There is also the probability that where jobs are hard to find for men they could be hard to find for women as well. This will depend on the structure of local labour markets.

The woman's employment outcome will also be affected by the types of employment available to her husband. If a man's period out of work does not extend beyond his eligibility for unemployment benefit, which allows for higher earning on the part of the wife, then a woman who already has a job would be wise to remain in employment. A calculated decision may be made about the probability of the man's finding further employment eventually, and if the prospects are reasonably hopeful then the woman will remain employed throughout his time out of work. If she gives up her job she cannot be sure of finding another once her husband is re-employed. If, however, his unemployment looks likely to be long term, then the woman's incentive to remain in employment is considerably reduced, thus producing the association between male and female unemployment within households.

Morris with Ruane (1989) has speculated on the potential for change in the two-earner/no-earner pattern since the introduction in April 1988 of a rise in the flat rate disregard on part-time earnings (to £15 a week) for couples who have been unemployed for two years or more. This may, however, lead to competition between spouses over who has the right to earn, and hence dispose of, such additional income.

A full understanding of the disincentive effect requires an examination not just of benefit rulings but of their interaction with married women's position in the labour market. Unless a woman can earn substantially more than the household can claim in benefit, she may be deterred from earning at all. It is therefore the disadvantaged position and poor prospects of the majority of married women, as much as the disincentive effect, that will mean that a wife is unlikely to become a sole earner. The growing concentration of part-time employment among married women makes such an outcome even less probable.

We should also note that it has been to employers' advantage in the UK to construct jobs of a particular kind: workers earning less than £35 per week, who will usually be employed part time, require no national insurance contribution. They also offer flexibility and disposability, having reduced rights as employees, often without holiday entitlement or redundancy compensation. In short, in cases of long-term unemployment the woman's economic role will be constrained by an interaction between the gendered structuring of employment opportunities and the operation of the benefit system. The effect of this relationship has been to limit the financial incentive for the woman to take paid employment, and substantially reduce the viability of role reversal.

Single Parents

Another significant group of recipients of income support in the UK are single parents. We have seen for both the US and the UK that male unemployment may be a contributing factor in the emergence of such households, although it is clearly not the only influence at work. We have yet to consider the situation of lone mothers dependent on benefit and the effect of this on their labour market experience. In the UK and US single mothers depending entirely on income from paid employment total 38.4 and 52.3 per cent, respectively (Rainwater et al., 1986: 112). Those combining work and welfare total 22.5 and 20.7 per cent, respectively, and the welfare dependent account for 24.2 and 17.0 per cent.

UK material suggests that the motivation for earning is stronger for lone parents than for married women, with 85 per cent of the employed in the former group working from financial necessity as compared with 37 per cent of the latter; and 78 per cent working to earn money for essentials, as compared with 28 per cent (Martin and Roberts, 1984: 110). A higher proportion of lone mothers also fell into a high financial stress category (48 per cent as compared with 11 per cent). The question of motivation to work as opposed to relying on benefit nevertheless remains. Nixon (1977) examines this question through research on two groups of low-income lone mothers – those dependent on supplementary benefit and those working and claiming family income supplement (now family credit).

The working group tend to have smaller families, 62 per cent having one child as compared with 48 per cent of the non-employed group, and fewer have a youngest child of pre-school age (41 per cent as compared with 49 per cent). Child care is nevertheless an important issue for the working group, and as many as 43 per cent were able to leave their children in the care of a grandmother, and 33 per cent relied on a state nursery or nursery school. Such places are often dependent upon the applicant having employment and the general availability of work is clearly an important factor in the outcome. Evidence suggests that single mothers dependent on benefit (and not working) tended to decrease in areas where employment opportunities for both men and women were relatively favourable.

Of the single mothers who had withdrawn from employment, a significantly higher proportion were living in single-unit households, that is not sharing accommodation with other adults, with no likelihood of their receiving direct child care support from others in the household, notably grandparents. Against this, however, we must set the finding that the employed women are more likely to be householders and therefore to have direct responsibility for meeting housing costs. Finally, Nixon reports that whilst financial calculations were important in the decision to work, they would be weighed against the practical costs of doing so. Nevertheless, the social and psychological benefits are also extremely strong influences, especially where the margin between benefit income and earned income is a narrow one. Such findings suggest that the availability of benefit is not alone sufficient to dissuade women from working if other circumstances permit.

Rainwater et al. (1986) provide some data on the situation of lone mothers in the US. We should first note that the proportion of sole mothers relying only on employment for an income is higher in the US than the UK (by 13.9 per cent), though the numbers mixing benefit and employment are roughly the same at respectively 20.7 and 22.5 per cent (p. 112). One important factor in the US that has a bearing on whether or not lone mothers are employed is their previous work history. The probability of a lone mother working if she has worked in the past is 93–4 per cent, whilst if she has not worked the proportion is between 25 and 30 per cent. As in the UK a further important factor is the number of children and age of the youngest child. Among women receiving welfare, as the number of children increases the probability of the woman working decreases, but in cases of women with four or more children, 54 per cent work where there is a preschool child, as compared with 86 per cent of the mothers of larger families with only older children. Of the lone mothers who are totally benefit dependent, 38 per cent have large families with young children as compared to only 14 per cent with medium-sized and large families of older children.

The factors affecting the labour market behaviour of lone mothers are therefore similar in many respects to the influences acting upon married women. For both the UK and US the existence of welfare does not seem sufficient to deter women from working where their circumstances make it practically possible, although we have noted in previous chapters that there is some variation by ethnic identity in employment patterns of lone mothers – Bruegel, for example, has argued that the very low wages available to black women in the UK make benefit dependence for lone parents more likely. Similarly the existence of welfare seems to facilitate marital disruption in cases where the man cannot or will not provide for the needs of the household, but is unlikely to be a sole determinant.

Taxation and Labour Market Behaviour

Another aspect of statutory rulings that affects the labour market behaviour of women in general is taxation. Dex and Shaw (1986: 11) have commented on tax and employment legislation in the US and UK, and find the two countries to be alike in that: 'tax laws are based on the idea that a family has a husband/father at work and a wife/mother at home [and] it has been argued that these regulations offer married women some disincentive to being employed relative to men in both countries'.

The structure of personal tax allowances in the UK is such that a married man has approximately one and a half times the single person's allowance, whilst a wife's allowance is equal to that of a single person but can only be set against her own earned income. The implication of the married man's allowance is that husband and wife can be treated as one unit, which carries the assumption that the benefits of allowance will be received by the 'dependant' for whom it was made. This has been a focus for criticism, as has the inbuilt discrimination against couples in which the woman is not employed, through the loss of her personal allowance. Dex and Shaw argue that the married woman's allowance could be seen as encouraging part-time work up to the tax threshold, especially since the marginal rate of tax that applies beyond that threshold is high, being based on the couple's combined earnings. Indeed, working couples have become used to calculating whether or not it would be advantageous to elect for the wife's earnings to be taxed separately, for which they must make a specific request.

The necessity for such manoeuvres is soon to be removed, however, for from April 1990 husband and wife will be taxed independently on all sources of income, and the married woman will receive a single person's allowance to be set against her income from any source. The rate at which she is taxed above this income will be determined by her own level of earnings rather than the combined earnings of herself and her husband. There is still discrimination between husband and wife in that the married couple's allowance (which replaces the married man's allowance) is available first to a husband and only when he has insufficient income to absorb it, to a wife. Thus there remains a vestige of the assumption that it is the man who is responsible for maintaining the household, and the woman is in some sense dependent.

Changes in legislation regarding taxation in the US have similarly been concerned to establish a balance between the tax liabilities of single and married people. Between 1971 and 1981 the system in operation was felt to contain a marriage penalty in that the total tax bill was higher after marriage. In 1981 there was an attempt to counteract this by deducting

10 per cent of the earnings of the spouse with the lowest income in computing income subject to tax (Dex and Shaw, 1986: 13). Unlike the new UK legislation, then, the American system does not grant independent taxation for members of a married couple. What the two countries do have in common, however, is that each retains an element of the assumption that the married couple can be treated as a financial unit, such that advantages that accrue to one through the tax system are necessarily also experienced by the other. The problem with this assumption is that, as chapter 6 made clear, one powerful influence on many women's wish to seek employment has been their constrained access to or control over their husband's earnings.

Accommodations for Children

There is legislation in the UK that has no US parallel and is designed to at least acknowledge the possibility that all of the income entering the home is not necessarily equitably distributed. The traditional fear has been that the man, as breadwinner, would not necessarily honour his obligation to his wife and children and that some payment directly to the mother on behalf of the children was a desirable feature of any welfare system. It currently takes the form of child benefit (previously family allowance). There are two distinct arguments underlying this provision:

1 If wages are deemed inadequate and the payment of a 'family wage' sufficient to maintain a wife and children cannot be assumed, then there must be some form of benefit available to children of the low paid.
2 Regardless of wage levels, do not women need access to some independent income for use on behalf of their children?

In other words this provision is related to questions about both the level of the man's wage and the uses to which that wage may be put, and is particularly relevant in homes either with low wages managed by a whole-wage system, or in homes adopting an allowance system *whatever* the wage level.

There exists a further benefit in the UK designed specifically for low wage households with dependent children: family income supplement (FIS) (now family credit). There has been some contention about the manner of payment of this benefit. FIS was a benefit normally collected by the non-employed partner and therefore a means of direct access to additional income for them. Initially, family credit was to be paid through the wage and was thus seen as a step towards the integration of the tax and social security system. This proposal, however, raised questions about the targeting of benefit, and doubts about whether it would reach those 'dependants' in the household for whom it was intended, especially given that the payment was to include an allowance for school meals and milk. Spending on children commonly falls to the woman, but the early proposals meant that the allowance would go to the man via the wage-packet. In the face of criticism, however, payment by order book to be claimed by the wife was eventually conceded.

An accommodation for children that does exist in the US and is absent from Britain is the opportunity to set child care expenses against income tax. As chapter 4 noted, this has been one of the factors in explaining the higher rate of full-time employment for married women in the US. There are others, however, notably the inducement to employers in the UK to create part-time jobs. Whilst the effect of such jobs has been to facilitate the paid employment of women with child care responsibilities, the *explanation* lies in the ruling that excludes employers from national insurance contributions for employees earning less than £43 a week. The situation in the US is the reverse of this. Social security and unemployment insurance have been levied on all employees (with the exception of very short-term work) up to a certain ceiling. Dex and Shaw (1986) conclude: 'It is cheaper to hire one person whose earnings exceed the ceiling than to hire two part-time people to do the same job and pay them both less than the ceiling' (p. 13).

As we have seen, the existence of part-time employment has done much to encourage a 'double burden' of paid and unpaid work for married women in Britain. It offers employment whilst accommodating domestic obligations.

Social Networks and Domestic Life

The burden of the argument so far in this chapter has been to illustrate that the fashioning of systems of benefits and allowances necessarily makes assumptions about domestic organization, and also influences the behaviour of household members. In other words, the household is shaped to some degree by the 'statutory' environment in which it is located. It is not only the content of state family policy and provision that has such power, however, but the informal patterns of association that constitute the household's social environment will exert a strong influence on its internal dynamics, prospects and outcomes.

A good starting point for this discussion is the seminal work of Elizabeth Bott (1957) whose innovations in family sociology were noted in chapter 3. The core of her argument was that the elementary family – or, more specifically, the married couple – was to be seen as constituting a focal point within a network of social relations, the nature of which exerts considerable influence over the character of the marriage. Hence the association between network type and the organization of domestic life.

Bott's central hypothesis is that: 'The degree of segregation in the role relationships of husband and wife varies directly with the connectedness of the family's network' (p. 60). In other words, members of a couple who perform domestic tasks interchangeably or together are likely to have a minimally connected network, whilst those with task segregation will show greater network connectedness. Bott classifies the conjugal roles of the couples in her sample as segregated or joint, and conceives of their social network as a means through which factors such as type of locality, occupational status, family phase and so on exert their influence on these roles. Harris (1969), following Fallding (1961) refines the argument somewhat by suggesting that the critical factor is the extent to which the network favours group formation, on the following logic.

The development and maintenance of clear ideas and beliefs about gender role content and behaviour are more likely to occur in conditions of peer-group solidarity. It is also the case that the interconnectedness of the network provides the means by which deviation from agreed patterns is detected and controlled. There are a number of ways in which work in this tradition has helped to clarify the social mechanism mediating the relationship between the household and the labour market status or activity of its members.

Chapter 3 documented work in South Wales (Morris, 1985b) with 40 redundant steel-workers and their wives that showed a number of correlative features of network type, with particular implications for responses to unemployment. The research revealed three distinct patterns of social activity, distinguished in terms of the degree of group identity implied, and these are referred to as 'collective', 'individualistic' and 'dispersed'. A marked association was found between social activity and the division of domestic labour, with rigidity in attitudes and behaviour most likely to occur with collective social activity and flexibility most likely with individualistic social activity.

It also proved possible to identify certain implications for financial expenditure. Men with an individualistic network were less involved in social activity, and consequently had more predictable spending needs than other men. They were also freer from pressure against involvement in the domestic sphere, and as a result disagreement and misunderstanding about domestic expenditure was less likely. Whilst a more expansive male social life might be contained by the woman's retaining control of household income, this could lead to serious dischord, unless finance was provided through illicit earnings or through friendship and kinship support.

Support Networks

In so far as American research has focused on household networks, the central concern has been largely with the identification and explanation of patterns of perceived cultural difference between black and white household and family forms. Hofferth (1984), for example, documents the higher incidence of extended family households among blacks than whites and observes that a number of studies have shown that blacks have stronger kin ties than whites. The main debate seems to revolve around the question of whether this represents a distinctive black culture that the network then plays a part in transmitting and reproducing, or whether the more active kinship ties of the black population are simply a response to economic need.

Hofferth argues, however, that since black families are more likely to be single-parent families, the positive relationship between race and extended family types may simply be due to a higher black incidence of single motherhood. This she shows to be the case, finding that one-parent white families are more likely to participate in kin networks than comparable black families, but that among two-parent families black kin participation is higher. This suggests a *determining* role for family structure in network participation, but also provides some evidence of a cultural difference.

Such connections as are made between networks and gender roles focus upon the matriarchal character of the black family and the female centredness of its social networks, although in opposition to this view some researchers have characterized flexibility in the distribution of family maintenance responsibilities as indicative of an egalitarian allocation of roles. The counter-argument is a depiction of the black male as marginal to the family, but instrumental in socializing sons into deviancy. Similarly, the network is seen as self-reproducing in that kin-friend networks may actively resist marriage plans of particular individuals to ward off loss of a member, which could impair the overall welfare of the network (for a review of the argument, see Allen, 1978).

Two ethnographic studies referred to in earlier chapters provide illustrations of these arguments. Stack (1974) describes the supportive networks of a black ghetto community in the mid-West where she found:

> patterns of co-residence, kinship based exchange networks linking multiple domestic units, elastic household boundaries, life-long bonds to three generation households, social controls against the formation of marriages that could endanger the network of kin, the domestic authority of women, and the limitations on the role of husband or male friend within a woman's kin network. (p. 124)

Conversely, Liebow (1967) depicts the black male peer-group formed around street-corner activity, which supplies the unemployed black male with a positive image based on minimizing commitments and domestic responsibilities, and on the celebration of 'manly flaws'. Some caution is advisable here, however, since many 'behavioural patterns' of black and white males remain unstudied, and this suggests the possibility of stereotyping produced through an over-researched complex of associations.

Informal Activity

Male peer-group solidarity appears in another guise in both British and American discussions of opportunities in the informal sector of the economy. Whilst what has here been termed the 'statutory environment' of the household – state policy and provision – will have a strong influence on domestic life, so too will the informal means of evading statutory surveillance that are embodied in informal networks.

Economic activity that does not appear in national accounts of, for example, employment and productivity figures, or individual and household earned income, has been an increasing focus for speculation and debate. This area has been variously termed the black economy, hidden economy and informal economy – terms that are both vague and inaccurate. Not only is there a wide variety of activities subsumed under one heading, but the 'informal', being inextricably linked to the formal, should properly be termed a sector of the total, national economy.

The precise nature of the relationship between the formal and the informal, however, is by no means clear. Early speculation in Britain to the effect that the informal sector, at least potentially, offered a substitute for formal employment has now been rejected (Pahl, 1980, 1984). The argument against such a substitute function is that it is by definition most likely to occur in areas of high unemployment, but if local economies cannot generate formal employment then neither will they generate significant informal employment, whilst Pahl's (1984) findings suggest that informal activity will anyway be concentrated among those who have opportunities in the formal sector.

Conversely, however, high levels of unemployment in the UK have been argued to encourage the restructuring and casualization of some areas of employment (see Atkinson, 1984; Fevre, 1986; and for criticism Pollert, 1988), and informal sector activity has been shown in some cases to aid this process (see Morris, 1984b). In the US recent unemployment levels have not been so high as in the UK, and this might suggest that there will accordingly be less scope for the operations of the informal sector, or at least that this activity will be confined to 'moonlighting' by those in formal employment. This view neglects to take account of a large population of illegal immigrants, whose very presence, and not just whose economic activity, may be hidden from official counts. Their circumstances constitute a specific instance of the more general requirement for secrecy and trust involved in many of the operations of the informal sector.

Morris (1985b) and Harris et al. (1987) have emphasized the role of the informal network in conferring a moral identity on individuals such that they are deemed reliable in the receipt of information relating to opportunities for informal work. The network provides opportunity for the worker and a guarantee for the employer or client, who has to be assured that the worker will be available when required, will actually appear and will perform their task adequately, in the absence of formal means of redress. The source of security is the hope of future work and the nature of the social ties that brought client and worker together. The process is summed up by Harris et al. (1987: 131):

> Opportunities are made available and services offered on the basis of belonging to a social collectivity which serves both to distribute information and to confer upon its members a 'moral identity'. The worker is thus put in touch with an employer or client, while the employer is assisted in the search for appropriate labour, and any subsequent transaction is grounded in the social and moral ties which brought them together.

Lowenthal's US research (1981) on non-market transactions makes the same kind of points in a discussion of coping under financial duress: 'As people confront limited income and financial insecurity, as well as the desire to maintain or create supportive relationships in their communities, they will often engage in a system of economic transactions which are embedded in networks of social relationships' (p. 91).

The Household Connection

Very little research of this kind makes connections from the network into the domestic arena, though chapter 1 has mentioned one such development that spawned a wealth of research and debate in the UK on changing patterns of work. The initial argument was advanced by Gershuny and Pahl (1979, 1980), who suggested that economic change was revolutionizing household organization. It was suggested, for example, that in the workings of the informal economy the poor may be advantaged because of previously constructed support systems, and experience of hardship, and the possibility was floated that those with least incorporation into the formal sector might be best placed in the informal (Pahl, 1980), provided they had available the appropriate skills and a network through which to exploit them.

These early ideas were soon to be questioned by Pahl himself, and by work being carried out in a number of related areas. In his final account of his research findings in Sheppey (1984) Pahl in fact laid to rest the suggestion that informal activities of self-provisioning and communal labour exchange, or even illicit earnings, were the answer to decline in formal economic activity, and instead furnished evidence of an increasing polarization between working and workless households, a pattern likely to persist even as unemployment falls.

Morris's ethnographic research both in South Wales and the north-east of England (1894a, 1987c), however, found that there are men for whom informal economic activity provides a source of income which is at their disposal in a way that benefit, at least normatively is not. Whilst by no means supplying a substitute for formal employment, and by no means available to all the unemployed, informal earnings can be significant in a number of ways. Money earned in the informal sector may be used to finance some kind of male social activity; may be earned with a view to meeting some particular domestic cost; may be handed over entirely to the wife, who would almost invariably hand some back; or may simply be divided in half. Two general functions are identified (Morris, 1987c: 99):

1 The provision of some kind of male social activity outside the home, a dissociation from the wife and domestic activities during the day, and a substitution for employment.
2 The gaining of a fairly meagre amount of additional earnings that finance some degree of social activity without taking from the family purse.

In contrast, the spending patterns of women are bound up with their involvement in the domestic sphere, and the nature of informal aid they receive, as well as any illicit or legitimate income they earn, will tend to reflect this fact. Chapter 1 noted the early assumptions in the UK and US (Pahl, 1980; Thomas et al., 1980) that economic change would produce greater flexibility in household uses of time and labour, such that there would no longer be: 'a universal sex-linked division between the male "chief earner" in the formal economy and his unpaid dependent wife engaged in unremunerated housework. Nor is there such a rigidly sex-linked division of labour between men and women in the practice of domestic work' (Gershuny and Pahl, 1981: 86), and subsequent chapters have illustrated how far from reality such speculation has proved to be. Morris's material suggests the resources that are informally available in the face of unemployment are among the many influences that, far from encouraging change, in fact support established gender patterns. Both men and women will receive aid in cash or in kind from close kin or friends, but the source of the aid and the use to which it is put tend to acknowledge the different constraints on men and women imposed by a low household or domestic income. For the women in these studies there were also additional aspects of informality that served to shore up their traditional role.

Gendered Supports for Women

We have already noted that part-time employment for women is much more a British than an American phenomenon, and there are a number of statutory influences that work towards this end. The South Wales study noted above makes a link between this fact and the operation of social networks to supply employment information whilst also shoring up the female role.

Where there is a well-established pattern of female responsibility for domestic and child care tasks, a woman's paid work must either take account of her domestic obligations, or those obligations must accommodate her paid employment. Broadly speaking there are three possibilities:

1 Hours in paid employment must leave the woman free at appropriate times for the fulfilment of child care obligations.
2 An arrangement may be made with female friends and relatives whereby they assume some of the domestic labour, either for financial reward or on a reciprocal basis.
3 A husband may assume a share of the activities previously defined as the responsibility of his wife.

It is in deciding which of these possibilities is viable that the social network comes into play. This is not to suggest that there is no room for the notion of choice in our understanding of the entry into paid employment by married women; rather, decisions about work can only be understood in terms of constraints and possibilities that derive from the woman's location in a web of social contracts.

Entering paid work was found to be largely the result of exploiting informally acquired knowledge of suitable work opportunities; 'suitable' usually being defined as opportunities that did not interfere too severely with traditional patterns of domestic organization. Wives' participation was structured by their position in the traditional nuclear family-household, and the ability of their social contacts to provide, at the very least, information about the availability of suitable employment. Thus informal access to employment allows women with heavy domestic obligations who are seeking paid work to identify jobs that accommodate those obligations.

These data are in some ways reminiscent of the American work on the household strategies of the poor (Stack, 1974) and much of the research into black household structure and the position of single parents. Whilst the issue of part-time work is less central to women's employment in the US, there is ample evidence to suggest the importance of kinship support in facilitating paid work for women with children. In such studies, however, the effect is not to shore up the traditional domestic role of the married woman, as outlined above, but to accommodate the fact that the black male is often marginalized both in employment and in the family, such that the woman's role is expanded to that of household provider. This seems to be facilitated by assistance from a supportive and predominantly female social network. As we noted above, however, an over-attention to this complex of effects in research may well have neglected the alternative roles adopted by low-income males.

Access to Employment

One of the problems of using much of the data available in constructing an account of household–labour market relations is that a good deal of relevant material exists in discrete pockets. Thus there is an abundance of studies of, for example, the black American family, the unemployed male, female employment patterns and so on, but even where the data is presented in a manner that takes account of domestic circumstances and effects we are left without a means of connecting data in one area or about one population group with data about another. An alternative way of framing this problem is to ask why one household rather than another ends up with a particular 'strategy'. A number of constraining factors have at least implicitly been identified above. There is, however, a burgeoning area of research that could be tied more closely into concerns about family and household outcomes than has yet been the case: research on access to employment.

The notion of a survival strategy was first introduced by a literature concerned with third-world or ghetto poverty (Lomnitz, 1977; Peattie, 1968; Stack, 1974) that documents the routinized flow of information and aid across household boundaries. Such extra-household linkages have not been of central importance to current research focusing on the household, where concern with gender roles and the sexual division of labour have rarely made a connection with the social location of the home. Nevertheless, there is as we have seen a wide acceptance in both the UK and US of the importance of mutual aid, support networks, cross-generational assistance and so on in working-class districts, and the transfer of resources across household boundaries within middle-class extended families has also been documented (Bell, 1968; Litwak, 1960).

Grieco's (1987a, 1987b) research in the UK brings an extra dimension to this data by emphasizing links between family structure and employment prospects. She cites evidence to support the transmission of 'occupational property', but observes that in contrast to the working-class emphasis in studies of informal aid, the literature concerned with employment opportunities was 'restricted almost exclusively to middle and upper class families' (1982: 704). Her claim is that the transmission of occupational advantage also occurs within the working-class family.

If we broaden the application of this insight, of particular interest are the means by which different individuals are channelled into different sorts of jobs, or indeed into unemployment, and we find that information will play a crucial role. The best-known elaboration of this argument is through work in the US by Mark Granovetter (1974). Jobs that are formally advertised are, at least notionally, equally accessible to all potential applicants, although informal channels of influence can be brought to bear even in formal recruitment. Where jobs are not advertised, the dissemination of information and exertion of personal influence becomes crucial – even more so where illicit earnings are involved, that is in the informal sector of the economy. The realm of information and influence constitutes one area in which the social network of a household or individual is an important factor in establishing and maintaining links between household and the labour market, as well as mediating the effects of change in that market.

Recruitment Chains

The outcome of any given individual's effort to find employment will be partly a product of history, for time of entry onto the labour market can have a strong influence on future prospects by virtue of the prevailing employment structure (Morris, 1987c). Granted this, it is also the case that informal influences via social networks can play an important role through what Grieco (1987a: 33) describes as the interactions between job vacancy chains and social networks; 'grapevine recruitment'. She argues that: 'Networks play an important role in the filling of vacancies, both over distance and in the local labour market . . . the existing workforce pass employment information on to other members of their network, and use influence to put network candidates at an advantage over other candidates for the vacancy' (1987a: 36).

She cites a number of studies that provide evidence of the 'capture' of opportunity through 'the annexing of an entire chain of employment', and also suggests its importance is greatest in blue-collar occupations. A detailed study of this 'annexation' can be found in Dick and Morgan's (1987) study of a Yorkshire textile mill, and Whipp (1985) reports more generally on the connection between labour markets and the communities in which they operate. He emphasizes the family's role in work orientation, socialization, skill inheritance, training and so on, and in the 'capture, closure and control of job niches and pathways' (1985: 779).

The idea of preferential recruitment through informal channels is taken up by Harris et al. (1987) and a small case study documented by Morris (1984b) examining the effects of the South Wales steel redundancies. The study is partly concerned with the means by which redundant workers gained access to new employment, and found that methods of recruitment dictated not only which workers were successful in the search for employment, but also what kinds of work they eventually acquired. This is not to say that informal methods are characteristic of only particular occupations, or occupational levels, but there may be differences in their degree of importance in different areas of employment.

Scott (1982), writing on the 'old-boy' network in the UK, has argued how important informal links are in maintaining upper-class privilege, whilst in the US Granovetter has cited figures for a wide variety of occupations that clearly establish the importance of informal recruitment across a wide range of social strata. Blue collar studies show rates of 60–90 per cent; an engineering study found rates of 68 per cent and Granovetter's own work on professional, technical and managerial workers found that 56 per cent used personal contacts. Part of Granovetter's thesis is that there will be differences in dependence on strong ties (notably kin) and weak ties (acquaintances) according to age of the candidate and the type of job involved.

The young will have developed less far-flung contacts and be more likely to rely on kin; specialized jobs are more likely to pass along strong lines of contact; and so on. His general argument, however, is that weak ties pull in a far wider range of information and are therefore more valuable than strong ties. Grieco (1987b), however, argues that this ignores the preferential ordering of information, which will select some to receive before others, whilst Granovetter's argument seems to assume the perfect transmission of information. She cites Sheppard and Belitsky (1966: 97) for the US and Marsden (1982: 64) for the UK as instances of the importance of friendship and kinship in channelling information, and her own research makes the point for a number of different (though all working-class) occupations. Chapter 3 of the present work also documented the absence of informal links with the world of work where unemployment recurs within extended families, and where it is spatially concentrated. Research in the north-east of England (Morris, 1987c) found this pattern eventually to lead to the self-perpetuation of unemployment in particular sections of the population. Such concentrations also produced distinctive patterns of mutual aid and association, which confirmed the social and spatial segregation of the unemployed group.

Spatial Divisions

Space plays a part in household outcomes in a more general sense, however, as has been ably demonstrated by Massey (1984). The industrial make-up of local and regional labour markets can be important in determining which areas are most likely to benefit from recovery, and these will not necessarily be the ones that have suffered most from decline. Hence the 'social polarization' referred to earlier does not simply segregate one household from another, but produces sharp regional contrasts. In other words, there will be geographical variation both in the incidence of unemployment and the effects of recovery.

One characteristic of recession in the UK has been that, as with particular groups of workers, we find that particular regions have been more vulnerable to industrial decline and unemployment. It is generally true for both the US and UK that unemployment rates are highest in large metropolitan areas, but there is a regional variation above and beyond this tendency.

In the UK the poorest areas are Scotland, the North, Northern Ireland and Wales, with their traditions of mining, metal manufacture and ship-building, though there was what Townsend (1983) terms a 'Southward spread' of unemployment in the early 1980s to the previously more buoyant economies of the manufacturing heartland of the North-West, Yorkshire and Humberside and the Midlands. Even the most prosperous areas of the South-East were badly affected, though employment in services was better able to cushion job loss from other sectors than elsewhere in the UK. Not surprisingly, it is the South-East and areas with good access to the capital that have shown the most rapid recovery.

Through the years of high unemployment there were similarly marked contrasts in the US (Hanham, 1984). States with the highest rates of unemployment were located in a large bloc in the West, with isolated instances in the southern Mid-West and North-East. States with rates significantly below the national average are located in a large bloc in the centre and along the West Coast. Unemployment tended to occur where there was a large blue-collar work-force, high levels of unionization, a large black work-force, and low levels of female employment. In other words, as in the UK, the heavy manufacturing areas suffered most. This pattern, together with farm bankruptcies in the Mid-West, and oil closures in Texas, produced an overall spatial pattern that has been termed a two-coast economy.

The significance of spatial variation, both currently and across time, relates in part to both the nature of the response to unemployment and the probability of finding future employment. The varying economic structures that produce these patterns will also have different implications both for male and female job prospects, and for local ideas about the nature of gender roles. We might also expect extended family relations to play a different role according to regional and familial concentrations of unemployment, whilst previous experience of unemployment in the region generally will affect both the psychological impact and local perceptions of the problem.

Summary

There is clearly room for considerable variation in the way in which different households are articulated with their economic environment. Major influences will be the character of the local market for labour, and the nature and extensiveness of local social networks, which will pay a role both in the dissemination of information and influence in the search for employment, and in the formulation, expression and maintenance of group ideas and beliefs about gender roles. Whilst these networks constitute the immediate mechanism by which the household is articulated with its social environment, the history and current character of the labour market within which it is located will determine the nature of opportunities that are available, both in terms of employment and informal support.

The general point to emerge is that to understand the circumstances of any given household it is insufficient to deploy a rational, decision-making model that examines the labour power available and weighs the relative advantages of household members in domestic and paid work; an approach perhaps most clearly exemplified by Becker (1981). It remains to consider the way in which different individuals gain access to employment opportunities, and how that access relates to their location in a world of social contacts that, at least potentially, link the household with the labour market, as well as to combine this with an examination of other influences that operate in determining household outcomes. These influences have been identified as the normative or ideological constraints embodied both in local patterns of association, and in the statutory constraints built into a complex of provision and legislation that impinges upon, and carries assumptions about, the nature of life within the home.

10 Conclusion

This book began with a discussion of the recent fashion for 'household' research, which was attributed to concern on the part of social scientists to reach some understanding of the effects of economic change. This concern has sometimes taken the form of interest in how households cope in constrained financial circumstances, especially in the face of male unemployment, whilst married women's increased presence in the labour-force has prompted speculation about the changing nature of gender relations. Economic change is deemed to pose a challenge to the validity and viability of a model for household relations and domestic economy based on the earnings of a sole male breadwinner.

Briefly put, the evidence for both Britain and America indicates an absence of any significant change in established gender roles. Women do not, in significant numbers, take over from their unemployed husbands to become sole earners; unemployed men do not assume the housewife role; and married women's employment does not prompt a significant rise in domestic involvement on the part of husbands. So in what ways, if at all, has the nature of gender roles been shaken?

The archetypal household model that emerged from the development of an 'employment' society contingent upon industrialization was based upon the separation of home from work, and a gendered specialization of activities in these two spheres. Whilst women were never totally excluded from the work-place, and women's earnings were often crucial to poorer homes, male labour came to predominate in paid employment and the nuclear family household dependent on a sole male earner was one outcome. The emergent pattern of gender specialization has been theorized in terms of the fit between economy and society such that, in Parson's schema, women's association with the home through child-bearing and child-rearing made them the fitting partner to provide domestic support for the wage labourer. In Marxist-feminist terms the domestic worker came to provide the labour that turned the wage into the means of subsistence and guaranteed the daily and generational reproduction of the labour-force.

In so far as these approaches provide any account of how and why the division of labour became gendered it is with reference to the domestic obligations that accrued to women as mothers, their consequent disadvantage in the labour market and male workers' consolidation of their own labour market strength. With the fall in male employment and the rising presence of married women in paid work, the logic of this configuration appears to have been challenged, with men and women at least potentially freed from their traditional roles. Two notable approaches to understanding the resultant situation have emerged, which have in common an emphasis on the resources available to households in terms of time and labour. Thus one (American) approach examines comparative advantage in paid work and domestic work, respectively, with a view to understanding household outcomes; whilst the other (British) looks at the strategies of different households in exploiting the labour available to them.

Both of these approaches were based on the premise that there would be substantial change in domestic organization to accommodate the changes occurring in the economic structures of both Britain and America. In fact, the evidence is that no such fundamental change in gender relations has followed and the problem is less one of documenting varied domestic outcomes, than of explaining why change has been so limited. The important components in such an explanation have here been identified as institutional constraints in the functioning of both the labour market and the welfare state, normative constraints reinforcing and maintaining established gender roles, and the inequitable distribution of power within the household that enhances male power to resist change.

This latter point raises one aspect of the household not easily accommodated by any straightforward division of labour approach that takes the household as its unit of analysis; that is, neither in terms of power nor resources does the household function unproblematically as a unit. To understand fully the workings of the household we must therefore locate it within the web of institutional and social constraints and supports that influence its internal operations, whilst also opening up those operations for examination. This will mean the examination not only of the division of labour within the home, but also access to, distribution of, and power over household resources.

In the particular case of male unemployment there is little evidence of any renegotiation of gender roles in either the US or the UK, but rather both countries show a male defensiveness against any challenge to their traditional gender identity. This reaction is not confined to the men alone, however, and whilst there is some sign of flexibility regarding participation in domestic tasks, the woman's conventional load remains largely intact. One effect of the woman's traditional role is that she carries the main burden of budgeting, which often involves struggling not only to meet the collective needs of the household but also to control her husband's personal spending requirements. Her assumption of paid work in the place of the man is a rare occurrence in both countries, the US even more so than the UK, and it seems that welfare systems may have considerable bearing on the paucity of such arrangements. So too does male resistance.

Despite this general pattern there are a number of sources of variety in the experience of male unemployment, one important factor being stage in the life-cycle. Here a marked contrast is found between the UK and US, with vulnerability to unemployment high for men with dependent children in Britain but low for the same group in the States. The degree to which different sections of the population are affected can be an important differentiator in itself, as well as other essentially class- and ethnic-based contrasts. These largely have their source, however, in the degree of *vulnerability* to unemployment. Thus, the middle classes may suffer greater stigma and trauma, being part of a community in which unemployment is a rare experience, and a condition with which they conceivably have had no previous personal contact. They are, however, more likely to have greater financial resources to call on, and more room for reduction in their basic standard of living. Conversely, the unskilled working class, though more vulnerable financially are more likely to be situated in a community where unemployment is a common experience and mutual support is more likely to be forthcoming. What seems to be the case for all social groupings is a strong resistance to far-reaching change in gender roles.

Whatever the rise in married women's employment does mean, it has not resulted in a reversal of the traditional male and female roles, but has produced in both the US and UK a predominance of two-earner households. What this means for men's and women's respective roles, and for the internal dynamic of the household cannot be easily divined, however. America and Britain, for example, differ considerably in the level of part-time work for women. In the UK married women's child care obligations have led them to seek out part-time employment, which suits employers because of the lower costs to them in creating such jobs. US women, however, show less dependence on part-time work, can offset child care costs against income tax and show a much stronger attachment to the labour-force than British women, although present in slightly lower proportions.

It is the predominance of part-time employment for British women that, together with benefit rules and restrictions on 'additional earning', explains the absence of large numbers of role-reversal homes, whilst in the US no such clear-cut explanation is available. The generally shorter-term nature of male unemployment in the States may be one factor preventing any radical rethinking of the household division of labour. In cases of long-term unemployment it may be that the availability of welfare for single mothers in a far greater number of states, and at higher levels of payment than for unemployed men, has induced separation for some couples. Some interesting literature in the US has raised the more general question of whether marital strain or dissolution can be produced by the woman's employment, though there seems to be enormous scope for variety in responses, according to number of hours worked, size of the women's income, whether the man forgoes domestic services and so on. Such questions as this of course guide us towards an examination of the relationships inside the household and the topics of domestic labour and household finance.

Early approaches to domestic labour contained in exchange theory saw the traditional male and female roles as complementary components in a system of equal exchange, and yet it is clear from other work that the role of housewife carries less power and lower status within the home than that of earner, as well as presenting the incumbent with problems concerning the assessment of their performance, work satisfaction and work-based identity. Whilst male unemployment has done little to spread responsibility for what has been an all-but-exclusively female domain, the question has been posed of to what extent female employment brings about some redistribution of domestic labour. The general finding for both the UK and US has been that there may be a slight increase in male domestic involvement when the woman is employed, but this contribution by no means compensates for the additional labour she has assumed, or comes close to equalizing the domestic load. It was found by one American study that the proportional increase in the man's contribution to domestic labour was accounted for by the woman's reducing her domestic work time, not by the man's increasing his.

The roots of resistance to change are varied by class and occupational position. Amongst middle-class couples it seems that high earnings on the part of the man reduce amenability to participation in domestic duties, whilst on a practical level this position may be encouraged by the demands of jobs at the higher level of the occupational scale. And yet we find among working-class couples where high earnings are less likely to be an explanation for men's avoidance of domestic chores that there is a strong ideology supporting the separation of spheres, and rigidly gendered responsibilities. Support for this ideology seems often to be strengthened by male unemployment, as a means of warding off a perceived challenge to male identity. Thus it is not simply earning capacity that determines responsibility for domestic work. Receipt of a wage does not necessarily lead to a significant reduction of women's domestic role, and nor does the loss of men's earnings produce compensatory labour in the home. The existing situation can thus be explained only by some reference to a normative framework for ordering men's and women's respective roles, and possibly, it would seem, the relative distribution of power within the home

These findings question the validity of a 'comparative advantage' approach to the household's use of the labour resources at its disposal. Even when the comparative advantage of men and women in the market for labour and in domestic work are reversed, a reversal of their roles by no means necessarily follows. We are also led to question the degree to which a household 'strategy' will be constructed to exploit the apparent flexibility available to any given household, since responses will clearly be considerably constrained by normative ideas about appropriate gender roles, though there is evidence to suggest that the weaker the peer-group pressure to conform to these constraints, then the more flexible a man will be in his approach to domestic work. There is some indication in the literature, however, that participation in domestic labour is influenced by the distribution of power within the home, and this is a question not easily accommodated by approaches that, at least implicitly, emphasize the consensuality of household operations.

Nowhere are the pitfalls of this approach more apparent than in the study of household finance management. We have already seen some suggestion that power in a marriage derives from earning capacity, and this of course raises the question of whether women's earnings increase their power in the home. The answer in the case of domestic obligations seems to be largely negative, and indeed in the case of part-time employment women fashion their paid work to accommodate their unpaid labour in the home. With finance management, then, the questions of interest are: who earns the household income, who makes decisions about spending, who carries them out and do members of a couple have equal access to earned income? Although there is considerable variation between households in the methods of handling finance, one fairly consistent pattern emerges: spending decisions involving large amounts of money are taken by men, whilst day-to-day budgeting tends to be the responsibility of women. This distribution conforms to other aspects of the traditional distribution of responsibilities.

There are a number of ways in which position in the labour market comes to influence a household's financial arrangements. Simply put, these largely relate to size and source of income. The larger the income the more involvement the man has in household financial affairs, arguably because of the greater capacity for spending in large amounts – a characteristically male preserve. The smaller the income the closer total income is to the level required for minimal domestic needs and the more likely it is to be managed by the woman. This is especially true in cases of benefit dependence. Women's earnings at the lower level do little to affect these patterns, being commonly used to augment the domestic funds, though at a higher level of status and income women's employment brings a greater probability that there will be some shared element in the overall management of finances.

It is not simply that the labour market characteristics of particular households influence the organization of their finances, however, but the way in which couples organize their income will affect behaviour in the labour market. One clear example of this relationship concerns the motivation for male overtime working and the disincentive to additional earning where there is no direct personal benefit, that is when the wage packet was handed over intact. This is not, however, universally the case but varies with the worker's general orientation and degree of home centredness. The absence of any personally available fund and the commonly observed convention of handing benefit over to the woman is, of course, one strong argument *against* the contention that welfare payments constitute a major work disincentive for the unemployed male. He forgoes his right to, and control over, personal spending money.

The case of married women's employment provides another example of a labour market connection. Insufficient funds for domestic spending, caused variously by the husband's generally low earnings, or his intransigence about the amount he will give over to his wife, is what prompts many women to seek employment. The need or wish for independent funds by the woman will not necessarily bear a direct relation to the size of the man's income. What is rather at issue is access to that income, and its allocation to various areas of spending. These questions are of central importance to any understanding of the impact of unemployment for women, since one effect of increased labour market participation for married women has been the growth in numbers of two-earner households and the dependence of large numbers of homes on the woman's wage.

How the loss of this wage is felt, and by whom, will depend to a great extent on the use to which the woman's wage had been put. If, for example she had been augmenting inadequate housekeeping money, then the whole household may suffer, or she may herself be the only one to feel the stress of budgeting. Where the husband's wage is sufficient to meet all needs, and distributed appropriately, then the effects of unemployment will be felt more in terms of personal satisfaction and identity. One important factor in the outcome is the salience for particular women of the housewife role, and there is much speculation in early literature about the availability of a source of identity that is not employment based. Whilst there is some evidence of this in the relief expressed by women about having time for housework and with their children, this is more accurately interpreted as relief at respite from the 'double burden' of paid and unpaid work, rather than satisfaction with the housewife role. There is certainly evidence of the role of employment in defending women against depression and isolation.

The financial strains resulting from unemployment for women will vary considerably both by personal circumstances and level of income. Unemployment for single women is both psychologically and financially more threatening than for their married counterparts. Among married women, however, the financial pressure is likely to be greatest at the lower income levels, especially since low-earning women are likely also to have low-earning husbands. Thus overall household income will be low and women's earnings will be a major component in financing collective expenditures. In these circumstances it is difficult to separate out the role of women's employment in alleviating financial need and its significance in providing a source of independence. Even at higher income levels these issues can be blurred since women's wages may be crucial to the fulfilment of their domestic responsibilities, regardless of the size of the husband's wage. This makes statements about the relative significance of women's earnings problematic, though it should be noted that black women are not only more vulnerable to unemployment than white women, but show both a higher level of labour market involvement, and work longer hours. This has been partly attributed to the generally lower level of pay for black males.

The significance of women's earnings will depend not only on the level of husband's income but more importantly on the degree to which it is available for spending on collective needs. Where domestic spending is tightly constrained, women's unemployment will be felt most severely, especially if there is no recognition by the husband of the importance of his wife's wage. There is some indication of a tendency to see married women's earnings as somehow secondary; as a supplementary or luxury income rather than a necessity, which may mean a failure to appreciate the impact of their job loss. This being said, the effects of unemployment for married women have nevertheless received more attention than has unemployment for single women generally, and especially for professional single women, for whom employment and identity will be most closely related. Single parents are also a group whose circumstances merit special attention. For them even more than for other women the advantages of a wage must be weighed against the practical difficulties involved in paid work. Those who are employed are, however, more likely to be in full-time work and to feel the impact of unemployment most severely.

As with married women, an understanding of the employment position of young people will hinge to a great extent on the appreciation of their household circumstances, and particularly their role and responsibilities in the financial arrangements of the home. The central question here seems to concern the degree of parental indulgence accorded young people, and the general pattern is of fairly minimal contribution by young people to the running of the home, particularly so in the US. This indulgence seems to extend to both financial support and domestic services, and is particularly significant in cases of youth unemployment. Echoing findings on male unemployment we saw that it is the mother who usually bears the main financial burden of youth unemployment in that day-to-day budgeting for the household is commonly her responsibility. Considerable effort is made to offer material supports such that whatever contribution is made by young people is often more than returned. There is, however, a tension between the parental wish to keep them home and 'safe' and the responsibility of inculcating adult values and norms of behaviour.

Both the US and UK show similar concentrations of unemployment among the young, but the implications for family and household formation are rather different in the two countries. The major features of difference concern:

1 The availability of benefit other than contributory unemployment benefit in the UK, and therefore a guaranteed income, that is not provided by the American system of welfare.
2 The paucity of private rented accommodation in the UK, and its greater availability in the US where public sector housing is scarce.

The effect of these differences is to produce a pattern in the US of movement by young people in and out of the parental home according to their employment status, a pattern facilitated by the availability of private lets. In the UK, although an income to cover accommodation is assured from the age of 18 even without employment, the scarcity of private rented accommodation seems to produce greater dependence on the parental home. The most reliable means of access to an independent home where owner occupation is out of the question is actually through *family* formation, that is the birth of children, which validates a claim to public sector housing. In both the UK and US, however, there are advantages available to single parents that may discourage young women from committing themselves to an unemployed partner: in the US they have guaranteed maintenance through AFDC, whilst in the UK they have privileged access to public sector housing.

The effects of welfare provide but one instance of the constraints that fashion people's responses to changing economic conditions, but the identification of such constraints has served to temper expectations of variety and ingenuity in the 'household strategies' that emerge. The argument of this book has been that a full understanding of household–labour market relations must place the household in context by examining the statutory, social and ideological environment in which the connection is forged. Thus, for example, in America AFDC has been viewed as a possible threat to the marital stability of the unemployed, whilst in the UK income support for the unemployed acts as a disincentive to sole female earners. The result in both countries has been a tendency towards a two-earner/no-earner pattern rather than the anticipated role reversal.

Data presented in chapter 9 demonstrate in a number of different ways the importance of social networks in understanding the strategic outcomes for different households. Particularly significant is the channelling of employment opportunities through informal networks such that where there are social, spatial and familial concentrations of unemployment future work prospects will be poor. The network can, however, offer a source of mutual support in such circumstances, and has been found to be particularly important in access to opportunities in the informal sector; in the provision of child care, especially for single mothers; and in sustaining the gender identity of the male unemployed. More generally, the social network was found to be of significance in the degree of normative pressure to sustain gender roles, which appears to be greater where there is an extensive single-sex collectivity. The overall result for both the UK and the US is that economic change, and specifically the challenge to the nuclear family with a principal male earner, has been mediated for individual households by a web of constraining social, ideological and statutory influences that have militated against any significant challenge to established gender roles and identities.

References

Allatt, P. and Yeandle, S. (1985) *Family Structure and Youth Unemployment in an Area of Persistent Decline*, Report for the Leverhulme Trust.

—— (1986) 'It's not fair is it?', in S. Allen, A. Waton, K. Purcell and S. Wood (eds) *The Experience of Unemployment*, Macmillan, London, pp. 98–115.

Allen, W. R. (1978) 'Class, culture and family organisation', *Journal of Comparative Family Studies*, 10, pp. 301–13.

Anderson, M. (1971) *Family Structure in Nineteenth Century Lancashire*, Cambridge University Press, Cambridge.

Aneshensel, C. S. (1986) 'Marital and employment role strain, social support and depression among adult women', in S. E. Hobfoll (ed.) *Stress, Social Support and Women*, Hemisphere, Washington DC.

Angel, R. and Tienda, M. (1982) 'Determinants of extended household structure', *American Journal of Sociology*, 87, pp. 1360–83.

Angrist, S. S., Lave, J. R. and Mickelson, R. (1976) 'How working mothers manage', *Social Science Quarterly*, 56, pp. 631–7.

Ashton, D. (1986) *Unemployment under Capitalism*, Wheatsheaf, Brighton.

Ashton, D. M. and Maguire, M. J. (1986) *Young Adults in the Labour Market*, Research Paper 55, Department of Employment, London.

Atkinson, J. (1984) *Manning for Uncertainty*, IMS Report, Sussex University.

Atkinson, J. and Meager, N. (1986) *Changing Work Patterns*, IMS Report, NEDO, London.

Bahr, S. J. (1979) 'The effects of welfare on marital stability and remarriage', *Journal of Marriage and the Family*, 41, pp. 553–60.

Bakke, E. W. (1935) *The Unemployed Man*, Nisbet, London.

—— (1940a) *Citizens without Work*, Yale University Press, New Haven.

—— (1940b) *The Unemployed Worker*, Yale University Press, New Haven.

Barrett, M. (1980) *Women's Oppression Today*, Verso, London.

Barrett, M. and McIntosh, M. (1980) 'The family wage', *Capital and Class*, 11, pp. 51–72.

Barron, R. D. and Norris, G. M. (1986) 'Sexual divisions and the dual labour market', in S. Allen and D. Barker (eds) *Dependence and Exploitation in Work and Marriage*, Longman, London, pp. 47–69.

Becker, G. S. (1981) *A Treatise on the Family*, Harvard University Press, Cambridge, Mass.

Becker, G. S., Landes, E. M. and Michael, R. T. (1977) 'An economic analysis of marital instability', *Journal of Political Economy*, 85, pp. 1141–87.

Beechey, V. (1977) 'Some notes on female wage labour in capitalist production', *Capital and Class*, 3, pp. 45–66.

—— (1978) 'Women and production: a critical analysis of some sociological theories of women's work', in A.Kuhn and R. M. Wolpe (eds) *Feminism and Materialism*, Routledge and Kegan Paul, London.

Beechey, V. and Perkins, T. (1987) *A Matter of Hours*, Polity Press, Cambridge.

Bell, C. (1968) *Middle-Class Families*, Routledge and Kegan Paul, London.

Bell, C. and McKee, L. (1985) 'Marital and family relations in times of male unemployment', in B. Roberts, R. Finnegan and D. Gallie (eds) *New Approaches to Economic Life*, Manchester University Press, Manchester, pp. 387–99.

Ben-Porath, Y. (1982) 'Economics and the family – match or mismatch?', *Journal of Economic Literature*, XX, pp. 52–64.

Bergmann, B. R. (1980) 'Occupational segregation, wages and profits' in A. H. Amsder (ed.), *The Economics of Women and Work*, Penguin, Harmondsworth, Middx.

—— (1986) *The Economic Emergence of Women*, Basic Books, New York.

Berk, S. F. (1985) *The Gender Factory*, Plenum Press, New York.

Bernard, J. (1966) 'Marital stability and patterns of status variables', *Journal of Marriage and the Family*, 28, pp. 421–39.

—— (1972) *The Future of Marriage*, World, New York.

Berthoud, R. (1979) *Unemployed Professional and Executives*, PSI Broadsheet, XLV, no. 582, May.

Beveridge, W. H. (1909) *Unemployment: A Problem for Industry*, Longman, London.

Beynon, H. and Blackburn, R. M. (1972) *Perceptions of Work*, Cambridge University Press, Cambridge.

Binns, D. and Mars, G. (1984) 'Family, community and unemployment', *Sociological Review*, 32, pp. 662–95.

Blau, F. D. (1978) 'The impact of the unemployment rate on labourforce entries and exits', in *Women's Changing Roles at Home and on the Job*, National Commission for Manpower Policy, Special Report no. 26, pp. 263–86.

Blood, R. O. and Wolfe, D. M. (1960) *Husbands and Wives*, Free Press, Glencoe, Ill.

Blumstein, P. and Schwartz, P. (1983) *American Couples*, William Morrow, New York.

Booth, A., Johnson, D. R., White, L. and Edwards, J. N. (1984) 'Women outside employment and marital stability', *American Journal of Sociology*, 90, pp. 567–83.

Bott, E. (1957) *Family and Social Network*, Tavistock, London.

Bowen, W. G. and Finegan, T. A. (1969) *The Economics of Labourforce Participation*, Princeton University Press, Princeton.

Bradbury, K., Sheldon, D., Smolensky, E. and Smolensky, P. (1979) 'Public assistance, female headship and economic wellbeing', *Journal of Marriage and the Family*, 41, pp. 519–35.

Bradshaw, J., Cooke, K. and Godfrey, C. (1983) 'The impact of unemployment on the living standards of families', *Journal of Social Policy*, 12, pp. 433–52.

Braverman, M. (1974) *Labour and Monopoly Capitalism*, Monthly Review Press, New York.

Brenner, T. and Ramas, M. (1984) 'Rethinking women's oppression', *New Left Review*, 144, pp. 33–71.

Brown, B., Emerson, T., Falk, G. and Freedman, A. (1971) 'The Equal Rights Amendment: a constitutional basis for equal rights for women', *Yale Law Journal*, 80, p. 940.

Brown, C. (1984) *Black and White in Britain*, 3rd PSI Survey, Heinemann, London.

Brown, G. W. and Harris, T. (1978) *The Social Origins of Depression*, Tavistock, London.

Bruegel, I. (1979) 'Women as a reserve army of labour', *Feminist Review*, 3, pp. 12–23.

—— (1988) 'Sex and race in the labour market', unpublished paper presented at the CSE Sex and Class group.

Buck, L. and Shimmin, S. (1959) 'Overtime and financial responsibility', *Occupational Psychology*, 33, pp. 137–48.

Burchinal, L. G. (1965) 'Trends and prospects for young marriages in the United States', *Journal of Marriage and the Family*, 27, pp. 243–54.

Burr, W. R., Leigh, G. K., Day, R. D. and Constantine, J. (1979) 'Symbolic interaction and the family', in W. R. Burr et al. (eds) *Contemporary Theories about the Family*, vol. II, Free Press, New York.

Buss, T. F., Stevens, F., Redburn, F. and Waldron, J. (1983) *Plant Closings and Community Health*, Sage, London.

Cherlin, A. (1978) *Employment, Income and Family Life: The Case of Marital Dissolution*, National Commission for Manpower Policy, Special Report no. 26, pp. 157–78.

Clark, R. A., Nye, F. I. and Gecas, V. (1978) 'Husbands' work involvement and marital role performance', *Journal of Marriage and the Family*, 40, pp. 9–21.

Coleman, R. (1986) 'Social standing and income packaging', in L. Rainwater, M. Rein and J. Schwartz (eds) *Income Packaging and the Welfare State*, Clarendon Press, Oxford.

Coyle, A. (1984) *Redundant Women*, Women's Press, London.

Cragg, A. and Dawson, T. (1984) *Unemployed Women*, Department of Employment Research Paper no. 47, HMSO, London.

Daniel, W. W. and Stilgoe, S. (1977) *Where Are They Now?*, PEP, London.

Darity, W. A. and Myers, S. L. (1984) 'Does welfare dependency cause female headship', *Journal of Marriage and the Family*, 51, pp. 765–79.

Dennis, N., Henriques, L. and Slaughter, C. (1956) *Coal Is Our Life*, Eyre and Spottiswoode, London.

Dex, S. (1985) *The Sexual Division of Work*, Wheatsheaf, Brighton.

Dex, S. and Shaw, L. (1986) *British and American Women at Work*, Macmillan, London.

Dick, B. and Morgan, G. (1987) 'Family networks and employment in textiles', *Work, Employment and Society*, 1, pp. 225–46.

Edgell, S. (1980) *Middle Class Couples*, Allen and Unwin, London.

Ellwood, D. T. and Wise, D. A. (1980) 'Youth employment in the 1970's', in R. R. Nelson and F. Skidmore (eds) *American Families and the Economy*, National Academy Press, Washington DC, pp. 59–108.

Employment Gazette (1987) January, HMSO, London.

Ericksen, J. A., Yancey, W. L. and Ericksen, E. P. (1979) 'The division of family roles', *Journal of Marriage and the Family*, 46, pp. 301–13.

Fagin, L. (1984) *The Forsaken Families*, Penguin, Harmondsworth, Middx.

Fallding, H. (1961) 'The family and the idea of a cardinal role', *Human Relationships*, 13, pp. 329–50.

Farkas, G. (1976) 'Education, wage rates, and the division of labour between husband and wife', *Journal of Marriage and the Family*, 38, pp. 473–83.

Feinstein, K. W. (1979) *Working Women and Families*, Sage, Beverly Hills.

Fevre, R. (1986) 'Contract work in recession', in S. Wood and K. Purcell (eds) *The Changing Experience of Work*, Macmillan, London.

Finch, J. (1983) *Married to the Job*, Allen and Unwin, London.

Finn, D. (1988) 'Why train school leavers?' *Unemployment Bulletin*, Autumn, pp. 1–8.

Freeman, R. B. and Wise, D. A. (1982) *The Youth Labour Market Problem*, Chicago University Press, Chicago.

Geerken, M. and Gove, W. R. (1983) *At Home and at Work*, Sage, Beverly Hills.

General Household Survey (1986) HMSO, London.

Gershuny, J. I. (1977) 'Post-industrial society: the myth of the service economy', *Futures*, 10, pp. 103–14.

—— (1979) 'The informal economy: its role in post-industrial society', *Futures*, 12, pp. 3–15.

—— (1982) *Household Work Strategies*, presented at ISA conference, Mexico City, August.

Gershuny, J. I. and Jones, S. (1987) 'The changing work/leisure balance in Britain 1961–84', *Sociological Review Monograph*, 33, pp. 9–50.

Gershuny, J. I. and Pahl, R. E. (1979) 'Work outside employment: some preliminary speculations', *New Universities Quarterly*, 34, pp. 120–35.

—— (1980) 'Britain in the decade of the three economies', *New Society*, 3, January, pp. 7–9.

—— (1981) 'Work outside employment', in S. Henry (ed.) *Can I Have it in Cash?*, Astragal Books, London, pp. 73–88.

Gershuny, J. I., Miles, I., Jones, S., Mullins, C., Thomas, G. and Wyatt, S. M. E. (1986) 'Preliminary analysis of the 1983/4 ESRC time budget data', *Quarterly Journal of Social Affairs*, 2, pp. 13–39.

Gillespie, D. L. (1972) 'Who has the power?', in H. P. Dreitzel (ed.) *Family and Marriage and the Struggle of the Sexes*, Macmillan, New York.

Goldscheider, F. K. and Da Vanzo, J. (1985) 'Living arrangements and the transition to young adulthood', *Journal of Marriage and the Family*, 47, pp. 545–63.

Goode, W. (1960) 'A theory of role strain', *American Sociological Review*, 25, pp. 483–96.

—— (1964) *The Family*, Prentice Hall, Englewood Cliffs.

Goody, J. (1972) 'The evolution of the family', in P. Laslett (ed.) *Household and Family in Past Time*, Cambridge University Press, Cambridge.

Gould, S. and Werbel, J. D. (1983) 'Work involvement: a comparison of dual wage earner and single wage earner families', *Journal of Applied Psychology*, 68, pp. 313–19.

Gowler, D. and Legge, K. (1978) 'Hidden and open contracts in marriage', in R. Rappoport and R. Rappoport (eds) *Working Couples*, Routledge and Kegan Paul, London.

Granovetter, M. (1974) *Getting a Job*, Harvard University Press, Cambridge, Mass.

Grieco, M. (1987a) 'Family networks and the closure of employment', in G. Lee and R. Loveridge (eds) *The Manufacture of Disadvantage*, Open University Press, Milton Keynes.

—— (1987b) *Keeping it in the Family*, Tavistock, London.

Gray, A. (1979) 'The working class family as an economic unit', in C. C. Harris (ed.) *The Sociology of the Family*, Sociological Review Monograph, 28, pp. 186–213.

Gronseth, E. (1971) 'The husband provider role', in A. Michel (ed.) *Family Issues of Employed Women in Europe and America*, E.J. Brill, Leiden.

Hamill, L. (1978) *Wives as Sole and Joint Breadwinners*, Government Economic Workshop Service Paper, no. 13, London.

Hampton, R. (1980) 'Institutional decimation, marital exchange and disruption in black families', *Western Journal of Black Studies*, 4, pp. 132–9.

Hanham, R. Q. (1984) *The Changing Spatial Impact of Recession in the USA, 1960–83*, paper presented at a meeting of the Institute of British Geographers, Durham.

Hannan, M. T. (1982) 'Families, markets and social structures', *Journal of Economic Literature*, XX, pp. 65–72.

Hareven, T. K. (1977) *Family Time and Industrial Time*, Cambridge University Press, Cambridge.

Harris, C. C. (1969) *The Family*, Allen and Unwin, London.

—— (1983) *The Family and Industrial Society*, Allen and Unwin, London.

—— (1987) *Redundancy and Recession in South Wales*, Basil Blackwell, Oxford.

Harris, C. C. and Morris, L. D. (1986) 'Households, labour markets and the position of women', in R. Crompton and M. Mann (eds) *Gender and Stratification*, Polity Press, Cambridge.

Hartley, J. (1987) 'Managerial unemployment: the wife's perspective and role', in S. Fineman (ed.) *Unemployment*, Tavistock, London.

Hartman, H. (1979) 'Capitalism, patriarchy and job segregation by sex', in Z. R. Eisenstein (ed.) *Capitalist Patriarchy and the Case for Socialist Feminism*, Monthly Review Press, New York.

—— (1981) 'The family as the locus of gender, class and political struggle', *Signs*, 6, pp. 366–94.

Hayghe, H. (1981) 'Husbands and wives as earners', *Monthly Labour Review*, February, pp. 46–53.

Hays, W. C. and Mindel, C. H. (1973) 'Extended relations in black and white families', *Journal of Marriage and the Family*, 35, pp. 51–7.

Hedges, J. N. and Barnett, J. K. (1972) 'Working women and the division of household tasks', *Monthly Labour Review*, 95, pp. 9–14.

Hertz, R. (1986) *More Equal than Others*, University of California Press, Berkeley.

Hesse, S. J. (1979) 'Working women: historical trends', in K. W. Feinstein (ed.) *Working Women and Families*, Sage, Beverly Hills.

Hiller, D. V. and Philliber, W. W. (1986) 'The division of labour in contemporary marriage', *Social Problems*, 33, pp. 191–201.

Hofferth, S. L. (1984) 'Kin networks, race and family structure', *Journal of Marriage and the Family*, 46, pp. 791–806.

Homer, M., Leonard, A. and Taylor, P. (1985) 'The burden of dependency', in N. Johnson (ed.) *Marital Violence*, Routledge and Kegan Paul, London.

Honig, M. (1974) 'AFDC income, recipient rates and family dissolution', *Journal of Human Resources*, IX, pp. 303–22.

Hughes, J. J. and Perlman, R. (1984) *The Economics of Unemployment*, Wheatsheaf, Brighton.

Hunt, P. (1978) 'Cash transactions and household tasks', *Sociological Review*, 26, pp. 555–71.

—— (1980) *Gender and Class Consciousness*, Macmillan, London.

Hutson, S. and Jenkins, R. (1986) 'Family relations and the unemployment of young people in Swansea', in M. White (ed.) *The Social World of the Young Unemployed*, PSI, London, pp. 37–53.

—— (1987) 'Coming of age in South Wales', in P. Brown and D. N. Ashton (eds) *Education, Unemployment and the Labour Market*, Falmer Press, Brighton, pp. 93–107.

Incichen, B. (1981) 'The housing decisions of young people', *British Journal of Sociology*, 32, pp. 252–8.

Jackson, B. (1982) 'Single parent families', in R. N. Rapoport, M. P. Fogarty and R. Rapoport (eds) *Families in Britain*, Routledge and Kegan Paul, London, pp. 159–77.

Jackson, P. (1986) *Unemployment and the Family*, memo 746, MSC/ESRC Social and Applied Psychology Unit, University of Sheffield.

Jephcott, P., Seear, N. and Smith, J. (1962) *Married Women Working*, Allen and Unwin, London.

Joe, T. and Yu, P. (1984) *The Flip-side of Families Headed by Black Women*, Centre for the Study of Social Policy, Washington DC.

Joshi, H. (1984) *Women's Employment in Paid Work*, Department of Employment Research Paper, 45, HMSO, London.

Jowell, R. and Witherspoon, S. (eds) (1985) *British Social Attitudes*, Gower, Aldershot.

Kandel, D. B. and Lesser, G. (1969) 'Parent–adolescent relationships and adolescent independence in the US and Denmark', *Journal of Marriage and the Family*, 31, pp. 348–58.

—— (1972) 'Marital decision making in American and Danish urban families', *Journal of Marriage and the Family*, 34, pp. 134–8.

Kandel, D. B., Davies, M. and Raveis, V. H. (1985) 'The stressfulness of daily social roles for women', *Journal of Health and Social Behaviour*, 26, pp. 64–78.

Kelvin, P. and Jarrett, J. E. (1985) *Unemployment*, Cambridge University Press, Cambridge.

Kempers, M. B. and Rayman, P. M. (1987) 'The meaning of unemployment in the lives of women', in L. Beneria and C. R. Stimpson (eds) *Women, Households and the Economy*, Rutgers University Press, New Brunswick.

Kenkel, W. (1969) 'Family interaction in decision making on spending', in N. Foote (ed.) *Household Decision Making*, New York University Press, New York.

Kerr, M. (1958) *The People of Ship Street*, Routledge and Kegan Paul, London.

Kessler, R. and McCrae, J. (1982) 'The effect of wives' employment on the mental health of married men and women', *Journal of Health and Social Behaviour*, 47, pp. 216–27.

Kiernan, K. (1985) *The Departure of Children*, CPS Research paper, 85–3, Centre for Population Studies, London.

—— (1986) *Transitions in Young Adulthood*, paper presented at the conference on Population Research in Britain, University of East Anglia, September.

Komarovsky, M. (1940) *The Unemployed Man and his Family*, Octagon Books, New York.

—— (1967) *Blue Collar Marriage*, Vintage Books, New York.

Kuhn, A. and Wolpe, A. M. (eds) (1978) *Feminism and Materialism*, Routledge and Kegan Paul, London.

Laite, J. and Halfpenny, P. (1987) 'Employment, unemployment and the domestic division of labour', in D. Fryer and P. Ullah (eds) *Unemployed People*, Open University Press, Milton Keynes.

Land, H. (1969) *Large Families in London*, Bell, London.

—— (1976) 'Social security and the division of unpaid work within the home and paid work within the family', *Social Security Research*, HMSO, London.

—— (1981) 'The family wage', in M. Evans (ed.) *The Woman Question*, Fontana, London, pp. 289–96.

Lein, L. (1979) 'Male participation in home life', *The Family Co-ordinator*, October, pp. 489–95.

Leonard, D. (1980) *Sex and Generation*, Tavistock, London.

Lewis, J. (1984) *Women in England*, Wheatsheaf, Brighton.

Liebow, E. (1967) *Tally's Corner*, Little, Brown and Co., Toronto.

Litwak, E. (1960) 'Geographic mobility and extended family cohesion', *American Sociological Review*, 25, pp. 9–12.

Lomnitz, L. (1977) *Life in a Mexican Shanty Town*, Academic Press, London.

Lopata, H. Z. (1971) *Occupation Housewife*, Oxford University Press, New York.

Lopata, H. Z., Miller, C. and Barnewolt, D. (1986) *City Women in America*, Praeger, New York.

Lowenthal, M. (1981) 'Non-market transactions in an urban community', in S. Henry (ed.) *Can I have it in Cash?*, Astragal Books, London, pp. 90–104.

Lupri, E. (1969) 'Contemporary authority patterns in the West German family', *Journal of Marriage and the Family*, 31, pp. 134–44.

Luxton, M. (1980) *More than a Labour of Love*, Women's Press, Toronto.

MacDonald, M. and Sawhill, I. V. (1978) 'Welfare policy and the family', *Public Policy*, 26, pp. 89–119.

MacDonald, M., Thomas, P. and Garfinkel, I., 'AFDC and family dissolution', Institute for Research on Poverty, University of Wisconsin, Madison, (unpublished).

MacGregor, S. (1981) *The Politics of Poverty*, Longman, Harlow.

McIntosh, M. (1978) 'The state and the oppression of women', in A. Kuhn and A. M. Wolpe (eds) *Feminism and Materialism*, Routledge and Kegan Paul, London, pp. 254–90.

—— (1981) *Households, Incomes and the Politics of Need*, paper presented at BSA Conference, April.

McLanahan, S. (1985) 'Family structure and the reproduction of poverty', *American Journal of Sociology*, 90, pp. 873–901.

MacLennan, E., Fitz, J. and Sullivan, J. (1985) *Working Children*, Low Pay Pamphlet no. 34, Low Pay Unit, London.

Mainardi, P. (1970) 'The politics of housework', in R. Morgan (ed.) *Sisterhood is Powerful*, Vintage, New York, pp. 447–54.

Malabre, A. (1980) 'Recession hits blacks harder than whites', *Wall Street Journal*, August 21.

Mallier, A. and Rosser, M. (1986) *Women and the Economy*, Macmillan, London.

Malpass, P. (1984) 'Housing policy and young people', *Youth Policy*, 11, pp. 15–21.

Marsden, D. (1982) *Workless*, Croom Helm, London.

Martin, J. and Roberts, C. (1984) *Women and Employment*, report on the Department of Employment/OPCS Survey, HMSO, London.

Martin, R. and Wallace, J. (1984) *Working Women in Recession*, Oxford University Press, Oxford.

Massey, D. (1984) *Spatial Divisions of Labour*, Macmillan, London.

Matthaei, J. (1982) *An Economic History of Women in America*, Harvester, Brighton.

McKee, L. (1987) 'Households during unemployment', in J. Brannen and G. Wilson (eds) *Give and Take in Families*, Allen and Unwin, London.

Meissner, M., Humphries, E., Meis, S. and Scheu, W. (1975) 'No exit for wives', *Review of Canadian Sociology and Anthropology*, 12, pp. 424–39.

Michael, R. T. and Tuma, N. B. (1985) 'Entry into marriage and parenthood by young men and women', *Journal of Marriage and the Family*, 47, pp. 515–44.

Michel, A. (1967) 'Comparative data concerning the interaction of French and American families', *Journal of Marriage and the Family*, 29, pp. 337–44.

Milkman, R. (1976) 'Women's work and economic crisis', in *Review of Radical Political Economies*, Spring, pp. 73–97.

Millward, N. (1968) 'Family status and behaviour at work', *Sociological Review*, 16, pp. 149–64.

Mincer, J. (1962) 'Labourforce participation of married women', in *Aspects of Labour Economics: A Conference of the Universities*, National Bureau Committee for Economic Research, Princeton University Press.

—— (1966) 'Labourforce participation and unemployment', in R. A. Gordon and M. S. Gordon (eds) *Prosperity and Unemployment*, John Wiley, New York.

Moen, P. (1979) 'Family impacts of the 1975 recession', *Journal of Marriage and the Family*, 41, pp. 561–73.

—— (1983) 'Unemployment, public policy and families: forecasts for the 1980s', in *Journal of Marriage and the Family*, 45, pp. 751–60.

Molyneux, M. (1979) 'Beyond the domestic labour debate', *New Left Review*, 116, pp. 3–27.

Monthly Labour Review (1984) Bureau of Labour Statistics, Washington DC.

Morgan, D. H. J. (1975) *Social Theory and the Family*, Routledge and Kegan Paul, London.

Morris, L. D. (1984a) 'Redundancy and patterns of household finance', *Sociological Review*, 32, pp. 492–593.

—— (1984b) 'Patterns of social activity and post-redundancy labour market experience', *Sociology*, 18, pp. 339–52.

—— (1985a) 'Renegotiation of the domestic division of labour', in B. Roberts et al. (ed.) *New Approaches to Economic Life*, Manchester University Press, Manchester, pp. 400–16.

—— (1985b) 'Local social networks and domestic organisation', *Sociological Review*, 33, pp. 327–42.

—— (1985c) 'Responses to redundancy', *International Journal of Social Economics*, 12, pp. 5–16.

—— (1987a) 'The life cycle and the labour market', in A. Bryman and W. Bytheway (eds) *Rethinking the Life Cycle*, Macmillan, London, pp. 192–206.

—— (1987b) 'The household and the labour market' (ch. 6) and 'Domestic circumstances' (ch. 7), in C. C. Harris (ed.) *Redundancy and Recession in South Wales*, Basil Blackwell, Oxford, pp. 127–55.

—— (1987c) 'Constraints on gender', *Work, Employment and Society*, 1, pp. 85–106.

—— (1987d) 'Local social polarisation', *International Journal of Urban and Regional Research*, 11, pp. 333–52.

Morris, L. D. with Ruane, S. (1989) *Household Finance Management and the Labour Market*, Gower, Aldershot.

Mott, F. L. (1979) 'Racial differences in female labourforce participation', in K. W. Feinstein (ed.) *Working Women and Families*, Sage, Beverly Hills, pp. 85–101.

Moylan, S., Millar, S. and Davis, R. (1984) *For Richer, for Poorer*, DHSS cohort study of unemployed men, HMSO, London.

Moynihan, D. (1965) *The Negro Family: The Case for National Action*, Government Printing Office, Washington DC.

Mumford, E. and Banks, O. (1967) *The Computer and the Clerk*, Routledge and Kegan Paul, London.

Murphy, M. and Sullivan, O. (1986) 'Unemployment, housing and household structure among young adults', *Journal of Social Policy*, 15, pp. 205–22.

Nickols, S. Y. and Metzen, E. J. (1982) 'Impact of wife's employment upon husband's housework', *Journal of Family Issues*, 3, pp. 199–217.

Niemi, B. (1980) 'The female differential in unemployment rates', in A. H. Amsden (ed.) *The Economics of Women and Work*, Penguin, Harmondsworth, Middx., pp. 325–49.

Nowak, T. C. and Snyder, K. A. (1983) 'Women's struggle to survive a plant shutdown', *Journal of Intergroup Relations*, 11, pp. 25–44.

Nixon, J. (1977) 'Some factors affecting lone mothers' decisions to work', in DHSS *Social Security Research*, HMSO, London.

Oakley, A. (1974) *The Sociology of Housework*, Robertson, London.

Ostrander, S. A. (1984) *Women of the Upper Class*, Temple University Press, Philadelphia.

Pahl, J. (1980) 'Patterns of money management within marriage', *Journal of Social Policy*, 9, pp. 313–35.

—— (1983) 'The allocation of money and the structuring of inequality within marriage', *Sociological Review*, 31, pp. 237–62.

Pahl, R. E. (1980) 'Employment, work and the domestic division of labour', *International Journal of Urban and Regional Research*, 4, pp. 1–19.

—— (1984) *Divisions of Labour*, Basil Blackwell, Oxford.

Pahl, J. M. and Pahl, R. E. (1971) *Managers and their Wives*, Allen Lane, London.

Parsons, T. (1943) *Essays in Sociological Theory*, Free Press, New York.

—— (1949) 'The social structure of the family', in R. N. Ashen (ed.) *The Family*, Hayner, New York, pp. 241–74.

—— (1956) *Family, Socialisation and Interaction Process*, Routledge and Kegan Paul, London.

Payne, J. (1987) 'Does unemployment run in families?', *Sociology*, May, pp. 199–214.

Peattie, L. R. (1968) *The View from the Barrio*, University of Michigan Press, Michigan.

Perrucci, C. C., Perrucci, R., Targ, D. B. and Targ, H. (1985) 'Impact of a plant closing on workers in the community', in I. H. Simpson and R. L. Simpson (eds) *Research in the Sociology of Work*, vol. 3, pp. 231–60.

Pilgrim Trust (1938) *Men without Work*, Cambridge University Press, Cambridge.

Pleck, J. H. (1985) *Working Wives, Working Husbands*, Sage, Beverly Hills.

Pollert, A. (1988) 'The flexible firm: fixation or fact?', *Work, Employment and Society*, 2, pp. 281–316.

Popay, J. (1985) 'Women, the family and unemployment', in P. Close and R. Collins (eds) *Family and Economy in Modern Society*, Macmillan, London.

Popay, J., Rimmer, L. and Rossiter, C. (1983) *One Parent Families: Parents, Children and Public Policy*, Study Commission on the Family, Occasional paper no. 12.

Powell, D. H. and Driscoll, P. F. (1973) 'Middle class professionals face unemployment', *Society*, 10, pp. 18–26.

Prude, J. (1983) *The Coming of Industrial Order*, Cambridge University Press, New York.

Pruette, L. and Peters, I. L. (1934) *Women Workers through the Depression*, Macmillan, New York.

Rainwater, L. (1965) *Family Design*, Aldine, Chicago.

—— (1984) 'Mother's contribution to the family money economy in Europe and the US', in P. Voydanoff (ed.) *Work and Family*, Mayfield, Palo Alto, pp. 73–88.

Rainwater, L., Rein, M. and Schwartz, J. (1986) *Income Packaging and the Welfare State*, Clarendon Press, Oxford.

Rapoport, R. and Rapoport, R. N. (1971) *Dual Career Families*, Robertson, London.

—— (1976) *Dual Career Families Re-examined*, Robertson, London.

Reimers, C. W. (1984) 'Sources of the family income differentials between Hispanics, Blacks and White non-Hispanics', *American Journal of Sociology*, 89, pp. 889–903.

Reform of Social Security (1985) DHSS White Paper, HMSO, London.

Robertson, D. J. (1960) *Factory Wage Structures and National Agreements*, Cambridge University Press, Cambridge.

Robinson, J. P. (1977) *How Americans Use Time*, Praeger, New York.

—— (1980) 'Housework technology and household work', in S. F. Berk (ed.) *Women and Household Labour*, Sage, Beverly Hills, pp. 53–68.

Rodgers, H. R., Jr (1986) *Poor Women, Poor Families*, M. E. Sharpe, New York.

Rodman, H. (1970) 'Marital power and the theory of resources in cultural context', *Kolner Zeitschrift fur Sociologie*, Sonderheft, Autumn.

Rosen, E. I. (1987) *Bitter Choices*, University of Chicago Press, Chicago.

Ross, H. L. and Sawhill, I. V. (1975) *Time of Transition: The Growth of Families Headed by Women*, Urban Institute, Washington DC.

Rubin, L. (1976) *Worlds of Pain*, Basic Books, New York.

Safilios-Rothschild, C. (1970) 'The study of family power structure', *Journal of Marriage and the Family*, 32, pp. 539–52.

Sawhill, I. V. (1975) *Income Transfers and Family Structure*, Urban Institute, Washington DC.

Scanzoni, J. (1970) *Opportunity and the Family*, Free Press, New York.

Scheirer, M. A. (1983) 'Household structure among welfare families', *Journal of Marriage and the Family*, November, pp. 761–72.

Scholzman, K. L. and Verba, S. (1979) *From Injury to Insult*, Harvard University Press, New York.

Scott, J. (1982) *The Upper Classes*, Macmillan, London.

Sheppard, H. L. and Belitsky, A. H. (1966) *The Job Hunt*, Johns Hopkins Press, Baltimore.

Shimmin, S. (1962) 'Extra-mural factors influencing behaviour at work', *Occupational Psychology*, 36, pp. 124–31.

Siltanen, J. and Stanworth, M. (1984) *Women and the Public Sphere*, Hutchinson, London.

Snyder, K. A. and Nowak, T. C. (1984) 'Job loss and demoralisation: do women fare better than men?', *International Journal of Mental Health*, 13, pp. 92–106.

Social Security Bulletin (1986) vol. 49, no. 1, pp. 6–59.

Soldo, B. and Lauriat, P. (1976) *Living arrangements among the elderly in the US: a log-linear approach*, unpublished manuscript.

Solien, N. (1960) 'Household and Caribbean', *Social and Economic Studies*, 9, pp. 101–6.

South, S. J. (1985) 'Economic conditions and the divorce rate', *Journal of Marriage and the Family*, 47, pp. 31–41.

Stack, C. (1974) *All our Kin*, Harpers, New York.

Stamp, P. (1985) 'Balance of financial power in marriage', *Sociological Review*, 33, pp. 546–57.

Staples, R. (1985) 'Changes in black family structure', *Journal of Marriage and the Family*, 47, pp. 1005–11.

Stone, K. (1983) 'Motherhood and waged work: West Indian, Asian and White mothers compared', in A. Phizacklea (ed.) *One Way Ticket*, Routledge and Kegan Paul, London.

Strauss, M. A. (1962) 'Work roles and financial responsibility in the socialisation of farm, fringe and town boys', *Rural Sociology*, 27, pp. 257–74.

Thomas, C. E., McCabe, E. and Berry, J. E. (1980) 'Unemployment and family stress', *Family Relations*, 29, pp. 517–24.

Thomas, G., Wyatt, S. and Miles, I. (1985) *Preliminary Analysis of the 1983/4 ESRC Time Budget Survey*, SPRU, Brighton, mimeo.

Thrall, C. A. (1978) 'Who does what?', *Human Relations*, 31, pp. 249–65.

Todd, J. E. and Jones, L. M. (1972) *Matrimonial Property*, OPCS Social Survey Division, HMSO, London.

Townsend, A. (1983) *The Impact of Recession*, Croom Helm, London.

Tunstall, J. (1962) *The Fishermen*, MacGibbon and Kee, London.

Unemployment Bulletin (1988) Unemployment Unit, 9 Poland St, London.

Voydanoff, P. (1987) *Work and Family Life*, Sage, Beverly Hills.

Voydanoff, P. and Kelly, R. F. (1984) 'Determinants of work-related family problems among employed parents', *Journal of Marriage and the Family*, 46, pp. 881–92.

Waite, L .J. and Spitze, G. D. (1981) 'Young women's transition to marriage', *Demography*, 18, pp. 681–94.

Walby, S. (1983) 'Theories of women, work and employment', in Lancaster Regionalism Group (ed.) *Localities, Class and Gender*, Pion, London, pp. 161–76.

—— (1986) *Patriarchy at Work*, Polity Press, Oxford.

Walker, J. (1961) 'Shift changes and hours of work', *Occupational Psychology*, 35, pp. 1–9.

Walker, K. (1982) *Community Care*, Basil Blackwell, London.

Walker, K. and Woods, M. (1976) *Time Use: A Measure of Household Production of Goods and Services*, American Home Economics Association, Washington.

Wallace, C. (1987) *For Richer, for Poorer*, Tavistock, London.

Ware, C. (1977) Introduction, in Cantor, M. and Laurie, B. (eds) *Class, Sex and the Woman Worker*, Greenwood Press, Westport, Conn.

Warr, P. and Jackson, P. (1984) 'Men without jobs: some correlates of age and length of unemployment', in *Journal of Occupational Psychology*, 57, pp. 77–85.

Wheelock, J. (1986) *Unemployment, Gender Roles and Household Work Strategies on Wearside*, EEC report.

Whipp, R. (1985) 'Labour markets and communities', *Sociological Review*, 33, pp. 768–91.

White, L. K. and Brinkerhoff, D. B. (1981) 'Children's work in the family', *Journal of Marriage and the Family*, 43, pp. 789–98.

White, M. (1983) *Long-term Unemployment and Labour Markets*, Policy Studies Institute, London.

Wilcocke, R. C. and Franke, W. H. (1963) *Unwanted Workers*, Free Press, Glencoe, Ill.

Willis, P. (1984) 'Youth and unemployment', *Youth Policy*, 2, pp. 17–24.

Wolfe, D. (1959) 'Power and authority in the family', in D. Cartwright (ed.) *Studies in Social Power*, University of Michigan Press, Ann Arbor.

Wood, S. (1981) 'Redundancy and female employment', *Sociological Review*, 29, pp. 649–89.

Woodward, J. et al. (1954) *The Dock Worker*, University of Liverpool, Social Science Research Series.

Yeandle, S. (1984) *Working Women's Lives*, Tavistock, London.

Yogev, S. (1981) 'Do professional women have egalitarian marital relationships?', *Journal of Marriage and the Family*, 44, pp. 865–71.

Young, M. (1952) 'Distribution of income within the family', *British Journal of Sociology*, 3, pp. 305–21.

Young, M. and Willmott, P. (1957) *Family and Kinship in East London*, Routledge and Kegan Paul, London.

—— (1973) *The Symmetrical Family*, Routledge and Kegan Paul, London.

Zweig, F. (1948) *Labour, Life and Poverty*, Gollancz, London.

—— (1961) *The Worker in an Affluent Society*, Heinemann, London.

Index

adults, young 147–65
  domestic labour and 150–2
  employment of 156–61, 162
  housing and 159–61
  incomes of 147–50, 152–4
  marriage of 163–5
  unemployment among 151–2,
    154–64, 195–6
  see also children
Asians, female employment
    among 75, 76

benefit, unemployment *see* welfare
blacks
  domestic labour among 99
  extended families of 53–4
  female employment among 23,
    71–6, 119–20, 143–5
  female headship among 168–9
  household formation by 156–7
  household incomes of 74, 143–5
  single-parent 72, 73
  support networks among 53–4,
    178–9, 183
  unemployment among 52–4, 57,
    143, 144
  youth unemployment among 155,
    158, 159, 162–3

children
  care of 64–6

domestic labour and 88ff, 98, 101,
    150–1
employment of 7, 23
female employment and 63–6, 69,
    72–6
female support networks and
    182–3
female unemployment and 144–6,
    164
housing and 160–1, 196
single-parent 169, 172–3
taxation and 176
welfare and 167–9, 172–3, 175–6
see also adults, young
class
  middle: domestic labour and 85;
    household finances of 119, 122;
    support networks and 56;
    unemployment among 49–50, 56,
    141
  social: domestic labour and 98–100,
    101; female employment and 122;
    gender roles and 192; support
    networks and 54–6; unemploy-
    ment and 48–51, 191
  working: household finances of
    110–12, 113, 119, 120–2; support
    networks and 55, 58–9;
    unemployment among 22–41, 42,
    44–9
cohabiting 114, 158

conflict, domestic *see under* stress
contact, social, female unemployment
   and 133–5, 142

divorce 64

economy, informal 179–82
educational levels
   domestic labour and 99, 101
   domestic power and 107
employment
   access to 183–8
   child 7, 23
   female 12–14, 23, 60–79; Asian 75,
      76; attitudes to 142–3; black 23,
      71–6, 119–20, 143–5; children
      and 63–6, 69, 72–6; divorce and
      64; domestic labour and 35–6, 78,
      80–102, 191–5; domestic power
      and 121–2; gender roles and
      68–9; Hispanic 74; household
      finances and 113–14, 117–22,
      191–5; increase in 30; marriage
      and 12–13, 62, 63–72, 77–8,
      141–2; part-time 65–70, 171, 176,
      191–2; in services 12; social class
      and 122; social contact and
      133–5, 142; stress and 94–6;
      support networks and 182–3;
      taxation and 65, 67, 174–5, 176;
      welfare and 70–1, 170–2
   full 10–12
   households and 14–16, 30–1
   industrialization and 6–8, 12
   informal 179–82
   life-cycle and 44–8, 191
   male black, marriage and 76
   in manufacturing 12
   part-time 65–70, 171, 176, 191–2
   in services 12, 67
   young-adult 152–61
ethnic minorities *see* Asians, blacks,
   Hispanics
exchange theory 82–3

families *see* households

family
   extended 53–4
   functional theory of 4–5
   nuclear 4–5, 23, 28–9
fertility, female 63
finance, household 3–4, 6–8, 39–40,
   85–6, 103–22, 193–5
   female employment and 113–14,
      117–22, 191–5
   gender roles and 105, 108, 110–15,
      116
   middle-class 119, 122
   types of 109–10
   working-class 110–12, 113, 119,
      120–2

gender roles 5–6, 17–38, 40–1
   class and 192
   domestic labour and 5–6, 17–21,
      28–9, 80–102, 150–2, 189–93
   female 130–1
   female employment and 68–9
   financial decision-making and 105,
      108, 110–15, 116
   male-stereotype 29–30, 31–2
   social networks and 58–9, 97, 98–9,
      177, 193

health, unemployment and 26
   see also stress
Hispanics 74, 143–5
households
   black 52–4, 57, 74, 99, 143–5,
      168–9, 178–9, 183
   children and 147–64
   domestic labour in 5–6, 17–21,
      28–9, 80–102, 150–2, 189–93
   employment and 14–16, 30–1,
      113–14, 117–22, 183–8, 191–5
   finances of 3–4, 6–8, 39–40, 85–6,
      103–22, 181–2, 193–5
   formation of 156–7, 159–63
   Hispanic 74, 143–5
   incomes of 74, 103–22, 143–5,
      189–97: domestic labour and 90,
      96, 99, 100

industrial 4–5, 7–8
life-cycle and 44–8, 88–90, 98, 113,
  191
nuclear-family 4–5, 23, 28–9
power in 102
pre-industrial 6–7
research focus on 2–3
single-parent 54, 72–6, 144–6, 162,
  167–9, 172–3, 178
social context of 165–88
social networks and 176–83
strategies of 19–21, 103
stress in 50, 52, 58, 75, 77–8, 94–6,
  114, 120–1, 152
unemployment and 14–16, 22–41,
  45, 49, 52–4, 57, 123–46,
  154–61, 194–6
welfare and 159, 165–73, 194,
  196–7
young adults and 147–64
housework *see* labour, domestic
housing 159–61, 196

identity
female 130–1, 133, 134
male 22ff, 29–30, 139–40
income
domestic power and 104, 105,
  107–15
female: household finances and
  113–14, 117–22, 191–5; male
  image and 139–40; poverty and
  137
household 103–22, 189–97: black
  74, 143–5; domestic labour roles
  and 90, 96, 99, 100; female
  contribution to 74, 117–22,
  143–5, 194; female
  unemployment and 131, 135–40,
  194–5; Hispanic 74, 143–5; male
  unemployment and 22–9, 38–41,
  45, 49; welfare and 159, 165–73,
  194, 196–7; young adults and
  147–64
informal 181–2
single mothers and 73–4

support networks and 54–5
industrialization, employment
  and 6–8, 12
isolation
female unemployment and 133–5,
  142
structural 4
labour, domestic 5–6, 17–21, 28–9,
  80–102, 150–2, 189–93
children and 88, 89, 91ff, 98, 101,
  150–1
class and 85, 98–100, 101
educational level and 99, 101
female employment and 35–6, 78,
  80–102
household income and 90, 96, 99,
  100
life-cycle and 88–90, 98
male unemployment and 32–8,
  87–90, 97, 100
social networks and 58–9, 97, 98–9,
  177, 193
theories of 17–21, 82–4
young adults and 150–2
life-cycle
domestic labour and 88–90, 98
employment prospects and 44–8,
  191
financial decision-making and 113
living standards, unemployment and
  38–9
loneliness, female unemployment and
  133–5, 142

manufacturing, employment in 12
marriage
black male employment and 76
changing nature of 85
female employment and 12–13, 62,
  63–72, 77–8, 141–2
household formation and 156–7
stress in 50, 52, 58, 75, 77–8, 94–6,
  114, 120–1, 152
taxation and 174–5
welfare and 167
young 163–5

marriage (*cont.*)
  youth unemployment and 157–8
minorities, ethnic *see* Asians, blacks,
  Hispanics

networks
  social: employment and 182–8, 197;
    gender roles and 58–9, 97, 98–9,
    177, 193; households and 176–83
  support 54–6, 57–9: black 53–4,
    178–9; class and 54–6, 58–9;
    female 182–3; single-parent
    families and 178

parents, single
  female employment and 72–6
  female unemployment and 144–6
  financial stress and 73–4
  household structure and 162
  male unemployment and 54
  support networks and 178
  welfare and 167–9, 172–3
patriarchy, domestic labour and 83
poverty, female incomes and 137
power
  domestic 102: educational levels and
    107; female employment and
    121–2; income and 104, 105,
    107–15; social status and 104, 107
  theories of 83–4, 104–6

segregation, social, long-term
    unemployment and 56–7
services, employment in 12, 67
society
  households and 165–88
  industrial 4–5, 7–8
  pre-industrial 6–7
status
  marital, female unemployment
    and 141–2
  occupational: early marriage and
    163; unemployment and 28,
    140–1
  social, domestic power and 104, 107
  see also class

stress
  domestic 75: female employment
    and 77–8, 94–6; financial
    decision-making and 114, 120–1;
    male unemployment and 50, 52;
    social networks and 58; youth
    unemployment and 152
  female: female employment and
    94–6; female unemployment and
    134, 135, 142
  financial, single mothers and 73–4
  male 96–7

taxation
  children and 176
  female employment and 65, 67,
    174–5, 176

unemployment 8–9, 10–12
  black 52–4, 57, 143, 144, 155, 158,
    159, 162–3
  class and 22–41, 42, 44–9, 56, 141,
    191
  domestic labour and 6, 28–9
  duration of 37, 45–6, 47–8, 56–7
  female 123–46, 164, 191, 194–5
  health and 26
  household income and 39–40
  households and 14–16, 22–9, 30–1,
    123–46, 194–5
  living standards and 38–9
  long-term 37, 47–8, 56–7
  male 22–59, 77–8, 87, 88–90, 97,
    100, 170–2, 190–1, 192
  occupational status and 28, 140–1
  short-term 37, 47–8
  spatial patterns of 186–7
  vulnerability to 191
  welfare and 165–73
  young-adult 151–2, 154–63, 195–6
unions, male dominance of 61

wage, family 4, 6, 7–8
welfare 70–1, 126–7, 166–9
  children and 167–9, 172–3, 175–6
  as a disincentive to work 170–2